Pelican Books
In a Critical Condition
*Reading Australian Literature*

John Docker was born in Sydney in 1945, and grew up in
Bondi. He attended the barracks-like Randwick Boys High
School. In 1963 he went to the University of Sydney to
study English literature, which turned out to be a time of
bitter dispute within the department of English. At the
unripe age of 21 he followed Professor S. L. Goldberg to the
University of Melbourne's English department, where he
completed his MA in English literature. The ensuing
culture shock led to the writing of his first book, *Australian
Cultural Elites*, in the early 1970s. He has had two periods
of work and study in London. Between 1975 and 1980 he
researched and wrote a doctoral thesis at the Australian
National University, on Australian literature and social
thought in the 1890s. He has taught at the University of
Sydney, Macquarie University, the NSW Institute of
Technology, the University of NSW, and most recently, in
media studies at Canberra CAE. He is currently
researching for a book on television drama.

*Gavin Edwards,*
*Canberra 1984.*

John Docker

# In a Critical Condition
Reading Australian Literature

PENGUIN BOOKS

Published with the assistance of the Literature
Board of the Australia Council

For my parents
Elsie and Ted Docker

Penguin Books Australia Ltd,
487 Maroondah Highway, P.O. Box 257
Ringwood, Victoria, 3134, Australia
Penguin Books Ltd,
Harmondsworth, Middlesex, England
Penguin Books,
40 West 23rd Street, New York, N.Y. 10010, U.S.A.
Penguin Books Canada Ltd,
2801 John Street, Markham, Ontario, Canada
Penguin Books (N.Z.) Ltd,
182-190 Wairau Road, Auckland 10, New Zealand

First published by Penguin Books Australia, 1984

Copyright © John Docker, 1984
Foreword copyright © Humphrey McQueen, 1984

Typeset in Caledonia by Dovatype, Melbourne

Made and printed in Singapore
by Richard Clay (S.E. Asia) Pte Ltd

**CIP**

Docker, John, 1945-.
In a critical condition.
Reading Australian literature.

Includes index.
ISBN 0 14 02.2567 6.

1. Australian literature – 20th century –
History and criticism. 2. Criticism –
Australia – History. I. Title.

A820'.9

# Contents

After a brief struggle, the Leavisites and New Critics scale the heights of Fortress Criticism. The new régime proclaims new edicts, rules and procedures for literary criticism. Chief legislators include G. A. Wilkes and Vincent Buckley. Even A. A. Phillips obeys some of the new laws.

Gloom, doom, alienation, and horror, according to Manning Clark, H. P. Heseltine, and Leon Cantrell.

The reader again meets maestro Manning Clark, who is pulling strange rabbits out of the History Hat. Out comes Peter Coleman! Out comes Humphrey McQueen!

Time has passed. After two decades the Leavisite and New Critics' Régime is showing signs of wear. Within Fortress Criticism the rules never seem to change. The inmates are becoming restless and the warders jittery. Governor Kramer attempts to maintain order.

In which an ageing New Criticism receives unexpected and often unrecognised support. Help, in the form of post-structuralism, is flown in from Paris.

In which the author proposes that criticism be freed to consider literature in all its aspects, context as well as text, the historical, political, social, and ideological as well as the metaphysical.

The author faces death at a seminar on Roland Barthes.

# Acknowledgements

For helpful comments on particular chapters I'd like to thank Ann Curthoys, Susan Dermody, Terry Sturm and Michael Wilding. Barbara O'Brien gave me invaluable practical assistance.

In 1980 the Literature Board of the Australia Council granted me a Senior Fellowship, and it was during that year that the bulk of the book was written.

For permission to reprint parts of various essays I thank *New Literature Review*, *Arena*, *Meanjin* and *Overland*. The prologue first appeared in *Meanjin*, no. 4, 1981 and parts of chapters four and five were in *New Literature Review* 6, 1979 as 'University Teaching of Australian Literature' and 'The Politics of Criticism: Leon Cantrell and the Gloom Thesis'.

I would very much like to thank Penguin's Bruce Sims for his editorial suggestions and my warmest thanks to Alan Walker for the index.

# Foreword

by Humphrey McQueen

Because literary criticism has earned its low reputation, a book explaining why most criticism is worthless must itself be in some danger of not being widely read; the sole aim of this foreword is to speed up the rate at which Australians will find out how necessary a book John Docker has produced. His work also deserves the attention of people whose first area of interest is not literary criticism, for example, anthropologists, historians and political scientists. In pursuing one thread of academic organisation, Docker helps us to see many other things. First, we glimpse parallels with other professions, their cultish beliefs and rites; secondly, there are the points where literary matters express social changes or political patterns.

The third and most important reason why readers outside the confines of Australian literary criticism need Docker's work is because it looks at those social processes which shape memory and hope, and gives insights into past and future. Despite attempts by critics to freeze fiction into a concern with metaphor or allusion, literature still offers us some means of understanding experience through action. But if generations of student teachers are told that literature has no use beyond amusement, then generations of their pupils, in turn, are in danger of losing even more of that expansion of the possible which literature can disclose. The more we deny imagination's links to life, the more we limit our choice of realities. It is at this level that literary criticism scores its most profoundly political results.

John Docker allows to literature those creative powers which its authors draw upon when writing. Homer and Shakespeare and Tolstoy knew that politics could be a passion as tumultuous as any love affair; Flaubert re-wrote the 'fate' of his characters according to the condition of their bank balances. It is only critics far more than novelists and poets who keep politics and economics at arm's length.

Henry Lawson replied to his 'Cultured Critics' by accusing them of picking on his faulty punctuation while being 'blind' to those aspects of his writing that asked how humankind should behave. Lawson was wrong. His cultured critics were not blind to the social question. If they concentrated their fire on his use of dashes instead of semi-colons, it was because they saw his wider purposes all too clearly. Lawson ended by telling his critics to 'keep out of the tracks we travel' until their voices carried farther than college walls. Again he was mistaken. More than is the case today, professors were then employed to teach the gospel according to profit and loss. Eighty years later, John Docker finds that the cultured critics are still out on the track turning the signposts around. The big question remains: is criticism pointing towards or away from civilisation? The weight of Docker's evidence shows criticism as an obstacle.

Australia happily has critics who have never been able to grasp how literature could be produced out of handed-down metaphors. Of these critics the finest is Dorothy Green, whom Docker aptly praises and whose selected essays are soon to be published by Penguin. Green pays close attention to texts precisely because she accepts that authors write when they have something to say; she wants to find out what that something is so that she can better know if and when to act upon an author's understanding of the world. Form without meaning dies just as surely as intelligence thrives on our ability to appreciate life.

Orthodox academic critics will claim that what they write is literary while Docker is being political. The fact is that Docker has turned the searchlights onto that '-ism' – criticism – which likes, as Raymond Williams noted, to be looked upon as the '-ism' which is so non-ideological that it is not an '-ism' at all, in contrast to structuralism with its difficult discourses on theory, or Marxism with its foul language of class.

Docker's own style presents yet another challenge to the reigning lightweights. He is conversational while the fashion runs in favour of wilful imprenetrability. He is anecdotal while one prejudice would deny authors their very existence. Worst of all – best of all – Docker uses his own experiences as part of his argument. He tells us about getting drunk, feeling pissed off, laughing at a seminar audience. By relating such responses he alerts us to sources which 'proper' critics suppress from their accounts. The tang of Docker's prose is as salt to the wounds he inflicts on the body of criticism.

Another of Docker's achievements is that grace with which he introduces international debates followed by the pace at which he can spin off these debates to their relevance for Australia. He takes these steps without diminishing either the significance of the overseas ideas or the importance of the local works to which other critics have applied them. How welcome is Docker's approach after the usual ones which offer lumps of theory in one section followed by barely understood bits about Australian experience in another part, at the expense of both.

I put John Docker's manuscript down with a touch of impatience because it had made me anxious to read at once those works which his writing will help to make possible. In the bush, a fire is often needed to germinate native seeds. Docker's book has similar creative powers. It will clear out much rubbish and crack open hard kernels. The hunting and harvesting becomes available for all those who are not paid to be blind.

Humphrey McQueen, 1983

# Prologue

# How I became a teenage Leavisite and lived to tell the tale

Departments of English must often have been a baffling and frustrating experience to the generations of students who have passed through them since the enlargement of universities after World War II. The secrets and rituals of the mysterious activity called literary criticism are certainly transmitted to honours students in their senior years, mainly because most honours students are favoured by staff resources and attention. For most pass students – let alone for non-university people – the mystery remains, as a kind of vague irritant.

The dominant assumptions of a department are usually presented to its students as if they are universal, as if all teachers in whatever area in all departments in all universities all over 'know' their subject in the same way. One sign of this is that departments, for example, of English or History, rarely offer to students in early years courses in theory or methodology which will raise basic questions about the variety and contingency of intellectual approaches; usually courses like this might be given only to fourth-year honours students.

All university departments of anything have their own distinctive character, though many might seem peculiarly characterless and ghostly, composed of staff who are noticed mainly as they disappear into their rooms, or nod at each other in corridors, or chat in the tea-room. Most teaching departments are not very interested in holding staff-postgraduate seminars, and even when they're held most staff don't turn up. Staff will publish for a variety of reasons, particularly in the competitive atmosphere created by demands for promotion,[1] but rarely acknowledge each other's work. (It's almost a convention that staff don't say to each other, Oh, I've seen your latest publication and it's very interesting and stimulating and sure to create a stir in Spenser or something studies.) Nevertheless, despite this fragmentation and the fleeting quality of personal relations in the corridors – and despite that other phenomenon, amazing mutual hatreds and hostilities between this or that staff member – departments usually (but not always) teach within a uniform conceptual framework, a common paradigm or problematic.

Sometimes, however, sharp intellectual rather than personal differences are present in departments, and students can be faced with choosing sides. The humanities faculty in the NSW Institute of Technology has been the arena of one such struggle, as was the Philosophy department at Sydney University. The Sydney English department in the early 1960s also saw remarkable scenes of internecine bitterness and hostility, made even more dramatic because one side was warring within itself while trying to ward off the common rival. An analysis of this struggle might help illuminate something of the mystery of English departments; for once, unstated assumptions were forced out into the cold fresh air. In any case, I was, as a nineteen-year-old student, caught up in it myself.

The Sydney English department troubles began when S. L. ('Sam') Goldberg came up from Melbourne University, with various trusted lieutenants, to become professor of English. Goldberg and his troops were followers of the English critic F. R. Leavis, himself given to vigorous public brawling, as in his famous controversy with C. P. Snow over the relative virtues of positivist science as against literary culture.

F. R. Leavis is undoubtedly a monumental figure in the development of 20th-century criticism. Born in 1895 in Cambridge, he became a teacher there, influencing many to take up his concerns and to shape themselves in his aggressive mould. In books like *New Bearings in English Poetry* (1932) and in essays in the journal *Scrutiny*, which Leavis edited from 1932 to 1953 – essays which later formed the basis of famous books like *The Common Pursuit*, *Revaluation*, and *The Great Tradition* – Leavis tried to redraw the maps of received criticism. On one front he took arms against an older conservative orthodoxy that was established at the universities in the 1920s and '30s, an orthodoxy that still favoured weakly sentimental verse of a late-Victorian cast. Instead Leavis pointed to the excitement of the new poetry of the age like that of Gerard Manley Hopkins, Ezra Pound, T. S. Eliot, and argued that its force and verve demanded new criteria and standards not only for 20th-century poetry, but for the whole development of English poetry since the 16th century. As Leavis acknowledged, he was in part applying the insights of T. S. Eliot's critical essays in *The Sacred Wood* (1920), particularly the stress on poetry as fusing intellect and emotion. Pre-19th-century poets like Donne and Marvell (the 'line of wit'), Dryden and Pope could now be restored, poets whose merits had been slighted by 19th-century critics like Matthew Arnold for being too rational or cerebral (an orthodoxy followed as well in Australia by critics like the *Bulletin*'s A. G. Stephens, as in his well-known judgement on the verse of Christopher Brennan that it was too much of the mind, too little of the heart).

In these terms Leavis can be seen as a courageous pioneer of modernism in university criticism, applied first to poetry then to the novel, as in Conrad, George Eliot, James, and Lawrence. Certainly he received little encouragement from the critical establishment he took on at the time. Academic preferment came niggardly in his direction, and his followers often had to pick up what must have seemed like minor posts in colonies on which the sun was setting fast – a vast diaspora of prickly Leavisites.

Leavis fought as well on another front, against the prevailing Marxist approaches to criticism and cultural history, in some ways, however, meeting Marxism on a common ground. Leavis and the Leavisites agreed with Marxism that a purely internal approach to literary criticism was not desirable – though such an approach was the staple of their teaching method – and produced their own kind of cultural history, one that brought into primary focus an apocalyptic concern for the plight of civilisation. Civilisation was being destroyed by industrialism and a narrow Benthamite utilitarian ethos, creating a debased 'mass civilisation' which only a dwindling 'minority culture' could do something about saving. Criticism, in departments of English, was the central agency of preservation. Critics could develop in themselves the values of responsiveness, vitality, fineness, intelligence, vigour, subtlety, and wit that are created in the best literature. At the same time they would need to have a scalpel-like sense of which literature and which criticism *don't* realize such values. How urgent, then, were the tasks of the true critics! How contemptible were those who were thwarting them! – who were indeed helping to hasten the decay of civilisation!

Given this sense of historical occasion, it's not difficult now to remember why Leavisism seemed so attractive over a decade-and-a-half ago. The doctrine gave a sense of great power and authority to being a critic. The critic was not a mere follower of writers, penning commentaries in their wake, nor but a writer manqué. Now the critic was taking the initiative by saving civilisation itself, keeping alive its traditions and vitalities. Again, Leavisism was a method and a vocabulary which offered keys to the understanding of all literature. The greats of literary history were no longer inaccessible; they were all available now for analysis and value-judgement. Henry James could be judged subtle and fine, but lacking – compared to George Eliot – in vigour. Leavisites were always constructing hierarchies, judging writers against an implicit scale of which writer maximised – 'realised' – which and how many possibilities of life, a calculus of possibilities which ranged from talismanic terms like fineness to vitality. Further, Leavisism allowed entry into analysis of poetry, that seemingly most opaque of literary arts. A poem had to be a unified whole; its explicit meanings, however, could be modified or contradicted by other elements in this whole, by its tone or rhythm. The explicit urgings of the poem might be embodied in weak or notional or unconvinced or febrile rhythms, so that its real meanings lay in those parts more forcibly or intensely created.

It certainly wasn't an unpleasant feeling to regard oneself as part of civilisation's needed creative minority. This kind of élitism gave Leavisites the confidence, if not outright arrogance, to decide on any literature that ever came before them, and on any other piece of criticism – or piece of critic – they felt was inadequate and so endangered the historical mission of criticism: not unlike the harshness with which many leftwing groups judge each other.

Many of the Leavisites were fervent students in their early twenties, and excited enough because some staff had bothered to get to know them, let alone invite them to join the chosen. This was a rare thing at Sydney University, traditionally remote toward its students, although the Andersonians are a major exception to this usual ghostly aloofness, and in this sense invite comparison with the Leavisites in terms of forming an active movement. Both movements felt empowered with an intellectual approach that could handle all areas of knowledge and life, and both thought their doctrine should also be a lifestyle, a single experience. Both were impatient and dismissive with disciplines not their own, considering that other disciplines were hardly worth thinking about. For each, philosophers and critics were kings.

Leavis's influence on his many admirers was not a simple one, and there could be different Leavisite strands and outposts, each equally truculent and all guns blazing. In his three to four years at Sydney University Professor Goldberg was opposed by various dissident Leavisites, mainly quite young staff and some students, who felt his peculiarly Melbourne stress on metaphysical rather than moral values was precious, that Goldberg liked James Joyce too much, that more tough-minded writers like Thomas Hardy should be made central, and so on. Goldberg's *Melbourne Critical Review* (to be changed to *The Critical Review*) was opposed by the dissident Leavisites in their own journals, like *Harpoon* and, later, *Chauntecleer*.

The young dissident Leavisites – lecturers like John Wiltshire and students like Terry Collits, Richard Nichols, and Tom Burvill – tended to group themselves around Howard Jacobson, the young lecturer who had come from Leavis's Cambridge college, Downing, and found himself in some bitter opposition to the Goldbergites; eventually he returned to Cambridge to sell things at the local market. A favourite term of this group was 'vulgar', which tended to be thrown at anything or anyone that moved. I recall a fourth-year seminar where we all had to read some Marx and Engels – a paragraph or two for close analysis from the *Communist Manifesto* – to decide on its literary and intellectual worth. Jacobson suddenly decided that Marx and Engels' prose lacked all merit – 'this is vulgar', he said. 'Look at it. It displays a second-rate sensibility', and who were these Marx and Engels to criticise the English aristocracy, like Disraeli, who, after all, was a lord. (Jacobson himself displayed a first-rate case of English nationalism and chauvinism, that Leavis shared in his relative lack of interest in Joyce and Yeats. Jacobson and those he spellbound were wont loudly to suspect anything not English: French, American, and Irish literatures were hardly worth glancing at. By contrast, the Goldbergites, while they'd made the pilgrimage to Cambridge, or Oxford, as in Goldberg's case, were more cosmopolitan and inclusive in their sense of the great tradition.)

Something in my family background, not uninfluenced by the *Communist Manifesto*, leapt out of me, and I protested about this dismissal in one word of writing which had changed the face of the world for over a century. I said it was superb writing – as it manifestly is – but Jacobson repeated the verdict, no it's vulgar. Then the discussion moved on to other passages from other writers up that day for judgement. The tiny incident is revealing both of the superlative narrowness and ignorance of traditional literary critics – Leavisites are hardly alone in this – but also of the way Leavisites focus on the moral (or metaphysical, as in the case of the Goldbergites) at the expense of the political realm and of political writing, of polemic and rhetoric. Suspicious of the political, they couldn't see that the *Manifesto* is everywhere alive with moral and metaphysical implications.

For the young Leavisites, dissident and non-dissident, these were heady days. The doctrine had to be lived. They were to foster complexity and vitality, both in seminar and extra-seminar discussion (seminars would often repair for tea and coffee after) and by non-university activities, for example, by imagining themselves like Birkin and Gerald in Lawrence's *Women in Love*, and having life-enhancing wrestling matches on the floor at parties. There was also a Leavisite wedding, where passages were read out from *Women in Love* – obviously a key text – and the young couple were left after to consummate their relationship in a way befitting the novel's chief characters. People fervently liked each other and just as fervently might distrust the sensibility of another in the various grouplets and fall out. All was intensity and tension.

At the same time the Leavisites as a whole clashed badly with the older Sydney members of the department. The élitism of the Leavisites blended in well with pre-existent Melbourne cultural traditions stressing the social function of knowledge and the educative role of intellectuals, the assumptions of a journal like *Meanjin*.[2] But these attitudes didn't go down at all well in Sydney when Professor Goldberg brought them along for display and dissemination. The older Sydney lot felt aggrieved at the confidence of the new group, and how, as they saw it, it was dominating key areas of teaching and making them marginal. They also felt that the Sydney English department had its own traditions, descending from former giants like Sir Mungo MacCallum and le Gay Brereton and Waldock, in 17th-century English studies and in Australian literature, which shouldn't be scorned. They also discovered that these Sydney traditions were wonderfully pluralist, and didn't allow of moralising and forcing people to accept great traditions and strict canons of literary worth. In their eyes, to relate literature to 'life' was importing non-literary (contextual) standards: criticism was rather a matter of describing strictly literary qualities, and everything that moved the Leavisites, they judged not to be literary and so no business of the critic. The Sydney critics historically aligned themselves with an unexalted empiricism and supposed high standards of scholarship. Their ideal critic was one who went to Oxford and collated a minor 17th-century text, or went to London University to study the concerns of a 19th-century novelist: but usually nothing spectacular, rarely any original theorising, since this would be rude in a colonial; the Sydney scholars were to help tidy up the margins of knowledge.

At the same time, in a journal like *Balcony*, which sprang into existence fully-armed in March 1965 to combat the Leavisites, the links between this kind of empiricism in Sydney literary criticism and Sydney philosophic traditions, were dusted and brought forward for use, especially Andersonian pluralism and its offshoot Libertarianism: in particular the Andersonian and Libertarian opposition to élites setting values for the rest of society, the sins of solidarism and moralism.

As it happened, the older Sydney members could muster more friends higher-up in the university power structure than the intruders from Melbourne. The English department split into Leavisite versus anti-Leavisite groups, and thence into offering alternative A and B courses to students.

The drama drew to a close, mainly because its chief player, Professor Goldberg, probably with some joy, took up a chair in the Melbourne English department; he and his lieutenants trooped back there. The strident young anti-Goldbergite Leavisites also took themselves off south, mainly to La Trobe, where they were to regroup, join hands with other non-Goldbergite Leavisites still in captivity in Sydney, and in 1970 begin to produce *Chauntecleer*, a journal which hoped to show that the correct Leavisite approach could cope with all the demands and challenges of the barbaric contemporary world in which they found themselves.

A little shaken, the Sydney English department resumed its time-honoured course. In terms of basic challenges to its ruling critical concepts, the Sydney department was probably more lastingly affected by the politicisation of intellectuals during the Vietnam War. Staff members like Stephen Knight, Michael Wilding, and Terry Sturm wanted to teach courses which try to discover the shaping effect of political and ideological assumptions on literature, though Knight and Wilding were also drawn by the strong pull of Sydney Libertarianism, which suspects any attempt at wideranging theories of being monistic.

I experienced these years of comedy and trauma personally, since I enrolled in the Sydney English department as an undergraduate in 1963, just as Professor Goldberg was beginning to compete for the hearts and minds of first-year students by introducing new courses and insisting on more frequent tutorials and close study of texts. I also became quite a fervent Leavisite, and in seminars would enter into the debates with whatever passion I could muster. I was so convinced that I followed Professor Goldberg to Australia's Leavisite heartland, the Melbourne English department.

This was a remarkable shock in every way. I was, undoubtedly, like all my kind, arrogant and abrasive, but I was also, to say the least, young, shy, naïve and socially inept. While I had been a Friday night drunk at various pubs for a number of years, including the Royal George, the site of the Sydney Push and various libertarian excitements, I had in fact lived the usual suburban student's life at home with my parents in Bondi. My mother deemed me so young that when I caught the Melbourne train she cried on the platform. In Melbourne, in Carlton, opposite the cemetery and in the shadow of the huge blocks of flats, I established a household with a fellow ex-Sydney postgraduate and Goldbergite. Here we tried to live, with rudimentary-to-nil notions of relating and housekeeping, and I could go from our semidetached, with dust ankledeep in the hallway, to the university, to begin an MA on T. S. Eliot's super-difficult *Four Quartets*, and to offer fine and subtle perceptions to my students in the part-time tutoring I was doing.

I found nothing in Melbourne's intellectual culture that was not alien. Everything seemed too genteel. Professor Goldberg and Jock Tomlinson and Maggie Tomlinson and the other Goldbergites (actually I'm not sure if there were any other Goldbergites) were certainly very kind; there was sherry most afternoons at five, where everyone seemed nervous and tense, although a courteous atmosphere reigned: I was struck by the men standing conspicuously for any woman who entered the room. There was University House, and a civilised lunch with members of the department, where everything they considered amusing, witty, funny, adroit, and droll I found dull and simple; everything they felt was a stimulating thing to say about literature I thought marginal and uninteresting. Further, the department, it didn't take long to realise, was fairly split (with one or two notable exceptions perhaps, like Chris Wallace-Crabbe) by an almost ethnic level of tension, between the Goldbergites and Professor Vincent Buckley and his followers, who were or wanted to be Irish, went in for creative writing, were interested in contemporary Australian and American poetry, and were very political in a kind of throwback Cold War way. The Goldbergites tended to be critics only, and felt that literature revealed truths far more important than the passing shows of politics.

The young Buckleyites also, I felt, quickly made it known that we young postgraduate boatpeople should have stayed in Sydney with the other battered (in so far as any Leavisite's confidence can be disturbed) remnants there of Goldberg's original landing party and colony. We were gross visitors to the higher south. It was criminal of Sam to bring us down; we should have been shoved off the fleeing ship.

Another shock was the discovery that departments of the same thing could have radically different teaching methods in different universities. One young Buckleyite postgraduate, almost shaking with the intensity of his calling, invited me to sit in on one of his tutorials, and unselfconsciously put on a most remarkably authoritarian performance as a teacher. He would commence a point, a statement, ask if anyone disagreed or had any problems with it, then make his next point, and so on. Teaching methods at Sydney University had been more Socratic, based on discussion.

Starting with incidents like these I soon began to swim in a deep pool of nostalgia and idealisation, for mother Sydney (or perhaps my Sydney mother). Its intellectual sub-cultures were refreshingly cynical – 'knew more about life' – I would bitterly feel, than all this self-proclaimed and slightly revolting high-minded intensity, this posturing and exhibition of sensibility.

By the end of the first year of my MA I was disillusioned with the Melbourne Leavisites, and in general in a bad way – altogether less than happy, getting very drunk too often, flaking on (disapproving) people's floors, fond of imagining suicide on a disused pier near where I was then living at Albert Park and finding in the most unlikely places lines about soft and easeful death, and given to rushing to Sydney during vacations to bore my Sydney friends silly by getting hopelessly drunk and claiming I was unintense and unhighminded and 'flexible' about all things. The terrors and fatuities of exile . . .

My friend and fellow Sydney exile Ian Lennie and I set to to try and work out the bases of the Leavisite scheme.[3] The whole project seemed based on close study of the inner workings of a text – 'practical criticism'. But that text was also alleged to represent something about the period or age it was written in: it might, like Marvell's witty verse, indicate the fineness of early seventeenth-century civilisation; or George Eliot or D. H. Lawrence might reveal persisting values and virtues in non-industrial rural English society. So that before you knew it the Leavisite critic was not talking about the text at all, but about something else – about qualities of vitality or energy or fineness which were held to characterise the best in an age's spirit. A disliked text, however, would show that a period or phase of society was but vulgar or thin or coarse. Texts became symptoms.[4]

The Leavisite analysis of a text, that is, was always dissolving into a version of cultural history and the evaluation of culture. It struck me as a theory very much influenced by an apocalyptic mood about the decline of civilisation, shared by Pound and Eliot and Yeats as well as by Leavis, a thought which I also tried to work out, in a rough and rudimentary way, looking back, in my MA thesis. The notion of a writer or work representing an age seemed the most absurd of all the Leavisite propositions. How could one writer or work represent a whole society? What of everything else that was happening in that society? In particular, because the Leavisites seemed habitually to idealise the past, what of all the features of pre-modern society that indicate social misery?

The notion of literature being an index of the quality of a period was also hopelessly circular. The critic perceives certain qualities in a work which reveal the essence of a society: we know the essence of a society because we can perceive it in the literary work. Left out of this equation is any actual historical knowledge, the remotest knowledge about the economic, political, and ideological modes of the society some such work was supposedly representing and illuminating. And the notion of a unified essential spirit of a culture or period also seemed hopeless. Why couldn't different works reveal quite different – perhaps contradictory – aspects of a culture?

Another thought was that the Leavisites tried to apply their terminology – stultifyingly repetitive as it was – to all literature. But terms like vitality and energy seemed very much rooted in the English romantic movement. The whole Leavisite project was based on assumptions which its practitioners showed every sign of not knowing were assumptions, believing them to be universally true. They were not only ignorant of history, but philosophically ignorant of themselves. They were unprepared to see their own critical concepts as themselves historically formed and contingent.

From all this I decided to become more and more historical in my own approach, to see literary criticism as well as literature as always part of broader contexts – of cultural history, the history of ideas, the impact of ideology. In particular I felt that 'tradition' was a necessary and crucial concept: you shouldn't, in analysing a work, go straight from the text to the society. Rather, you try to work out how a text is part of a certain tradition: for example, how the ruling ideas that structure Lawrence's fiction also belong to, are shaped by, the romantic tradition, with its stress on natural vitality (including sexuality), and its frequent identification of women with the natural world. One could then work out something of why romanticism was so attractive a tradition – for example, in its anti-industrialism – and how particular writers were always altering and reshaping this tradition in response to contemporary situations through which they were living.

In this way I was regaining contact with an inherited Marxism, while wishing to retain the strength of the Leavisite critical method. An original attraction of the Leavisite approach was that it promised to make available what Marxists so far had been unable to provide – at least in so far as I'd perceived Marxist attempts at aesthetics in the communist tradition. Leavisites could analyse (it appeared) the details and detailed movement of a text, its very tone and rhythm, its ironies and ambiguities and the way it functioned as a self-sufficient whole. In particular, Leavisites were very good (it seemed) at analysing poetry – while Marxists are usually fairly hopeless at poetry and tend to race to the novel or drama for analysis and as the basis for their generalisations.

So that when I arrived back in Sydney in the summer of 1968-69, I wasn't too shattered, the pieces were coming together again. I took up residence (shared a house) in Balmain and pondered on the whole Leavisite episode, which now seemed a very contradictory experience. I'd worked through from the Leavisite position to my own approach (text-based and contextual), and could now try and apply it to the predominant challenges of Sydney intellectual life: the Libertarianism (and behind it, Andersonianism) of many of my drinking companions at the Forth and Clyde in Balmain and the Newcastle near the Quay; the development of the counter-culture, drawing upon the romantic tradition for key notions, like closeness to nature and natural instincts and feelings, dislike of rationalism and utilitarianism, interest in subconscious states; and the theories associated with the new liberation movements that sprang up during the Vietnam War. The Leavisite experience had been the Oedipal stage, but the later Vietnam War years provided the real intellectual apprenticeship.

To go ahead and implement my new approach, however, I had to learn one thing the Leavisites neglected to teach, that is, methods of research. Why do research when it was exhausting enough responding to a text with all your sensitivities and intelligence at full bore? My friend Ann Curthoys was invaluable here; as an historian she was puzzled and pained by my lack of even the most rudimentary skills at research, and had almost to take me by the hand and show me around Mitchell Library. A typical conversation.

'Do you know how to take proper notes?'

'Yes, of course I do . . . Well, what do you mean, proper notes.'

'Proper notes. You know, take notes of what you're reading.'

'Yes, well of course I know that.'

(Jesus. Gulp. Sounds like hard work. Why don't I stay a Leavisite.)

'Do you know how to use a card system?'

'Yeah. Bibliography cards.'

'No. A proper card system.'

'No I don't.'

(Hate getting grilled.)

'Jesus. What do you bloody critics do?'

(What is all this. Wouldn't know real research if he fell over it. Probably just bloody lazy. Moron literary critic.)

One conviction I did bring away from life and fanciful death in the unsunny south was how different were the intellectual cultures of Melbourne and Sydney. I didn't think too coherently about this difference until I began giving tutorials in Australian literature at Macquarie University. For the session on Kenneth Slessor I read his prose essays, and was struck by the similarities between the social and political theory of Norman Lindsay as Slessor describes it, and the theories of the Sydney Libertarians whom I'd got to know at the Forth and Clyde and the Newcastle: and how different again was this kind of social thought from Melbourne intellectual traditions. I wrote an article comparing Lindsay's and the Libertarians' thought, but neither *Australian Literary Studies* nor *Politics* felt able to chance either the politics or literary side of it, and it was then that it was suggested to me that I should write what became *Australian Cultural Elites* as the only way of developing the argument in the one place. It would also give me room to develop ideas and approaches suggested by the whole problem of Sydney/Melbourne differences, in particular, that these differences, while not blanket, were so sharp that all the cultural history that usually went on as if you could talk about all Australian culture in one breath was nonsensical. Australian culture was *not* unified, it displayed conflict and diversity that had to be explained in part by the different histories of its two major cities. There was, I thought, a general principle here also: that culture is always a drama, a drama of differences, conflicts, contradictions, tensions, antagonisms.

In 1972 I resigned from Macquarie University to write *Australian Cultural Elites*. A brilliant career was behind me.

# 1
# The Australian Background[1]

In Australian cultural criticism the radical nationalists are the most influential school of 'contextualists'. These people – writers, historians, and critics including Nettie Palmer, Vance Palmer, A. A. Phillips, Stephen Murray-Smith, Ian Turner, Russel Ward, Geoffrey Serle – have been influential both because they have so often been felt to be persuasive, and because they have so often been opposed by alternative – especially Leavisite and New Critical – accounts.

They have consistently occupied the radical end of the wider pioneer legend of which their thinking is a variant.[2] Where at its conservative end the pioneer legend can celebrate rural values of the squatter or individualistic small farmer kind, the radical nationalists have upheld the lower-class experience of outback itinerant workers as the basis of the national character or mystique, to use Russel Ward's term. Ward's 'typical Australian' is eloquently evoked in the first few pages of *The Australian Legend* – stoical, sceptical, independent, against affectation, concerned for his mates, a rolling stone without the impediments of a family.

According to the myth the 'typical Australian' is a practical man, rough and ready in his manners and quick to decry any appearance of affectation in others. He is a great improviser ever willing 'to have a go' at anything, but willing too to be content with a task done in a way that is 'near enough'. Though capable of great exertion in an emergency, he normally feels no impulse to work hard without good cause. He swears hard and consistently, gambles heavily and often, and drinks deeply on occasion. Though he is 'the world's best confidence man', he is usually taciturn rather than talkative, one who endures stoically rather than one who acts busily. He is a 'hard case', sceptical about the value of religion and of intellectual and cultural pursuits generally. He believes that Jack is not only as good as his master but, at least in principle, probably a good deal better, and so he is a great 'knocker' of eminent people unless, as in the case of his sporting heroes, they are distinguished by physical prowess. He is a fiercely independent person who hates officiousness and authority, especially when these qualities are embodied in military officers and policemen. Yet he is very hospitable and, above all, will stick to his mates through thick and thin, even if he thinks they may be in the wrong. No epithet in his vocabulary is more completely damning than 'scab', unless it be 'pimp' used in its peculiarly Australasian slang meaning of 'informer'. He tends to be a rolling stone, highly suspect if he should chance to gather much moss.[3]

That such a figure is typical may seem very suspect now, given the perspectives of the Vietnam War and the liberation movements. How can such a 'typical Australian', who is male, speak to the women of Australian society? Indeed, in its notion of men as rolling stones, doesn't it set up a dream and desire of escape from family life as such, a primary focus of women's historical experience? How can an ideal type forged in the 19th century act as an ideal type for postwar Australia's ethnically diverse population?

The radical nationalists have been and remain, however, very important in their varied contributions to Australian literature, historical writing, historiography, cultural history, and in journals like *Meanjin* and *Overland*. Certainly in their accounts of Australian literary history they have dared to be adventurous and grasp at overall interpretations where conventional critics have often appeared cautious and inturned. Their ideas must initially be understood as a distinctively Australian variant of 'historicism'; before outlining the key assertions of the radical nationalist view, then, an excursion into 19th- and 20th-century European historicist ideas is necessary, as well as discussion of some pre-1950s cultural theories concerning Aborigines.

## Historicism

In brief, the 'historicist' view is against general laws of social development for all societies. Rather, the individuality or distinctiveness or uniqueness of a culture is stressed. This distinctiveness is usually sought in organic connections between a specific culture, language, and a natural environment. Such an organic connection is often expressed in a 'folk' substratum, which is seen as subsisting and developing most strongly in a rural setting: a rural society is the repository or guarantee of myths, legends, lore, and folk poetry, oral traditions which have grown in long and close association with a particular natural environment. An urban setting, however, tends to a kind of cultural impersonality, encouraging a cosmopolitanism and over-sophistication which destroy a people's individuality. Cities tend to be the same everywhere – only rural environments provide a culture's necessary distinctiveness or uniqueness.

This usage of 'historicism' is taken from writers like Georg Iggers, *The German Conception of History* (1968), and in particular René Wellek in his essay 'Carlyle and the Philosophy of History' in *Confrontations* (1965). It has been occasionally claimed, including by Iggers, that this particular version of historicism is a phenomenon peculiar to German intellectual history. But its ancestry is much more widespread, beginning with French, German, Italian, English and Scottish writers in the 18th century, amongst figures as diverse as Vico, Warton, and Southey. It did flourish in German historical thought from Herder and Goethe through the German romantics like Novalis to Ranke and beyond; but it was also heavily influential in most European countries in the 19th century, a major figure in England, for instance, being Carlyle.[4]

Historicism is not necessarily or inherently nationalist or internationalist, racist or anti-racist. The concern for the culturally distinctive may lead to a preference for cultural variety and so a clearly internationalist stand. Later in the 19th century William Morris's utopian novel *News from Nowhere*, for example, is clearly influenced by historicist concepts of historical periods and change, and of the value of closeness to a natural environment, with a corresponding suspicion of large cities and an exclusively urban existence. The novel prizes the cultural diversity of different local communities: but at no stage does *News from Nowhere* suggest that any one community and culture is superior to others.

It was Herder, however, who made the fateful and in many ways – nazism included among them – disastrous connection between a specific culture, a specific language, and a specific nation and race.[5] This aspect of historicist thought, from Herder on, bred theories which explained differences in language and culture in terms of differences in racial origin. It spawned theories of the differences between northern and southern Europe, as in Madame de Staël's *On Germany* and Ruskin's essay 'The Nature of Gothic', that northern Europeans (designated as Teutonic or Nordic) were hardy, adventurous, inventive and imaginative, while southern Europeans, lolling in the sun below the Alps, were languorous and idle, and given to notions of a closed perfection which stifled further creativity. In response, Matthew Arnold in his *On the Study of Celtic Literature* (1867), defended the Celtic spirit as against the superiority of the Teutonic, a defence which was later very important in the Celtic Twilight and Irish literary nationalism, movements in turn which were influential on Australian cultural theorists and practitioners like Vance Palmer and Louis Esson. Ethnic terms such as the Celtic, the Nordic, the Teutonic, the Hebraic, were assumed to have high explanatory value in terms of social and cultural differences. A further development later in the 19th century and well into the 20th century, was the interest in heredity and eugenics, in figures like Galton and Karl Pearson, with their concern for the quality of a racial stock, a quality, it was often thought, that could be maintained only in rural areas, not in the cities. Here various anti-urban strands of historicism and of romanticism fuse closely together, in a view of the cities as necessarily corrupting the fibre of a race, producing a physically and spiritually debilitated people.

This kind of historicism also involved theories of evolution and historical periodicity. Societies evolve, but in no clear or predictable way, and the historicist view doesn't assume that history is unending, gradual progress. On the contrary, historical evolution is unpredictable and instead of a steady progression often reveals, in René Wellek's words, 'a dynamic evolution of alternating periods',[6] a view of history found in writers as varied as Warton, Herder, Goethe, Novalis, Southey, and Hazlitt. In this view, history is a story of alternating periods or epochs, like an age of belief followed by an age of unbelief, or an age of faith followed by an age of denial or scepticism, or an age of imagination followed by an age of reason. An associated view is that each new period comes in via a rebirth, a rebirth that could be painful and enacted in an historical moment of conflict and struggle, in a reversal of a previous period's guiding *Geist* or spirit. This could lead to an apocalyptic view of history: a society was either sunk in a particular spirit of, say, scepticism and disbelief, or on the verge of cataclysmic rebirth into a new spirit of, say, faith or imagination.

A theoretical consequence of the historicist view is that an age or epoch or period is seen as possessing an essential spirit, so that each period of a nation's life has also a unified 'national physiognomy' and national character. Wellek writes that probably Carlyle's most influential pronouncement (in a view largely derived from Herder's literary nationalism), lies in his advocacy of literary history as the history of the national mind. To discover the literary essence of a period, Carlyle argues,[7] is to discover that period's leading spiritual tendency – a view that was pursued enthusiastically later in the 19th century in England and which leads directly to the stance of modern critics like Eliot, Pound, and Leavis that literature is a revelation of a society's general state of vitality or decay.

## Australian versions of historicism

Important strands of Australian literature and literary criticism can be seen as particular interpretations of all or some of these elements of European historicism in terms of Australia's specific experience and history as a colony and ex-colony. An early and remarkably clear statement of historicist attitudes in the 19th century can be found in Marcus Clarke's 1876 preface to Adam Lindsay Gordon's poems. Clarke is claiming to offer a response to the Australian mountains. He writes that the dominant note of Australian scenery is Weird Melancholy. The Australian mountain forests strike us, Clarke says, as 'funereal, secret, stern. Their solitude is desolation. They seem to stifle, in their black gorges, a story of sullen despair.' Where in 'historic Europe' every bit of ground is happily hallowed in legend and song, and the soul among sylvan scenes is soothed and satisfied, in Australia, 'placed before the frightful grandeur of these barren hills, it drinks in their sentiment of defiant ferocity, and is steeped in bitterness'.

This may appear as the expression of a bruised sensibility in an alien to our shores, the cry of the permanent émigré unable to adapt to and put down roots in Australia's natural environment. Yet Clarke ends his famous preface on a more optimistic note, an optimism based on a belief in historicist doctrine. Every continent, Europe, Asia, America, Africa, Clarke argues, has its distinctive natural environment and so its distinctive cultural spirit. Just so, the interior of the Australian continent will be the cradle of a distinctive consciousness. 'In Australia alone', writes Clarke, 'is to be found the Grotesque, the Weird, the strange scribblings of nature learning how to write.' For the dweller in the wilderness, the 'phantasmagoria of that wild dream-land termed the Bush interprets itself, and the Poet of our desolation begins to comprehend why free Esau loved his heritage of desert sand better than all the bountiful richness of Egypt.' [8]

Interestingly, A. D. Hope's early and curiously anti-neocolonialist poem 'Australia' (1939) follows the argument and language of Clarke's preface very closely. The poem opens by describing Australia as 'A Nation of trees, drab green and desolate grey', which darken her 'hills, those endless, out-stretched paws of Sphinx demolished or stone lion worn away'. Like Clarke, Hope appears to find the Australian interior hopelessly depressing, 'the last of lands, the emptiest'. Yet like Clarke again, Hope ends his poem on an optimistic and historicist note:

Yet there are some like me turn gladly home
From the lush jungle of modern thought, to find
The Arabian desert of the human mind . . .

Like Clarke's feeling about Esau's heritage of desert sand, the Australian interior will yield a new, distinctive, national 'spirit' which will mark it off from the spirit of European 'civilisation'.

An historicist – and romantic – assumption shared by Clarke in his preface and Hope in this poem is that it is outside the cities that a true creative spirit of a national culture is nurtured. Hope refers scathingly to Australia's 'five cities, like five teeming sores', and both Hope and Clarke write as if it is the unique natural world of Australia itself – the 'savage and scarlet as no green hills dare', the 'strange scribblings of nature learning how to write' – which will yield Australia's unique cultural identity.

Hostility to the cities, in which historicism and romanticism fuse, has been and remains a very influential attitude in Australian literary practice and cultural theory. The view that the true national spirit and true national character will be fostered in the unique natural world of the Australian interior, away from the corrupting and suffocating reach of the cities, is present, for example, in many statements made by A. G. Stephens as editor of his reviews journal the *Bookfellow*. Stephens argued (from the conservative end of the pioneer legend) that Australia urgently needs British racial stock to people its rural areas and so build up its national fibre – a kind of rural eugenics.[9]

Hostility to the cities is not confined to any one political view, conservative, liberal, or socialist. Such hostility can be seen in an unfortunately little-known utopian novel by S. A. Rosa called *The Coming Terror, or the Australian Revolution* (1894), a work clearly influenced by the American Ignatius Donnelly's *Caesar's Column*. Rosa belonged to the Australian Socialist League, an off-spring of William Morris's English Socialist League, and in the novel he toys with ideas drawn variously from Morris's communitarian anarchist views and from opposing state socialist concepts. In Rosa's utopian vision, Australia will experience radical rural reforms, with land leased out by the state and people urged to 'earn their living from Mother Earth without crowding into the already over-populated cities'. A character, the lost explorer Dr Leichhardt, later refers to the cities as those 'coast settlements' which are 'evil, corrupt, and the abode of all forms of cruelty and fraud'.[10]

The historicist and romantic idea of rural life or the natural world as the only possible site of perfectible human relationships also pervades the popular poetry of A. B. Paterson, and of C. J. Dennis in *The Sentimental Bloke*. The same idea pervades the works of novelists like K. S. Prichard, Vance Palmer, and Patrick White, involving a dislike of cities and suburbia, and a vision of organic oneness with the natural world as central to individual and perhaps social fulfilment. (Such a promotion invites a critique from writers who question whether actual social conditions in the Australian countryside can sustain pro-rural idealisation and exhortation. This kind of questioning and critique – if often very ambivalently – can be seen in writers as various as Henry Lawson, Barbara Baynton, Miles Franklin, Joseph Furphy, and Steele Rudd, each of whom sought to focus on what they saw as the realities ignored by the myth. Lawson and Paterson quarrelled over rural realities versus idealisation in the *Bulletin* in the early 1890s.)

A major concern of historicist thought in Australia has been to work out how, in this new continent, the desired unity between the evolving culture and the natural environment can be created and developed. In a great deal of British historicist and romantic thought of the 19th and 20th centuries the problem was not so much the creation of this unity but of bemoaning its continuing decline: industrial society and the evils of urbanisation were destroying the culture-nature harmony that once led so vigorous a life in pre-capitalist, pre-industrial England. A frequent answer was medievalism, an answer common to thinkers as varied as Cobbett, Carlyle, Ruskin, and William Morris, which extended its reach into the 20th century in the cultural theories of Pound and Eliot. F. R. Leavis obeys an impulse similar to medievalism in searching for community and forms of spirit in 19th- and 20th-century English society that persist outside of the devastation wrought by industrialism.

In Australia the answer frequently has been to look to Aboriginal society as an example of *Gemeinschaft*, a community which has successfully adapted to Australian nature, an organic adaptation revealed in its life of myth and legend. The Jindyworobaks in the late 1930s and 1940s are an interesting case: their poetry almost seems to offer itself as too purely a doctrinal expression of the historicist paradigm. It's heartening, however, to see the revival of interest in the Jindyworobaks in recent years, an interest prompted in part by the upsurge of Aboriginal protest along with other protest movements following the Vietnam War.[11] In a newspaper review of the 1977 *Meanjin* Aboriginal issue Roland Robinson, describing himself as 'the last of the tribe of Jindyworobaks', welcomes the new interest in Aboriginal society. 'It is obvious', Robinson writes, 'that a source of culture and wisdom thousands of years old is at last influencing and enriching the arts in Australia', and he reports that in conversation Aboriginal poet Kath Walker agreed with him that white people were coming to see, 'in the security of the tribal Aborigines' culture, social structure, ecology and non-materialistic values, the answers to predicaments the civilised world faces . . .'[12]

Apart from the Jindyworobaks, the interest in Aboriginal society as expressing a nature-culture harmony is a persistent theme in writers like Vance Palmer, Katharine Susannah Prichard, Xavier Herbert, Judith Wright, and Patrick White. Such a persisting concern can be seen as an Australian intellectual tradition structurally similar or homologous to the British medievalist tradition.

## Modernism and primitivism

Further, in the 1920s, '30s, and '40s – a period whose conflicts and drama served as spur or animus to cultural theorists in the 1950s and '60s – we can notice an interlinked interest in the meanings of Aboriginal community and culture between writers, anthropologists, and artists. In *The Timeless Land* (1941) Eleanor Dark acknowledges a debt to professional anthropologists like Herbert Basedow, A. P. Elkin, and Phyllis Kaberry, as well as to Mary Gilmore and Daisy Bates, while Katharine Susannah Prichard in the foreword to *Coonardoo* (1929) also refers to Basedow's work. The Jindyworobak movement was based on Adelaide figures like Rex Ingamells, who was influenced by the rightwing nationalism of P. R. Stephensen's *The Foundations of Culture in Australia* (1935), as well as by the Aboriginal stories told by James Devaney in *The Vanished Tribes* (1929).[13] The Jindyworobaks were a prolific movement in Australian verse, and widely supported outside of Adelaide by writers and critics, as is clear from the many tributes to their success in the birthday issue of the *Jindyworobak Review 1938-1948*. And for this issue the artist Margaret Preston – whose work was exhibited in the Art Gallery of NSW in September 1980, at the same time as the ABC was screening *The Timeless Land* – did the cover, with an Aboriginal-influenced design, as well as contributing a congratulatory note 'On the Birthday of Jindyworobak'.[14] Preston also contributed a chapter to *Cultural Cross-Section* (edited by John Ingamells), one of the Jindyworobak volumes slammed by A. D. Hope as boy scoutish in his notorious review in 1941 in the new Sydney journal, *Southerly*.

Recent research prompted by the feminist movement of the 1970s has drawn attention to the strong presence of female writers and artists in the *entre deux guerres* period,[15] so it perhaps doesn't surprise that such women, asserting their own experience, should also be concerned for the identity and value of the cultures of other oppressed groups. In his *Literature and the Aborigine in Australia 1770-1975* (1978) J. J. Healey argues that the first quarter of the new century saw little interest in Aborigines in Australian literature compared to the fascination in 19th-century writers like Tucker, Mrs Praed, Harpur, and Boldrewood. Such fascination resurfaced dramatically, however, with the publication in 1929 of Prichard's *Coonardoo*, stimulating what became a flood of literary interest, in Xavier Herbert, James Devaney, Mary Gilmore, William Hatfield, Eleanor Dark, and Henrietta Drake-Brockman.[16]

Prichard's pioneering rediscovery of an Aboriginal theme for 20th-century Australian literature was stimulated by her contact with the Ngarlawongga people in 1926,[17] about the same time as Margaret Preston was revealing a pioneering interest in Aboriginal art. *Coonardoo* was the exciting work of a young and till then relatively unknown novelist. Margaret Preston, born in 1875, was by the 1920s well-known and well-respected, with a special number of *Art in Australia* devoted to her work in 1927. Her new Aboriginal interest represented, according to Bernard Smith in *Place, Taste, and Tradition*, a third phase of her career.[18]

Preston felt that her call for the relevance of Aboriginal art to modern design was such a departure that it needed careful explaining. This she did in an article in *Art in Australia* in 1925, 'The

Indigenous Art of Australia'. The editors of *Art in Australia*, Sydney Ure Smith and Leon Gellert, also felt it required comment. 'Much interest has been displayed,' they told their readers, 'in Mrs Margaret Preston's brilliantly successful application of Australian aboriginal art to modern designing.' Mrs Preston is the 'first artist to make the art of the Australian aboriginal a serious study, and already her knowledge and enthusiasm have seriously infected designers who have been struggling unsuccessfully to develop a distinctive national type of design'.[19]

Preston reminded her readers that 'primitivism' was a very strong movement in modern art, in the way, for example, that European artists in general draw on Javanese culture, that French sculpture has gained new life from the 'primitive natural forms' of Cochin China, and that art in Germany has renewed itself by recourse to its own peasant culture as well as to the 'native crafts' of Central Africa. 'Therefore', she explained, 'I feel no loss of dignity in studying and applying myself to the art of the aboriginals of Australia.'[20]

In this 1925 opening shot Preston felt that the indigenous culture shouldn't be merely economically exploited, that our 'relation and most intimate connection with our aboriginal art is almost mystic and religious more than merely commercial and industrial'. The editors of *Art in Australia*, however, wished to combine the two interests and activities. Introducing an issue in 1930 they saw, in a blinding moment of vision, the 'establishment of an Australian school of design, a school whose business it would be to train students to design the rugs and furniture, the cups and saucers and plates, the wallpapers, the textiles, everything in daily use. The possibilities are infinite and the establishment of great industries implied . . .' An admirable director of this school of design was at hand, they felt, in Mrs Preston, 'for besides being a designer of distinction and capable of original research, she is also qualified in the practical side of several crafts'.[21]

Preston's changing and varying commitments to Aboriginal art was lifelong, extending into the 1940s and '50s, as is clear from the paintings assembled in the 1980 exhibition. In an essay in the Jindyworobak collection *Cultural Cross-Section* which drew down upon it the wrathful Hope, Preston divided Australian artists into two broad groups, those who were experimental and innovative, and those who were 'non-inventive' and dwelling happily in the 'prison of traditionalism'. The principal need was to break away from academicism. 'Some artists have gone in the direction of geometry; others in the way of symbolism, and others are searching for new forms for a new country.' The work of these 'moderns' has affinities with and draws on modern European art, not least in their desire to 'base their art from the aspect of the Aboriginal art of Australia'.[22]

About the same time Preston was arguing, with a touch of Ruskin and William Morris, that Aboriginal art work 'never aims at perfection, but only a semblance of it'. Their drawings and rock carvings are a 'truthful art; they are realism in a wider sense than that recognized by European art'; they are in fact 'either hyper-realistic, naturalistic or symbolical'.[23] Such study of Aboriginal art contains, she felt, 'limitless possibilities for the artist'. The 'symbolism expressed through its tribal totems opens up a new world' – a reference which continues from her position in 1925 that totemism is 'one of the origins of art'. Aboriginal-influenced art, then, should not be tied to narrow ideas of time and place as in conventional western art; it can be abstract, geometric, symbolic, hyper-realistic, naturalistic, witty (the 1925 essay refers to 'some very amusing drawings' from north-west Australia).

We don't have to accept the Aboriginal theme in 1930s and '40s literature and art uncritically. The attraction for a start of Jindyworobaks like Rex Ingamells to P. R. Stephensen's conservative nationalism is hardly appealing. Nor were the Jindyworobaks uncriticised at the time. Hope's joke about the Jindies as the boy scout school of Australian poetry was coupled with an insistence on the European character of Australian culture: 'We have created a new European country in Australia and we belong to the European nations even though we do not live in Europe.'

Hope also chides Victor Kennedy, another contributor to the Jindyworobak cause. Kennedy had argued that our poets too often write as if they were still living in England and hence in a secondhand, imitative way. For the majority of Australians, Hope replies, the 'point of view and culture of the aboriginal is still more alien and remote', and the poet who tries to write 'like a second-hand abo' is no more likely to produce sincere work than the poet who writes like a secondhand Englishman.[24]

Yet Hope had not always seen the relationship between European and Australian cultural forms as simply and unproblematically as this. We have already observed that Hope's well-known pre-World War II poem 'Australia' ably illustrates the historicist idea of every society having a distinctive culture, based not on urban life but on its specific natural environment:

And her five cities, like five teeming sores,
Each drains her: a vast parasite robber-state
Where second-hand Europeans pullulate
Timidly on the edge of alien shores.

Yet there are some like me turn gladly home
From the lush jungle of modern thought, to find
The Arabian desert of the human mind,
Hoping, if still from deserts the prophets come,

Such savage and scarlet as no green hills dare
Springs in that waste, some spirit which escapes
The learned doubt, the chatter of cultured apes
Which is called civilization over there.

'Australia' is a 1939 poem, and we could be excused for wondering if the 'there are some like me' was referring to the Jindyworobaks, who were going strongly at the time.

In any case the Jindyworobaks, as we've seen, can be located in that Australian historicist tradition which also spawned the radical nationalists, one of whom, Geoffrey Serle, was later to use part of a line from Hope's 'Australia' for the title of his cultural history work *From Deserts the Prophets Come*. Perhaps Hope in his jibing review wished to sever any thought of so close an association with the Jindyworobaks and with literary nationalism that 'Australia' might have been implying. Hope's cultural attitudes seem very uncertain and shifting in the years of the late 1930s and early '40s, ranging from the, in effect, pro-Jindyworobak stress on Australian nature as renewing in this 1939 poem, to the pessimism about relationships with anyone or anything in 'The Wandering Islands' in 1943, to 'The Gateway' a year earlier, with its simple affirmation of woman as symbolic of the earth. It is the strand of 'The Gateway' which, I argued in *Australian Cultural Elites*, becomes predominant later, and leads to a stress on European symbolic forms that dramatise woman as the universe and man's desire to achieve transcendence in sexuality.

Further, the Jindyworobaks were criticised from the left in the middle 1940s by Bernard Smith in his *Place, Taste, and Tradition*, where he attempts a Marxist history of Australian art. Discussing how Aboriginal art might prove influential in Australian culture, Smith expresses dislike for the 'neo-Rousseauan romanticism common to the Jindyworobaks', which sees the Aboriginal as an 'idealised figure symbolic of the perfect cultural amity of man and environment'. Smith feels that the most pressing task is to arrest the extermination by 'our own predatory culture' of Aboriginal society, and he contrasts the Jindyworobak attitude unfavourably with the work of Vladimir Bergner, a young east European and a member of the Melbourne realist group along with Noel Counihan. 'For the first time in our history,' Smith argues of a series of paintings by Bergner in 1943 depicting Aborigines as suffering and oppressed, 'the aborigine has been painted realistically.'

Perhaps surprisingly, Bernard Smith doesn't aim and fire this realist criterion at Margaret Preston's work, nor does he question her association with the Jindyworobaks. Rather he writes approvingly that her interest in the application of Aboriginal art might prove to be a valuable strand in a truly Australian art, and he points out that her primitivism is an aspect of modernism as an international movement, citing the way modern American artists are interested in adapting Indian art forms.[25]

From the perspectives of the anti-racist thinking and movements of the 1970s and '80s, we might direct another criticism at writers and artists like Prichard and Preston, precisely at the point where their work seems most strong, admirable, and innovatory: their racial attitudes themselves, and contributing to these, their romanticism and evolutionism. These attitudes have to be related to the broader cultural context of the 1920s and '30s.

In the middle of 1980 a controversy blew up about the Aboriginal cartoons of Eric Jolliffe, in particular a cartoon of his depicting a young Aboriginal woman, who'd been given a bra and had placed it around her bum. The drawing presumably wished to show the woman as part of nature because Aboriginal, and hence as cheer-fully impervious to and free from the repression and conven-tionality of white civilisation as represented in the scanted gar-ment. The cartoon was seen as embarrassingly and culpably racist, including by an Aboriginal who wrote to the *Sydney Morning Herald* about it.

Jolliffe did, however, find a defender. In a letter to the *Herald* George Blaikie said he was puzzled by the charge of racism, since he'd always considered Jolliffe as anti-racist and extremely sym-pathetic to Aborigines. Blaikie pointed out that before Jolliffe's car-toons in the 1930s the ruling cartoon stereotype was 'The Smith's Weekly Abo'. In *Smith's Weekly* their cartoonist Stan Cross specialised (Blaikie said) in Jacky-Jacky jokes, where the 'Smith's Weekly Abo' was promoted as a bare-footed, flat-faced moron, clad in discarded white man's clothes. Jacky's wife was seen as a fly-bitten trollop in sorry shift and wrinkled stockings.

Jolliffe, an Englishman, had decided to challenge this stereotype. Cleverly, says Blaikie, Jolliffe took the comic concept of the Abor-iginal back to the native state: 'Off with the ragged clothes and away with the flies. Black girls became as beautiful as white models. Black men became athletic hunters with a sharp sense of humour.' Blaikie writes that among those who cheered Jolliffe in his one-man crusade were Kenneth Slessor, Lennie Lower, A. P. Elkin, and Bill Harney, and he unhappily concludes that if Jolliffe now abandons, because of these recent accusations, his 'life's work aimed at improving the image of "the noble Australian savage", then the Australian Aboriginal will have lost one of the best friends he ever had'.[26]

Whatever Jolliffe looks like in the 1980s, then, we can probably see his work as part of the broad stream of cultural attitudes from the 1920s on that includes Prichard and Preston and that sets out to rescue Aborigines from imprisonment in an image of squalor which is their own uncivilised fault. Instead, in a romantic way, the image is reversed. White civilisation is perceived as thin and artificial because it has lost touch with the vitality of the natural world, a vitality enjoyed by and symbolised in the noble Australian 'primitive'.

This kind of reading of Aboriginal life, heavily influenced by the kind of romantic assumptions about nature, sexuality, and modern society that we can see in D. H. Lawrence, is certainly present in Prichard's *Coonardoo*, and not least in its central figure. Coonardoo resides with her people on a station owned by Mrs Bessie and her son Hugh in the remote nor'-west of Australia. Her name itself ('the dark well, or the well in the shadows') symbolises water, fertility, the deep springs of life. She and Hugh grow up together as playmates, but on reaching manhood he acquires habits of solitude and a non-communicative independence: 'he had closed in on himself as most men of the country do'. Coonardoo, meanwhile, is also growing up and passes through a *rite de passage* to womanhood, a rite which Mrs Bessie realises is something 'impersonal, universal, of a religious mysticism' – the veneration which every Aboriginal woman, in her rhythmic closeness to the earth, has of 'the principle of creation, fertility, growth'. But while tied to the customs of her own people and become 'one of Warieda's women', Coonardoo would also like to be 'Hugh's woman': 'She, Coonardoo, had thought any girl would be proud and very pleased for Hugh to take her.'

As it turns out, this only happens once. Mrs Bessie had just died, and the Aborigines on the station wailed for her the day long, Coonardoo and the other women crying, sobbing, and beating their breasts with sharp stones. In his distress and bewilderment at his mother's death, Hugh finds himself drawing close to Coonardoo as he had when they were children playing together. Out mustering together – for Coonardoo is, like Mrs Bessie was, an excellent rider and works with the men – Coonardoo 'was like his own soul riding there, dark, passionate and childlike'. Resting at night, Hugh calls to Coonardoo, and she kneels beside him, 'her eyes the fathomless shining of a well in the shadows'. Hugh takes her in his arms. 'Deep inexplicable currents of his being flowed towards her', and he gives himself to the 'spirit which drew him, from a great distance it seemed, to the common source which was his life and Coonardoo's'.

The tragedy the novel sets out to dramatise is that Hugh won't fully give himself to Coonardoo, and so live in organic oneness with the surrounding earth, making whole his instincts and his consciousness. Generally Hugh resents the 'secret understanding' between himself and Coonardoo from their childhood; to his adult eyes his regard for her is but a relic of that long ago growing up together, and his present admiration of her riding skills: 'Every finer, less reasonable instinct he had stamped on, kicked out of his consciousness.'

Hugh marries Mollie, a European woman from the south, but Mollie with her conventional civilised notions is essentially alien to the land and being of the Nor'-West. He remains trapped in his isolated self, and in this environment that is death to the spirit. As the novel says, in language that curiously recalls both D. H. Lawrence and Norman Lindsay (although for Lindsay sexuality should embody not unity with Australia's natural environment but symbolic values of life and beauty which give the artist or other élite being momentary access to a higher and eternal consciousness) as well as looking forward to Patrick White:

. . . here in a country of endless horizons, limitless sky shells, to live within yourself was to decompose internally. You had to keep in the life flow of the country to survive. You had to be with it, and of it, in order to work, move as it did. After all what was this impulse of man to woman, woman to man, but the law of growth moving within them? How could a man stand still, sterilize himself in a land where drought and sterility were hell? Growth, the law of life, which brought beauty and joy in all the world about him? No wonder the blacks worshipped life, growth – sex – as the life source.

But this is a truth Hugh can't hold on to and realise within himself. He won't let his dry and narrow rationality and surface consciousness go, won't give himself to Coonardoo, to 'Something primitive, fundamental, nearer than he to the source of things: the well in the shadows.'

Hugh is less attached to his own child by Mollie than to Winni, 'his son of a whirlwind', the result of his brief union with Coonardoo when she became the 'one sure thing in his life when his mother went out of it'. Further, the split within Hugh between his mind and senses is reproduced within Winni, who at one point looks at Coonardoo 'with the eyes of his aboriginal intuition, instinctive wisdom, his white man's intelligence, reasoning'.[27]

*Coonardoo* is certainly a very moving and passionate novel, astonishingly frank about sexuality and remarkably pro-Aboriginal for its time. The primitive and instinctive function in the novel as admired terms, as concepts by which to criticise white society for wishing to have no other relationship with the land and its original inhabitants than exploitation. In Lawrentian and Patrick Whitean terms, whereas Aboriginal society is in touch with the deepest springs of life, whites are trapped in the superficial realm of mere consciousness and driving purposeless will – the kind of will that inspires and destroys Voss.

Yet the racial attitudes in *Coonardoo* are also curious and some-how evasive and elusive: as Althusserian Marxists might say (if there are still any around), the novel is full of 'absences', unspoken and silent assumptions. It is, for example, simply assumed that throughout her life Coonardoo – a young Aboriginal woman, initiated, happy with her people and its ways, married – would love Hugh, be always devoted to him, wanting ever to be his 'woman'. Further, it is assumed in general that the Aboriginals on the station will be loyal and devoted to Mrs Bessie and Hugh, working for them, serving them, sorrowing for them. Mrs Bessie and Hugh are shown as kind and fair station owners – apart from Hugh's cruelty to his own finer instincts and so to Coonardoo, who represents them and always reminds him of them. Yet why isn't there envisaged in the novel any conflict within Coonardoo between her attraction to Hugh (who nowhere appears anything but boring) and her com-mitment to her own people? And why isn't there envisaged any fun-damental resentment by these Aboriginal people towards the whites – kind as Mrs Bessie might be – who have dispossessed them of their land?

Coonardoo and Hugh aren't characters of course in any simple psychological sense. Coonardoo is the symbol of primitive natural vitality, Hugh of civilisation, of abstract intelligence and conscious-ness: and the two have to be united for European society to achieve fulfilment on this continent, for only such oneness will answer to the most profound human needs. Terms like primitive and civilised, nature and consciousness, are reversed in value; and in so structur-ing her novel Prichard joins the modernist impulse that looks to notions of traditional community and 'primitive' life as alternatives to a crippled modern world. Such theories also look forward to the

*négritude* movement in Caribbean and African literature, a movement which in many ways is analogous to Western romanticism.

The effect of this reversal of values is a kind of racism. By
admiring Aborigines and 'primitives' generally for being in essence
instinctive and natural, such romanticism denies to non-Europeans
rationality, intelligence, consciousness – denies to them precisely
the *wholeness* of mind and senses, instinct and reason, that the
Europeans can possibly attain (a point made by the Nigerian writer
Wole Soyinka precisely against the doctrine of *négritude*).

The denial of consciousness to the 'primitive' that we can see in
this quick glance at *Coonardoo* is also assumed by Margaret Preston
in her early thinking about Aboriginal art, and we can link the
denial to the kind of evolutionary race theory that Prichard and
Preston accepted and worked on in the 1920s. In her foreword to
the first edition Prichard quoted from Basedow's *The Australian
Aboriginal* to the effect that Aborigines were originally from India
and therefore caucasian, not mongoloid or negroid, and therefore
Aborigines stand somewhere near the bottom rung of the great
evolutionary ladder we have ascended.

Margaret Preston's thinking travels along similar lines. In 1925
she argues that in 'returning to primitive art it should be remem-
bered that it is to be used as a starting point only for a renewal
of growth', for later come the individuals who 'with conscious
knowledge (education)' use Aboriginal symbols to found a great
art.[28] In 1930 Preston was convinced that the making of cloth like
tapa, as done by 'neighbours of Australia', was beyond Aboriginal
racial capacity: 'although the maker of Tapa is a primitive, he is
a developed primitive and in advance of our own aborigines'. She
pointed out that 'every design by our aborigines is irregular; this
is the essence of their beginnings, for the minds of very primitive
beings are not capable of working on set lines'.[29] Like Gauguin,
Preston urged, modern artists must bring education and consciousness to Aboriginal design, a consciousness which Aborigines themselves must, because of evolution, lack.

Such thinking in Prichard and Preston looks back to the evolutionist assumptions of 19th-century anthropology, rather than
anticipating the structural-functionalist movement in anthro-

pology which reacted against seeing present societies as relics of past evolutionary stages – although 19th-century evolutionism lived strongly on in some Marxist anthropology and clearly influences Jack Lindsay in his book of essays *Decay and Renewal*.[30] Later Margaret Preston appears to have modified her anthropological views of the 1920s. In the early '40s she writes that Australian Aborigines have always been regarded as on the lowest branch of civilisation: 'That this is not the case, is shown by a study of their native art. Their rock paintings are true murals, and their geometric designs are spontaneous and symmetrical.'[31]

## The radical nationalists

The desired unity between Australian culture and the natural environment has also been located in the folk, popular, and literary culture of the 1890s, by the radical nationalist line of thinkers running from Nettie Palmer and Vance Palmer to A. A. Phillips and Russel Ward, together with recent representative works like Geoffrey Serle's *From Deserts the Prophets Come* (1973). In many ways the body of literary and cultural theory and historical analysis worked out by these writers is very clearly an attempt to present a particular interpretation of European historicism in terms of colonial and post-colonial experience. In this interpretation, colonial and post-colonial societies all go through various stages of evolutionary adaptation to their particular environments. Australian culture can be seen as going through stages of adaptation and maturation, like a plant[32]: from the pre-1890s colonial émigré culture, to the 1890s nationalist stage, and on to the post-1890s state of cultural maturity. Each stage prompts its own characteristic set of metaphors: in the émigré stage an alien European culture tries to impose European cultural forms, which fail to take root and wither in the unreceptive soil; in the nationalist stage, indigenous cultural forms evolve which send down strong, new roots which take hold; and in the next stage, these forms spread and flower and mature and become abundant.

In these terms, the growth of Australian culture is also very similar to stages of human maturation, from child through to adolescent to adult. We can see this idea at work in 'The Democratic Theme', a key essay in A. A. Phillip's 1958 *The Australian Tradition*. In the 'development of the Australian mind', Phillips writes, 'successive phases can be observed', and 'for each phase, a different decade is central to its development'. Phillips believes that 'the spirit of a time somehow finds the voice which is suited to express it'. Thus Lawson and Furphy express the spirit of the 1890s phase, a spirit which is at once 'socially and politically adventurous' and 'jingoistically assertive', swaggering with an 'absurdly youthful cockiness'. In the decade after the 1890s, the more sophisticated O'Dowd 'fitted most happily into his epoch'. With O'Dowd the 1890s writers began to grow up, in a 'maturing and intellectualising process . . .' Christopher Brennan, however, Phillips thinks, doesn't fit into the spirit of the times at all, and he wistfully regrets that Brennan's parents chose to mate when they did.[33]

In Australia the important place occupied in European historicist thinking by 'folk' experience and poetry is transferred first to the Aboriginal culture and then to the bush workers, so that the bush workers come to have the status of Australia's pre-industrial 'folk' – in effect they are white Aborigines, as Vance Palmer argues in *The Legend of the Nineties*.[34] Just as the Aborigines reveal and express their oneness with the land in songs, myth, and legend, so too do the bushworkers, in folk song, yarns, and ballads, and also in written literature, via the *Bulletin*. Thus in *The Legend of the Nineties* Vance Palmer writes that there 'was, in truth, nothing to hold people to the country until the dreams of men who had been born in it and conceived a mystical faith in its future with their first impressions gave it a spiritual core'. This was the achievement of the pioneers, Palmer says, and he compares these nomadic bush workers to the 'blacks (who) had woven the country's flora and fauna into their legends, let their imagination play about its hills and rivers, and taken its natural features into the ritual of their lives. It was not until similar impulses arose among the invading population – selectors, shearers, bushworkers – that there was any real possession of the country.' Such people established a necessary 'dream-time', says Palmer, for white Australians generally.[35]

In *From Deserts the Prophets Come*, Geoffrey Serle, talking about the relationship between the bushworkers and the *Bulletin*, makes a similar classic statement of historicist speculation and hope:

By late in the century the bushmen as a class had developed a range of radical nationalist assumptions, were confident in their environment, knew they had something to say, and said it in the *Bulletin* which also said it for them . . . The *Bulletin* tapped the folk undercurrent which had been running strongly for half a century or more. For a genuine folk culture had begun to emerge in the pastoral interior, which had three main forms – the song, the narrative ballad for recitation and the yarn . . . The pastoral folk culture had only a limited time to develop in isolation before the impact of industrial society first diluted and then eliminated it.[36]

Serle's view of the damaging effect of urban, industrial society is shared by writers like Nettie Palmer, Vance Palmer, A. A. Phillips, and Russel Ward: the distinctive spirit of a society can only be formed in rural life, not in the cosmopolitanism of the cities. In an essay on Latin American literature in *Meanjin* in 1947, Nettie Palmer urges South American writers to focus on the 'half-buried life of the pampas or the mountains', and feels that this 'interpretation of rural life . . . would throw light on the more shifting complexities of their cities: it would result in a general enrichment of national understanding.'[37]

A. A. Phillips applies this axiom to Australia in 'The Democratic Theme'. Talking of developments after the 1890s, Phillips feels that 'One powerful influence behind the dwindling self-confidence of the democrats was the growth of the city populations.' After all, declares Phillips in an historicist lament, 'Urban man is everywhere much the same; it was in the cradle of the Open Spaces that the individual Australian character had been nurtured. Its influence still affected the nation as a whole; but the city population was not the cohesive force which the scattered bushmen had been.'[38] In *The Australian Legend* Russel Ward also points out that people living in Australia's 'coastal cities' in the 19th century were very much like their English forbears. It was only 'on the western plains beyond the mountains', where the 'nomad tribe' of bush workers lived, that the 'national *mystique*' was formed.[39] A related consequence of this pro-rural emphasis is a dislike of the suburbs: the suspicion of industrial society and urbanisation is carried naturally over into a dread of that even worse phenomenon – suburbanism.

Historicism is not a confidently liberal view of history as unending progress. Particular writers like Ward may appear optimistic about Australian society, though it is a strange optimism that in *The Australian Legend* looks for a society's vitality in a distant and elusive 19th-century legend. The radical nationalist school is given to seeing history as European historicists have done, in terms of historical periods, often, in alternating moods of optimism and pessimism, hope and near-despair. In 'The Democratic Theme', for example, A. A. Phillips, after praising the 1890s, refers to 'the Australian spiritual recession in the 1920s', a period apparently of 'retreat into imitativeness',[40] and it was a common theme of Vance Palmer's that the inter-war period, and particularly the 1920s, was a cultural desert, a reversal of the 1890s. Palmer's alternating periods continue: along came the precarious early 1940s, where the basic Australian spirit showed through in plans for post-war reconstruction, war-time social cohesion, and the existence of a journal like *Meanjin*; by the late 1950s, another period of negation was setting in, with a suffocating loss of adventurous values.[41]

## Problems and limitations

What of the limitations of the radical nationalists' contextual approach to cultural history and literary criticism? The first problem is that it is contextual usually at the expense of detailed analyses of texts, which means also that it doesn't usually provide evidence for its assertions. It doesn't, that is, usually combine contextual and textual analysis in the one critical moment, and so as criticism in particular it remains unsatisfactory. A second limitation lies precisely in the historicist premise that a literary or cultural period can possess a single unified essential spirit, which in turn is the reflection of an essential spirit in the society or natural environment. In these terms, radical nationalist criticism tends to erect a rigid hierarchy of works, by raising to the top those writers like Furphy and Lawson who are held to reveal the true consciousness

of the time. But the aesthetic diversity, plurality, conflict, and contradictions of an age or period cannot be compressed in this way,
just as societies themselves exhibit not a single spirit or even a single
mode of conflict, but a multiplicity of conflicts and structures.
Some writers can't be hailed as representative of a presumed true
spirit of a period, and other writers viewed with suspicion as either
leftovers from a previous age or anticipations of a future period
of cultural expression.

Radical nationalism is also evolutionist in a fairly crippling way.
Literature is seen as evolving towards a goal, that of the mature,
confident expression of distinctive Australian values, and only those
works in a period – and particularly in the 1890s – are noticed
which articulate these true values: other writers, presumed outside
this evolving *Geist* or spirit, are ignored. But writers of a period
cannot be dismissed as irrelevant or marginal because they don't
contribute to an eventual goal they don't and cannot know about.

# 2
# The International Context

In 1948 Lionel Trilling presented the theory that the novel of social realism (which had flourished in America throughout the 1930's) was finished because the freight train of history had passed it by. The argument was that such novels were a product of the rise of the bourgeoisie in the nineteenth century at the height of capitalism. But now bourgeois society was breaking up, fragmenting. A novelist could no longer portray a part of that society and hope to capture the Zeitgeist; all he would be left with was one of the broken pieces. The only hope was a new kind of novel (his candidate was the novel of ideas). This theory caught on among young novelists with an astonishing grip . . .

As a result, by the Sixties, about the time I came to New York, the most serious, ambitious and, presumably, talented novelists had abandoned the richest terrain of the novel: namely, society, the social tableau, manners and morals . . .
That was marvellous for journalists – I can tell you that . . .

The – New Journalists – Parajournalists – had the whole crazed obscene uproarious Mammon-faced drug-soaking mau-mau lust-oozing Sixties in America all to themselves.

Tom Wolfe, *The New Journalism*: 'Seizing the Power'.

## Modernism

Modern criticism as a discipline, an organised body of knowledge, largely issues from that most remarkable and turbulent of eras, the late 1890s and early 20th century – in so many ways a period of crisis for industrial society, and for Victorian notions of evolutionary progress, of civilisation as inherently benevolent. In 'modernist' literature, the literature of famous names like Ezra Pound, T. S. Eliot, and W. B. Yeats in poetry, and James Joyce and D. H. Lawrence in the novel, we can see a questioning of any spirit of social optimism. The spirit of the new literature was more likely to be – given the strand of anti-utopian writing of the 1890s, the nightmarish science fiction of H. G. Wells, the speculative literature of disaster and lost continents, the early strain of remarkable horror films in the new cinema – a spirit stressing social cataclysm, pessimism, alienation, the bizarre, comic, grotesque, ironic, rather than suggesting forces that reconcile or harmonise, however eventually. (I am not describing all literature of the period, which was very diverse and contradictory – for example, a competing utopianism in the 1890s – only the 'modernist' strand.)

Modernist literature questioned all conventional 19th-century notions of what literature should be. In the symbolism of the 1890s, leading to the modernism of the early decades of the new century, we can witness a discarding of clear, continuous narrative surfaces; there was a strong interest in unconscious depths as primary to any notion of 'character', rather than an allegiance to character as acting in consciously willed, rational, self-determining ways; and such depths were to be captured and embodied by stretching the metaphoric resources of language in terms of symbol, myth, and image. There was also a rejection of the particular (non-symbolist) romantic notion of art as individual self-expression – art as expression of the personality and feelings of the author. Art itself became problematic; it was rejected as a given, a transparency. Modernism threw into the foreground the question, does art reflect social reality? How does it construct its world of meanings, and what is the relation of this created world to previous imaginative 'worlds' and to the social world beyond literature? If the literary work establishes a created world of its own, what is the relation of that world to the author? The telling of a story becomes a story itself, to be related to all other stories, and modernist literature frequently refers as much to itself as art, and so to all art, as to knowledge of society or history or nature.

Modern, or rather 'modernist', criticism, developed in close association with modernist literature, and in many ways such criticism was pioneered by the writers themselves. T. S. Eliot's own criticism, for example, stands behind much that became institutionalised later in the century, and his 1917 essay, 'Tradition and the Individual Talent' – along with other essays republished in *The Sacred Wood* (1920) – was to be a seminal work for British critics like F. R. Leavis and William Empson, and for the American New Critics like John Crowe Ransom and Cleanth Brooks.

*The Sacred Wood* is polemical, concerned to castigate 19th-century critics, as well as important critics of the day like Arthur Symons, for various errors like seeing criticism as a matter of recording the critic's impressions. For Eliot, criticism should observe more closely the actual nature of artistic production, how a poet produces a poem. What is the relationship of the personality of the poet to the poetry itself? How does present poetry relate to past literature? Much of 'Tradition and the Individual Talent' is concerned to advance his own 'programme for the *métier* of poetry', to advise young poets on how in future they ought ply their craft; Eliot wrote as if he were a hundred years old and stood for a thousand years of poetic wisdom.

As young poets you should learn, Mr Eliot tells them, to regard your minds and personality as rather like platinum in a chamber containing oxygen and sulphur dioxide: these go on to form sulphurous acid. But the platinum remains unaffected, 'inert, neutral, and unchanged', a catalyst and no more. Same goes for the poet, for the 'more perfect the artist, the more completely separate in him will be the man who suffers and the mind which creates'. The poet's mind is in fact a receptacle for storing up numberless feelings, phrases, and images, and the important thing is the combination of these in artistic production, and the variety of types of combination that make up literature as a whole.

There is, the young male poet is informed, a great deal, in the writing of poetry, which must be conscious and deliberate. But what is really important is that the combination, the concentration, of feelings, emotions, and experiences – including emotions which the poet has never experienced – 'does not happen consciously or of deliberation'. The result is that

the poet has, not a 'personality' to express, but a particular medium, which is only a medium and not a personality, in which impressions and experiences combine in peculiar and unexpected ways. Impressions and experiences which are important for the man may take no place in the poetry, and those which become important in the poetry may play quite a negligible part in the man, the personality.[1]

What counts is the 'intensity' itself of the artistic process, the pressure and the complexity of the fusion of unexpected feelings, images, thoughts: and in so combining, a 'new art emotion' is produced, which has no necessary or interesting relation to the actual emotions of the poet, which might be, consciously, quite other. Further, Eliot argues in a way reminiscent of his contemporaries on the Continent the Russian formalists, with their theory of making the familiar strange, that the point is not ceaselessly to hunt for different, 'eccentric', or 'new emotions' to express, but to combine 'ordinary' and 'familiar' ones in 'peculiar and unexpected ways'.

There is self-sacrifice for our young male poet, who should, Eliot intones towards him, give in to 'a continual surrender of himself as he is at the moment to something which is more valuable', that is, to tradition. In short, he's got to develop the 'historical sense':

the historical sense involves a perception, not only of the pastness of the past, but of its presence; the historical sense compels a man to write not merely with his own generation in his bones, but with a feeling that the whole of the literature of Europe from Homer and within it the whole of the literature of his own country has a simultaneous existence and composes a simultaneous order.

This is an unusual sense of 'historical', since Eliot in fact is talking of a purely literary tradition. It's very reminiscent of the way the Russian formalists thought about literary history: works belong to a strictly literary series, and change occurs when a generation over-throws the ruling conventions of a previous generation; no convention disappears, and any convention can rise again along with other conventions or sub-literary genres (like the mystery novel) to do some subverting and overturning. As Eliot tells his young poet:

He must be aware that the mind of Europe – the mind of his own country – a mind which he learns in time to be much more important than his own private mind – is a mind which changes, and that this change is a development which abandons nothing *en route*, which does not superannuate either Shakespeare, or Homer, or the rock drawing of the Magdalenian draughtsmen.

If he wants to be a poet beyond his twenty-fifth year, he must develop consciousness of the past – the literary past – and should continue to develop this consciousness throughout his career; and it is this 'historical sense' which makes a writer 'most acutely conscious of his place in time, of his contemporaneity'.

Eliot is also not short on advice for people who want to be critics beyond their twenty-fifth year: 'Honest criticism and sensitive appreciation is directed not upon the poet but upon the poetry.' But a poem is never alone, for the critic, following the poet, has to realise a 'conception of poetry as a living whole of all the poetry that has ever been written': any one poem refers back and forwards to all poetry: any one art work refers to all art.

. . . what happens when a new work of art is created is something that happens simultaneously to all the works of art which preceded it. The existing monuments form an ideal order among themselves, which is modified by the introduction of the new (the really new) work of art among them. The existing order is complete before the new work arrives; for order to persist after the supervention of novelty, the *whole* existing order must be, if ever so slightly, altered; and so the relations, proportions, values of each work of art toward the whole are readjusted . . .

Given this conception, we are not to be perturbed if we find that the 'past should be altered by the present as much as the present is directed by the past'.

A bold synopsis of 20th-century Anglo-American literary theory

The work of modernist writers does not provide the only context for the emergence of departments of English about the turn of the century. In many humanities disciplines – anthropology, the structural linguistics of Ferdinand de Saussure, Freudian psychoanalysis – there was a widespread movement away from the various predominant 19th-century approaches. For example, in anthropology there appeared structural-functionalism, which opposed a previous evolutionist approach to 'traditional' societies by people like Tylor and Frazer. The 19th-century approach tried to collapse these societies into their more or less distant or ancient origins: whereas structural-functionalism will assume a traditional society is a self-enclosed entity, existing in a kind of ahistorical present, where every aspect functions not as a mere survival of the past but as part of a living whole.

New Criticism and Leavisism, the predominant 20th-century critical approaches in English, American, and Australian universities, seem the equivalent to structural-functionalism in anthropology. In a similar way they strike out against previous approaches which saw a literary work in terms of its context: the way 19th-century critics used to collapse a work into problems of the author's personality; or would try to see a work as the expression of national character or the national mind, or racial or ethnic origins; or saw the imagination as referring to the writer's own emotions and feelings outside the work; or felt that criticism was a purely subjective matter of recording the impression on the critic's own emotions of receiving the work. These contextual approaches – biographical, genetic, expressionist, historicist, impressionist – varied throughout the 19th century, but they were rejected by the Leavisites and New Critics because they never focused on the literary work as a text, as an entity existing in and for itself. They were 'extrinsic' approaches.

In contrast to 19th-century criticism, then, what we usually think of as modern text-centred criticism has an overall distinctiveness and unity. This doesn't mean that 20th-century criticism of this kind has not witnessed various schools competing for attention, arguing against each other at times sharply and bitterly, and ready at times to deny the name of critic as such to opponents. This is no more than to say that such modern criticism – conceived in its broadest aspect – is a tradition, and like other intellectual traditions is full of variations and differences and conflicting elements: but on the whole exhibits fundamentally shared positions, assumptions, and rules.

Of course the 20th century has seen other approaches beside the Leavisite and New Critical; there've been Marxist and existentialist and psychoanalytic approaches, often very important and influential, particularly on the Continent. This is not to suggest a simple line of demarcation between English, American, Australian New Critics – trapped in Anglo-Saxon empiricism, always unadventurous, unsoaring, like a wingless bird – and Continental thinkers, who inhabit a paradise of grand theory and speculation and generalisation. For one thing, Leavisism and New Criticism derive just as much from Continental sources – from German romanticism and French symbolism – as from the English romantic tradition. For another, New Criticism has its rough equivalents on the Continent, particularly in Russian formalism, Czech structuralism in the 1920s, and recent French structuralism and semiotics: similarities I go into in the chapter on the new formalism.

What are the basic rules of Leavisism and New Criticism? First of all, the Don'ts, usually called a Fallacy. Any critic – or, more likely, any young bewildered pass student – who ignores these Fallacies gets donged with the full weight of Leavisite and New Critical scorn.

*The Imitative Fallacy:*
*literature as reflection of social reality*
A key rule of Leavisism and New Criticism is the autonomy of the text. It's no use, if you're a student (I'm recalling my own experience in first year) doing an essay on Byron, including things about Byron's life and personality, or the hectic times he lived in, or his radical social beliefs. You have to focus on Byron's poetry itself. For Byron's poetry does not, says the Imitative Fallacy, simply reflect or imitate or describe or transcribe a reality (personal, social, political) outside of itself. Rather, the poetry creates its own 'reality', its own perceptions and interpretations – its own 'truths'.

In general, these truths, this reality, constitute the 'universe' or – a very, very favourite word – the 'world' of the text, and critics will characteristically refer to the moral or the imaginative world of a writer. Linked terms here are 'organic' and 'whole' and 'unity': in the world of the text, the various aspects function as part of the whole; all parts are organically related.

### The Intentional Fallacy: the death of the author

The origins of New Criticism and Leavisism lie deep within the history of European romanticism, with its dislike of rationalism. In particular such criticism abides by the romantic stress on the importance of the imagination and the subconscious in artistic creation. In this view, the imagination is always drawing on an author's subconscious. But this subconscious is not merely personal, for it is a realm of universal truths, about the natural world, about natural feelings, instincts, intuitions, about the very essences of human existence. In literary creation, the imagination combines insights from the subconscious and the conscious mind. But because such creation is always partly subconscious we can never say, look, the author 'intends' her or his poem to be about something or other. For authors can never know what is going to be produced by their imaginations. For this reason, the author's whole waking personality and known emotions and public attitudes – including possibly social and political and ideological attitudes – are a dangerous guide to the real created meanings of the work, so dangerous that they have to be jettisoned as unreliable, as extrinsic and contextual.

What matters is the literary or poetic personality revealed and active in the text, not the irrelevant 'real' personality of the authors themselves. The notion of the 'author' becomes problematical, and leads to a special language. The literary personality, that belongs to, that is in and of the text, is referred to as the 'persona' or 'mask' or 'voice'. Leavisites and New Critics will often talk as if the text is doing its own imagining, thinking, and feeling: 'The poem suggests . . .'; 'the novel implies . . .' Further, critics will often try to avoid saying, for example, that 'Byron argues in his poetry that . . .' because such terminology might suggest that literature is a rational discourse or argument, that it has a content separable from its form. Critics would rather say that the work 'dramatises' (or 'realises' or 'enacts') various 'themes', whether these be a perception or state of feeling, or a conflict of perceptions and feelings.

New Criticism and Leavisism are not lazy inheritors of the romantic tradition. They are very selective in what they take over and develop. In particular, they oppose one fairly prominent side of romanticism, the view that literature is self-expression (the Intentional Fallacy). New Criticism and Leavisism have in fact a firm philosophical basis, though their practitioners would shudder at the thought that they might represent a philosophical system. For New Critics and Leavisites, literature is a drama, the arena where are created the dilemmas and problems of experience which are the crucial and primary ones for humanity, however unrecognisable they may be to anyone else as life's major problems.

In the Leavisite and New Critical view, the ideal literary work is always exploring conflicting and contradictory possibilities of experience, like the real and the ideal, art and life, appearance and reality, humanity and the natural world, mind and body, imagination and intellect, thought and feeling, the unconscious and consciousness. The work, by its use of images and metaphors and symbols and myths, tries to reconcile and harmonise these conflicting possibilities. And they can be reconciled, in the synthesising power of the imagination via the image and symbols and so on – but only for a moment. What the drama of the work as a whole does, however, is to hold in balance these tensions and dualities. Because, finally, such contradictory moral and metaphysical ideals and possibilities can never be reconciled, the work must always be ambiguous, ironic, paradoxical.

The work's quality and interest lies in exploring these potentialities with a kind of creative poise that doesn't commit itself to any one possibility alone. However much a writer may be involved politically or socially outside her or his work, the text itself presents a self-sufficient imaginative world beyond social and political choice and commitment.

It's certainly easy to fall under the spell of Leavisism and New Criticism, once their rules have been assimilated and internalised. Particularly seductive is the stress on the work as 'exploring' or being 'exploratory', and so on the ideal critic as explorer. You come to a work and say, well, let's find the key tensions and dualities here;

look, there's a tension between (say) art and life, between art as fixed and eternal, and life as always changing; you can see the tension and opposition in these images and symbols and in the overall rhythmic patterning. Doesn't it create well the attraction and vitality of life as against art, and the serenity of art as against life, but isn't it so finely ambiguous and ironic in denying either can be supreme in value; the poem is so subtly open about the possibilities it is exploring. A superb poem in fact. Beautifully exploratory. Must write something about this, and particularly stress in my article how 'exploratory' this poet is.

The New Critical and Leavisite project has certainly been liberating for criticism, particularly in its insistence on the autonomy of the text, the text's freedom from history and its own creator. New Criticism and Leavisism allow for the detailed inner investigation of the text's actual workings and modes and aesthetic shape and dramatised meanings. Further, the stress on detailed study of texts is necessary as only such detailed analysis can provide evidence for an argument. The notion of a work 'dramatising' its themes is also liberating because it directs attention to the fact that literature is literature and not something else, that there is a specific aesthetic mode of apprehending reality, and that evaluation of literature – a hoary, horny problem – must take into account how well or how badly themes are dramatised, are created for us.

But the New Critical and Leavisite project also has major limitations, which have a lot to do with its philosophical base and origins. These origins are special indeed, going back to Kant, and Kant's thought, so crucial to modern aesthetic theory, that dualities like thought and feeling, mind and body, and so on, can only be made whole, reconciled in art; further, Kant considered that such reconciling (in what later came to be termed symbols) was a contemplative act. The mind that is revealed in the work plays over – explores – the metaphysical dualities that ravage yet activate our desire for wholeness and harmony, a wholeness assumed and felt to be the true goal of life. This philosophical desire has on the one hand a lot in common with mysticism, and on the other has stimulated the aesthetic ideals of 19th- and 20th-century romanticism, symbolism, and modernism.

Despite their special origins and character, New Criticism and Leavisism nevertheless try to present themselves, not least to their own practitioners, as possessing a critical language that can apply to all literature at all times. The result is rather like an elephant chewing up a game park: to every object is applied the same fixed vocabulary (myth, metaphor, symbol, irony, play of mind, tensions and oppositions, unresolved dualities, ambiguity, ambivalence, paradox). So that New Criticism and Leavisism are always reproducing the work in their own image: what such criticism *sees* is itself. In narrowing literature down to only those works, or those aspects of works, felt to be most susceptible to their own approach, New Criticism and Leavisism have become exclusive and reductive, an effect most evident in university courses.

## Criticism in conflict in the 1950s

So far I've boldly outlined the primary rules and formulas in the mainstream teaching of literature in departments of English. Such underlying rules and formulas also, of course, were interwoven with shifting historical, political, and ideological contexts, and it is to one such, crucial for our overall narrative, that we can now turn – the 1950s. The full blast of the Cold War as it swept the intellectual arena will be discussed in chapter three; here we can study one of its ramifications, its effect on the received model of Anglo-American literary criticism.

In the 1950s the reign of Leavisism and New Criticism was challenged by important members of the rising new left, in particular the historian E. P. Thompson – best known for his massive *William Morris* (1955) and, later, in 1963, *The Making of the English Working Class* – and the cultural critic Raymond Williams, an ex-Leavisite himself and author of *Culture and Society* (1958).

In the years of the Cold War a principal so-called end-of-ideology theme was that English society, in the dawning post-war prosperity, with the welfare state working and classes converging, should be left to itself in its happy consumerism. People could perhaps be deepened by contact with religious experience. But they shouldn't be disturbed by ideology, by ideas of political change and social transformation. Thompson and Williams reacted against this insistent claim that the English people were (and should be) essentially politically passive. In separate ways, in books of the 1950s like *William Morris* and *Culture and Society*, Thompson and Williams tried to demonstrate the historical strength and resourcefulness of past critiques of industrial capitalist society, whether radical and socialist as in Morris, or conservative as in Ruskin, Carlyle, or Cobbett. In particular, they stressed that the English romantic tradition was rich in alternative visions to industrial society and to utilitarianism: it was a tradition that inextricably and inescapably possessed social, political, and ideological dimensions. The further implication was that this romantic tradition was still alive and well and couldn't be suppressed. There was no sharp post-war, Cold War, end-of-ideology break with the turbulent past. Ideology and utopian desire were present, active forces.

There were of course differences between Thompson and Williams in the 1950s. Thompson was much more the Marxist; Williams was a literary critic approaching radicalism by transforming Leavisism in a left direction. In *William Morris* Thompson was contesting not only conventional Cold War views but also what he perceived as the economism of orthodox communist theory, the economism which played down the vital historical importance of moral values – moral values he saw developed in romanticism in general and Morris in particular. As Thompson records in his postscript in 1976 to the book, he himself was still suspicious in the 1950s of fully recognising the importance of utopianism, given that since Engels utopianism had been largely written off in official Marxist theory as unscientific.

Another difference between Thompson and Williams is that Thompson came to feel that Williams, in dealing in *Culture and Society* with thinkers like Carlyle, Lawrence, Tawney, Eliot, and Leavis, was not evoking the intellectual traditions that in English history can be found in more popular, radical and artisan cultures – the task of evocation he so magnificently addressed himself to in *The Making of the English Working Class*.[2]

The political dimensions of romanticism, and its utopianism in particular, that Williams and Thompson stressed in the 1950s, were principal targets of suspicion, dislike, scorn, and abuse for those influenced by Cold War attitudes. The Cold War view was that utopianism (the desire to transform society in the direction of an alternative idea of community) had moved the world to commit the crimes of fascism, nazism, and communism. Utopianism was the beast of ideology which had already sprung on civilisation and tried to savage it. Now it had to be caged, tamed, and forgotten, and anyone still attracted to it was but an example of psychological weakness and personality disorder (the authoritarian personality, etc.). Utopianism had to be opposed by scepticism and realism, by the pragmatic, wise and sophisticated knowledge that the utopian desire to help and change humanity always led to authoritarianism and totalitarianism and thence to disaster.

Yet it was – or appeared to be – an embarrassing fact that romantic and post-romantic literature since Blake had criticised and denounced industrial society, and had sought alternatives to it, in imagination, intuition, instinct, emotion, sexuality, in how these might be embodied in medieval or other notions of society. More: the writers we usually take to be the founders of modernist Anglo-American literature and literary criticism, Eliot, Pound, Yeats, Lawrence, were caught up in an early 20th-century apocalyptic mood, struck by the plight of civilisation, and searching for a vision whereby their metaphysical concerns could be realised in social forms, so that Western industrial society – found to be so grievously lacking in true values – could be saved.

These great modernists, the precursors of the New Critics of the 1950s, were attracted to social, political, and ideological theories – indeed often to fascist ideas. They were utopians! This was embarrassing, but Frank Kermode came to the theoretical rescue.

In 1957 Kermode published *Romantic Image*. (Kermode was later, in 1966, to distinguish himself as an editor of *Encounter* by denying all knowledge of *Encounter*'s relations with the CIA and by threatenening to sue the *New Statesman* if it dared mention such an unlikely and preposterous connexion.)[3] *Romantic Image* is a polemical essay offering an historical interpretation of the essence of romanticism and of the criticism it yielded. Kermode's argument is that, for good or for ill, modern Anglo-American criticism is based on the romantic inheritance, particularly as it is manifested in the 1890s, in French symbolism and in its equivalent in the poetry of the Image in England – in 1890s figures like Ernest Dowson and Lionel Johnson, and, first and foremost, in Yeats. I won't go into Kermode's treatment of the 1890s here except to note that in this period he locates a flowering of the true nature of the romantic tradition, a tradition that in England goes back through Pater, Arnold, Hazlitt, Wordsworth, Keats, and Coleridge to Blake.

True poetry is concerned with the Image, a mode of perceiving reality that is neither merely emotional nor merely cerebral. The Image yields 'joy' for poets, but it also cuts them off from society, so that poets are always suffering, they must necessarily be lonely, haunted, and victimised. However much they may be attracted to the ordinary world of action, including political action, they must – to be true to their pure artistic impulse and gain the Image – really remain contemplative. They must search into themselves for imaginative resources and access to vision.

For Kermode, this *is* romanticism, 'the tradition' – something as unlike the character of Raymond Williams's lineage as you'd ever wish to see. To be truly artistic, truly literary, is to be metaphysical, to be divorced from and opposed to the world of social 'action' and politics. To be political, to be involved in 'action', is to be inartistic, impure and non-literary.

This symbolist doctrine of the Image was transmitted to the 20th century by Yeats, Pound, and Eliot, and thence to modern Anglo-American criticism in general. Kermode says in his conclusion that he might be thought of as working with a hackneyed, obsolescent idea of the artist as different and separate. But look what happens when we try and make poetry political, as in the 'propaganda poetry of the 1930s', like Auden's of that period: it hasn't survived, and doesn't deserve to. Whereas symbolism, with its stress on metaphor, offers an aesthetic approach that is adequate not only to poetry, but to all literature – for example, to the modern novel as exemplifying the 'possibilities of complex symbolic relations', or in Wilson Knight's symbolist readings of Shakespeare's plays.

We can, argues Kermode, be happy about all this – this is all for the good. But the French symbolism/romantic Image inheritance has left modern criticism a problem in terms of literary history and historiography, which Kermode discusses in chapter eight, ' "Dissociation of Sensibility": Modern Symbolist Readings of Literary

History'. In terms of the symbolists and early modernists, the modern world is split between mind and feeling, emotion and intellect, intuition and imagination as against mechanical rationality. The symbol, the Image, would reconcile this split in moments of imaginative perception. This is fine, but the modernists like Yeats or Pound or Eliot then looked to previous ages when this split, they felt, hadn't been. This search for an ideal community culminated in T. S. Eliot's famous pronouncement in his 1921 essay 'The Metaphysical Poets', that the 'dissociation of sensibility', the split between thought and feeling, occurred somewhere in the early 17th century.

Such an historical doctrine may have helped nourish early 20th-century poetry, says Kermode, but as a doctrine for literary history it is and has been harmful and 'useless'. Indeed, as Kermode writes in his conclusion, we must 'kill the symbolist historical doctrine of dissociation of sensibility as publicly as possible'. The trouble, Kermode feels, with symbolism as literary history is that it is too narrow and exclusive. It sets up a canon, whereby modernist poetry is compared to 17th-century metaphysical poetry, and to Jacobean drama. Symbolism tends to celebrate short poems that realise the Image, more than longer poems or works. The result is that Donne is puffed up to the exclusion of Milton and his long poems. Such a bias can no longer be tolerated, says Kermode. We have now to devalue Donne, see that his poetry, rather than combining sense and feeling, depends on 'dialectical conjuring', 'slight but totally destructive perversities of analogue', and that his images are narrowly logical or pseudo-logical.

Indeed, says Kermode, we shouldn't take Donne as an example of the undissociated sensibility at all. This honour should go to Milton, unhappily dethroned and despised in favour of the 17th-century metaphysicals. Milton was the 'main sufferer in the great experiment of projecting on to an historical scale a developed romantic-symbolist theory of the Image'. We should now recognise that Milton is a supreme example of sensuous, passionate thought, that his poetry can be assimilated to Yeats' belief in the pure Image. In this way, we don't have to dismiss poets and literary periods, for example, the 19th century, as stricken by dissociation of sensibility, and falsely raise others to pantheon status. Criticism can now be fully professional (reading everything in terms of image, symbol, metaphor), treating all literature with a single approach. So Kermode can conclude his chapter on literary historiography: 'Somehow, and probably soon, the age of dissociation – which is to say, the age that invented and developed the concept of dissociation – must end.' Which sounds very much like a pronouncement, in aesthetic terms, of the end of ideology. All will now be well. Poetry, we will recognise, is concerned with a solitary, contemplative vision of truths that are not ideological and don't lead to political action. At the same time, literature is not so irrational as to be divorced from rational discourse and as to lead to possible utopian involvements in the political realm; nor will it be unhealthily pessimistic or anarchistic. It will 'still, of course, be Symbolist', but the

new poetic would be remote from the radicalism of Blake, have little to do with the forlorn hopes of Mallarmé, and less with the disastrous *dereglement* of Rimbaud. We have perhaps learnt to respect order, and felt on our bodies the effect of irrationalism, at any rate when the sphere of action is invaded by certain elements of the Romantic *rêve*.'

Literature will be seen as not so estranged from society as to be apocalyptic in the manner of Eliot and Pound, condemning western society. Rather, critics will see in literature – as in the exemplary Yeats – an effort to reconcile the Image and the poet's isolation from ordinary life. The 'new poetic' will be a 'waking poetic, respecting order'.

Perhaps F. R. Leavis and Leavisism are the great exceptions to this new critical orthodoxy that Kermode is seeking to establish, and Leavisism interestingly does not appear amongst the critical positions our maestro nudges and pushes about while legitimating his own sense of 'order'. Leavis and Leavisism span the periods before and after World War II, and Leavis and Leavisites continued what E. P. Thompson and Raymond Williams would describe and evoke as the moral critique of industrial capitalism, of utilitarianism and narrow Benthamite rationality. They still carried on about the plight of civilisation, the theme that end-of-ideology ideologues like Kermode wished to expunge from critical discourse. As a recent book by Francis Mulhern on Leavisism suggests, *Scrutiny* in its last days was becoming demonstrably hos-

tile to the entire political and social universe of post-war Britain
– to all those tokens of freedom and prosperity on which the
ideological defence of the west was now coming to depend. At the
same time, Mulhern argues, *Scrutiny* was certainly anti-communist
in the 1950s, and so in that sense was compatible with Cold War
ideology.[5]

In some ways the trajectory of *Scrutiny* and the Leavisites
reveals a curve similar to that which goes from Eliot to Kermode.
In the 1930s the Leavisites were engaged in argument with Marxist
social and aesthetic theories, and Leavis could declare in *Scrutiny*
that 'economic communism' was a necessity. Q. D. Leavis was
applying a sociological approach to literature that she acknowledged owed a great deal to Veblen, and L. C. Knights revealed a
strong historical approach, as in his *Drama and Society in the Age
of Jonson*, that owed a great deal to Tawney.[6]

Yet Leavisites were to become more and more insistent on judging literature in terms of moral and metaphysical criteria. Further,
L. C. Knights turned more and more towards a criticism that, like
the American New Critics, saw all literature in the narrow Col-
deridgean terms of image, metaphor, and symbol.[7] Also, in Australia, the Melbourne Leavisites certainly bent Leavisism towards
a preoccupation with the metaphysical in the 1950s and '60s. They
even felt Leavis himself hadn't gone far enough in this direction,
and that this was one reason Leavis had never explored Shakespeare fully – the ultimate repository of metaphysical depths and
truths.[8]

## And then there were the Americans

In *The Critical Twilight*,[9] John Fekete has argued that American
New Criticism exhibits a curve similar to that we've been witnessing in British criticism. Fekete's example is John Crowe Ransom,
a father-figure to both the southern agrarians like Allen Tate and
Robert Penn Warren, and to the New Criticism that emerged from
southern agrarianism in the latter 1930s and became prominent in
American universities in the 1940s and '50s.

Southern agrarians like Ransom in the 1920s and early 1930s constructed full-blown social, political, and aesthetic theories which recall, in terms transported to the American south, the historical theory of dissociation of sensibility favoured in Europe by modernists like Pound, Yeats, and Eliot. An anti-capitalist critique held a central place. In this view, humanity in urban, industrial society was fragmented, had lost wholeness and harmony because of the dominance of science and rationality, which had made feelings and emotions – all that we know as sensibility – unnaturally shrink. Industrial society means exploiting nature, not living with it, and it means reducing personality to merely economic functions.

Yet the answer to this plight of American civilisation, this disaster that the false doctrine of industrial progress is leading us into, is so near at hand. Fekete quotes Ransom admiring American plantation society in the agrarian manifesto *I'll Take My Stand* (1930). The south in the 18th century exhibited

social arts of dress, conversation, manners, the table, the hunt, politics, oratory, the pulpit. These were arts of living and not arts of escape; they were also community arts, in which every class of society could participate after its kind. The south took life easy, which is itself a tolerably comprehensive art.[10]

This kind of agricultural society permits a subtle, sophisticated association of people and play of feeling and intellect. The America of the pre-bellum south is in fact the traditional, ancient centre of civilisation that writers like Eliot dream about and look for in medieval or early 17th-century society in Europe: in Ransom's words, the southern communities are the 'chief instance of the stationary European principle of culture in America'.[11]

As Fekete argues, the agrarian campaign, launched in the 1930s by *I'll Take My Stand*, with its besotted idealisations of racist plantation society, failed, and Ransom by the late 1930s was narrowing the broad ideological concerns of agrarianism down to the aesthetic field of New Criticism. Ransom was the decisive figure in this transition. He began to tone down his previously strong radical-conservative anti-industrial critiques, to accommodate his thought to science, rationalism, and liberal progress, and to drop the T. S. Eliot-like theme of the crisis of civilisation. By the end of the decade Ransom was calling for New Criticism to be established in universities as a fully professionalised criticism, a call which coincided with the institutional expansion of universities in the 1940s and '50s. In 1939 Ransom himself moved to Ohio and founded the *Kenyon Review*, which he edited for twenty years and which acted as a permanent manifesto of New Criticism.

Yet the very institutional success of New Criticism, Fekete reports, stunned and dismayed even Ransom himself, who in 1952 declared in the *Kenyon Review* that while close verbal analysis has secured its place and tenure, it has also bogged down in an excruciating impasse, with cold-blooded critics of poetry working away in what appears to be the merest exercises with words. Nevertheless, by then New Criticism had become the dominant pedagogical tradition, particularly in the textbook productions of other New Critics like Cleanth Brooks, and while the myth criticism of Northrop Frye loomed in the latter 1950s, New Criticism – with its procedures that analyse literary works as 'autotelic', as self-enclosed wholes impervious to social and ideological implications and historical explanation – remained firmly entrenched, a staple fare so natural that for critics its origins in radical social critique (however conservatively directed) became lost and invisible.[12]

In the 1950s New Criticism, now massively institutionalised in departments of English, found an ally, the famous New York moralist Lionel Trilling.

Whereas Ransom emerges from a highly conservative tradition, Trilling's bearings originally ran all the other way. The New York critic's journey through the literary politics of the left in the 1930s takes him, as it took journals like the *Partisan Review*, from closeness to the Communist Party and thence attraction to Trotskyism, to a postwar entry into a celebration of liberalism: into an accommodation with mainstream American society, and with New Criticism itself (Fekete notices Trilling in 1949 as a senior fellow of the Kenyon school of English, along with names like F. O. Matthiessen and John Crowe Ransom).[13]

It's strange rereading Trilling now in the context of the Cold War years and end-of-ideology movement of the latter 1940s and the '50s. His *The Liberal Imagination* (first published in April 1950) was one of those texts most 'around' in my undergraduate days, in some ways a counterpart about fiction to the poetry-centred analyses of Cleanth Brooks's *The Well-Wrought Urn*. Yet, then, I didn't have a clue about the political implications of Trilling's title. Why was it called the *liberal* imagination? Shouldn't we, if we're talking of literature, expect the title to be the *romantic* imagination? What does Trilling mean by this paradoxical-sounding rearrangement of received historical categories? Why the insistence on a non-literary term? What's going on?

In his 1949 preface to *The Liberal Imagination* Trilling begins the show by announcing that in the United States of the present time, liberalism is not only the dominant but indeed the sole intellectual tradition. Marxism, it appears, no longer effectively exists as a post-World War II presence, for the only rival to liberalism Trilling can observe in action is conservatism. But while strong conservative 'impulses' abound, these are not 'ideas'. For, 'as the experience of Europe in the last quarter-century suggests', in the modern situation 'it is just when a movement despairs of having ideas that it turns to force, which it masks in ideology'.

Ideology, then, represents the moment when intellectual movements degenerate into force, into non-ideas, and liberalism is the only tradition to survive intact the last quarter of a century of conflict; the others, presumably the Marxist as well as the conservative, are now ideological, not intellectual. Yet we shouldn't be complacent about liberalism, which has to be approached in a 'critical spirit'. For liberalism has always been in danger of drifting towards a denial of the emotions and the imagination.

The great liberal John Stuart Mill early saw this historical danger, and he enriched the liberal tradition by opening it up towards conservatism. Mill realized, says Trilling, that an affection for poetry was necessary for a proper sense of 'variousness and possibility' in life – the essence of the liberal imagination – and in particular Mill was receptive to the conservative thought of the great romantic poet and philosopher Coleridge.

So, from the middle part of the 19th century, in Trilling's historical scheme, a conjuncture was effected between liberalism (Mill) and romantic conservatism (Coleridge). One went into the other: liberalism, which wishes to 'organise the elements of life in a rational way', is combined with sentiment, emotion, imagination. We can now, Trilling happily avers, comprehend with the Coleridge of *The Ancient Mariner*, 'that the world is a complex and unexpected and terrible place which is not always to be understood by the mind as we use it in our everyday tasks'. The result will be that liberalism, informed by the tragic truth of conservatism, will influence 'ideas', guide moral sentiment, and so help shape 'political actions and institutions' towards the direction not of a narrow rationality but towards variousness, possibility, complexity, and difficulty. The importance and very historical mission of literature is that it is the repository of these qualities, and indeed we can say that modern literature's 'job' is one of 'criticising the liberal imagination', making sure it never descends to mere reason, mere rationality.[14]

If literature and the liberal imagination can have a moral influence on political and social institutions, we shouldn't, however, take this to mean that literature possesses a utopian desire for radical social change. On the very very contrary. In 'Manners, Morals, and the Novel', first published in the *Kenyon Review* in 1948, and presumably the essay mocked by new journalist Tom Wolfe in the epigraph to this chapter, Trilling calls for the novel to devote itself not to the world of tangible, direct and immediate social reality, but to 'moral realism'.

What we then find is that the novel over the last two hundred years or so, and indeed really since Cervantes and *Don Quixote*, is anti-utopian, is a long critique of utopianism. The novel encourages a questioning not so much of social conditions as of ourselves: it will 'lead us to refine our motives and ask what lie behind our good impulses'.

It is probable that at this time we are about to make great changes in our social system . . . we must be aware of the dangers which lie in our most generous wishes. Some paradox of our natures leads us, when once we have made our fellow men the objects of our enlightened interest, to go on to make them the objects of our pity, then of our wisdom, ultimately of our coercion. It is to prevent this corruption, the most ironic and tragic that man knows, that we stand in need of the moral realism which is the product of the free play of the moral imagination.

Fortunately, the novel is on our side, in its essential aesthetic character: it has been the 'literary form to which the emotions of understanding and forgiveness were indigenous, as if by the definition of the form itself'.

The novel, by encouraging, as does *Don Quixote*, the 'wildly conceiving, the madly fantasying', by teaching us the 'extent of human variety and the value of this variety', will show that reality is not as our conventional education has led us to see it – will defamiliarise, as the Russian formalists were wont to say. The 'real reality' is not the world of tangible reality after all – the lesson of Cervantes – and, says Trilling, 'all prose fiction' is a variation on the theme of *Don Quixote*. Rather, the real reality is questioning our social reforming motives to show that attempts at radical change will end tragically. Sure, 'people change, practical reality changes' when they and it come into the presence of the moral imagination: but they change in the direction of introspection, of deepened impulses.[15]

The 1950s must have been a harrowing time for Trilling, an old radical warhorse now wishing to find in postwar American illiberal society a safe field for quietly munching and mooching. So many pitfalls still! Marxism could be forgotten, but what about all those novels that wish to take society as their object? Easy: they don't really belong to the essential novel form itself at all. Forget about them, and let's hope they're never rediscovered. Trilling, determined now to be upfront about his own critical method, offers to his students his version of modern literature. Except it's not just his own version, for the teacher decides that what they'll get is modern literature's actual 'characteristic element'. To find this defining feature, the typical young male student Trilling has in his mind's eye embarks on a journey which seems to begin at Sir James Frazer's *The Golden Bough*, and then stops at various other ports – at Nietzsche's *The Birth of Tragedy* and *The Genealogy of Morals*, at Conrad's *Heart of Darkness*, Thomas Mann's *Death in Venice*, Freud's *Civilization and Its Discontents*, Diderot's *Rameau's Nephew*, Dostoevski's *Notes from Underground*, Tolstoi's *Death of Ivan Ilyitch*, and some Pirandello plays. From all these stops sufficient freight is brought on board to yield a full cargo of the essential impulses of modern literature.

There's a reference to the romantics as well, in particular to Blake, but it's a Blake who leads to Nietzsche, not the Blake of radicalism and political vision, the Blake who figures in E. P. Thompson's *The Making of the English Working Class*. Reading modern literature is like looking into Blake's hell, into an abyss of anti-civilisation and an assault on the 'commonplace, commonsense mind'. For what modern writers from Diderot and Blake on desire 'is not merely freedom from the middle class but freedom from society itself'. Modern literature is not concerned with society, rather it wants to question what we mean by society and civilisation. It reveals that the 'essential metaphysical activity of man' is constituted not by ethics but by art, and that art is concerned with the kind of states that Frazer said are fundamental to all humanity. By establishing that faith and ritual and the mysterious are 'indigenous' to the human condition, Frazer provided a bridge to the modern attraction to extreme mental states, to rapture, ecstasy, and transcendence, which nowadays are achieved by 'drugs, trance, music and dance, orgy, and the derangement of personality'.

Then in Nietzsche, Trilling's students will be informed, in Nietzsche will be found a theory of the social order that dismisses all ethical impulse from its origins. The 'basis of society is to be found in the rationalization of cruelty: as simple as that'. Also, Nietzsche has 'no ultimate Utopian intention' in saying this, no hope of revising the essence of the social order. Nietzsche shows that the basis of tragic art lies in Dionysian rapture, in a 'sadic' and masochistic frenzy. True, Nietzsche insists that all this frenzy needs the taming hand of Apollo to be placed on it before it becomes art, but still Nietzsche's thinking leads straight to the 'canonisation' in modern literature of the 'primal, non-ethical energies'.

Perhaps the final port of call to which Trilling's itinerary *should* bring his students is Kermode's *Romantic Image*: they could then complement Trilling's account of modern fiction and drama with Kermode's account of modern poetry. Of course there are still lots of differences. Kermode follows Eliot and theorists like Wellek and Warren in their *Theory of Literature* in proposing a symbolist reading of literature, including the novel and drama; and Kermode allows the modern poet some joy in the Image as well as suffering, whereas for Trilling modern literature is a version of 'terror'.[16] Yet both wish to canonise a certain element in modern literature – to do with metaphysical states and awareness – as *the* modern element, and then canonise only those authors, or those aspects of authors, whose work most embodies it. As usual, to canonise a certain line or aspect, to read literature in only one kind of way which is held to be appropriate to art or 'modern literature' as such, is to exclude, to narrow down, to impoverish.

Both Kermode and Trilling wish to push literature as far away from the ideological and political as possible, towards religion. Kermode insists on the historical connexions of the Image with the supernatural and with magic; Trilling tells his students and us that the questions asked by modern literature are 'not about our culture but about ourselves'. It asks us if we are 'saved or damned – more than anything else, our literature is concerned with salvation', and indeed no literature 'has ever been so intensely spiritual as ours'. Trilling adds that he does 'not venture to call it actually religious', but it's almost, it's part of the 'great modern phenomenon of the secularization of spirituality'.[17]

Overall, we can notice a curious aspect of the argument about the nature of romanticism – over, in fact, the character of English literary and cultural history – between radicals like E. P. Thompson and Raymond Williams and Cold War liberals like Frank Kermode. For it is the radicals, Thompson and Williams, who wish to see English literary history as a broad and wideranging activity, full of heterogeneity, diversity, contrast, and conflicting attitudes.

Thompson in his book on the romantic William Morris points to the diversity of his literary interests – in the value of medieval communities and the Icelandic sagas, his notions of socialist community, his attraction to anarchism and libertarianism, his linking of art to pleasure, his subtle and humorous visions of possible utopias. Williams in his *Culture and Society* shows how diverse romanticism is, embracing as much the radical democratic vision of a Blake, hailing the American revolution, as the conservative vision of a Coleridge or Carlyle. Coleridge thought society should be an organic whole guided and shaped in its values by an educated elite, a 'clerisy', an idea developed in his own way later by Leavis; Carlyle thought society ought to be as organised as a medieval monastery, inspired by strong leadership. It was the radicals like Thompson and Williams who were insisting on the historical presence of romanticism as having all sorts of bearings in philosophical, political, and ideological terms, whether these were socialist or conservative. But it was Cold War critic Kermode (and, we can add, Trilling) who wished to thin down the cultural heterogeneity of romanticism to a narrow *literary* movement, whereas Thompson and Williams drew out romanticism as a rich *cultural* formation.

Further, it was radical Raymond Williams who in *Culture and*

*Society* pointed to the breadth of the cultural theories of the great early modernist critics like T. S. Eliot and F. R. Leavis – whereas Kermode ignored Leavis and, in the case of Eliot, wished to get rid of Eliot's theory of dissociation of sensibility, the theory of a long post-Renaissance crisis in Western civilisation, a gathering split between intellect and feeling. Kermode in effect wanted to get rid of Eliot's radically conservative social and historical theory, in the interest of saying that only metaphysical themes and perspectives were essential to modernist criticism. For Thompson and Williams romanticism is multifaceted, indeed Janus-faced, capable of looking all ways at once; for Kermode (and Trilling) romanticism has a single set expression.

In the early 1960s H. P. Heseltine extended Lionel Trilling's arguments about the centrality of 'terror' in modernist literature to Australian literature. We can leave discussion of this claim to later in our evocation of the gloom thesis. Here, we can observe that it was part of a debate in *Meanjin* with A. A. Phillips over the essential Australian cultural tradition. The debate, later featured in the *Meanjin* collection *On Native Grounds*, is in many ways a culmination of a decade of critical and historiographical argument, conflict, and contestation, similar to what we have witnessed in Britain in the 1950s between radical thinkers like E. P. Thompson and Raymond Williams, and Cold Warriors like Frank Kermode, over the nature of the English romantic heritage: arguments in which the Cold War theorists tried to establish that the nature of literature itself excluded social/political/ideological/utopian concerns, and was inherently moral, metaphysical, religious, sacred.

In Australia in the 1950s, Vance Palmer's *The Legend of the Nineties* appeared in 1954, and Russel Ward and A. A. Phillips published *The Australian Legend* and *The Australian Tradition* in 1958, Phillips's essays having previously appeared in journals like *Meanjin* and *Overland*. Against their kind of radical nationalist arguments, and struggling for intellectual supremacy with them, were those presented by James McAuley, Australia's most spectacular literary Cold Warrior, and by *Quadrant* writers generally, including Vincent Buckley, as well as by that most ambivalent of cultural figures, Manning Clark. My tattered copy of *Quadrant* for Spring 1957 includes Clark as an editorial advisor, along with other literary and critical names like A. D. Hope and Leonie Kramer.

# 3
# The Cold War

The present becomes history so quickly. Tertiary students now, perhaps born in 1964 or '65, turn blank faces towards their teachers if they happen breezily to mention recent figures in Australian political history. Gough Whitlam – who's he? Bob Menzies? And what is this Cold War s/he is rabbiting on about that happened before we were born?

In chapter two I tried to relate the Cold War to the politics of criticism; in this chapter I'll confront directly the phenomenon in terms of the intellectual politics it helped generate, and the relation to this of one of Australia's foremost 'metaphysical' poets, James McAuley. In particular we can notice the influence of 'end-of-ideology' theories. Early in the Cold War, in the late 1940s and early '50s, end-of-ideology meant that since Russian communism was now the chief enemy, we – liberals and conservatives alike – should sink any prior political differences, and confront the common enemy, at the same time rooting out and exposing its willing or unwitting agents (communists, Marxists, leftwing unions and sections of the Labor Party, left-liberal intellectuals) in our own society.

Later in the 1950s and early '60s end-of-ideology took on more sociological and cultural meanings. In the wake of the prosperity and high employment that was developing, we should understand that the old divisions between an impoverished proletariat and a prosperous middle class were gone. Those divisions had fed the Marxist delusion which predicted that class divisions would get sharper and sharper in modern history, leading to the possibility of revolution.

Now we can see that the proletariat is disappearing, with the rise of the new white collar occupations. Most people were now middle-class and enjoying themselves in the new suburbs. The language of class and class conflict was dead. Some commentators and writers like Donald Horne and Craig McGregor celebrated this end of ideology as a new hedonism; some like Patrick White or Barry Humphries or Vance Palmer in *Meanjin* abhorred it as a new spiritual emptiness. But the phenomenon itself was taken, by right and left, to be true and to be the major startling historical fact of the second half of the century.

It is, however, to the manifestations of the earlier phase of end-of-ideology that we can now turn.

## The intellectual atmosphere

In many ways World War II had left western intellectuals shattered and unnerved: how could Europe, supposedly the repository of civilised values, of freedom and democracy and tolerance, have spawned the barbarism of fascism and nazism, with their totalitarianism and rampant racism? The shock and dismay had many healthy intellectual responses, in particular leading to critiques of the kinds of social Darwinist, eugenicist, and race-obsessed thinking that had been so institutionally important in western societies. During and after the war books came out like Richard Hofstadter's *Social Darwinism in American Thought* (1944), or, in literary studies, revaluations of the 19th-century stream of thought that promoted racial analyses of history and society and culture, as in the revered Matthew Arnold's attempted exclusion of the semitic from European culture, and his identification of ethnic categories with social and cultural qualities.[1]

World War II indeed presented a crisis for western intellectual traditions. In 1944 Eric Russell Bentley brought out *A Century of*

*Hero Worship*, where he tried to work out how far a tradition of heroic vitalism – in Carlyle and Nietzsche in particular, but also in Wagner, Shaw, Spengler, and D. H. Lawrence – aided the triumph of the modern dictators. This theme was also taken up in *Debates with Historians*, by the prominent Dutch historian Pieter Geyl (who had been imprisoned by the Nazis in Buchenwald). In essays collected and published in 1955, Geyl is concerned – like Bentley, whose book he acknowledges as influencing him[2] – to look at received greats of history like Carlyle and Ranke, and to ask to what degree their 19th-century teachings and dicta flowed into the 20th century and contributed to its major 'anti-liberal revolutions', the fascist, the nazi, and the communist. How much are thinkers like Carlyle and Ranke pioneers of national socialism?[3] And what of the whole romantic tradition to which Carlyle in particular is related, that emphasises instinct, intuition, imagination, as the primary qualities of humanity and society? What happens to this tradition when it sees these instinctual qualities embodied in great men, as in Carlyle glorifying Frederick the Great (which earned him an admiring notice from Bismarck), or the Cromwell who destroyed 'the papistical Irish', or the Governor Eyre who exacted savage revenge in Jamaica after a black uprising? Doesn't this lead directly to Hitler?

Both Carlyle and Ranke were influenced by German romanticism and philosophical idealism but whereas Carlyle drew on aspects which stressed instinct and intuition, Ranke was influenced by the side which directed the mind to be open to reality in all its manifold manifestations and appearances. In Ranke's famous phrase, echoing Herder,[4] each society or period was 'unmittelbar zu Gott', immediate to God: the past has to be considered in and for itself, as the working out of God's ideas for the world.

For the writing of history, Geyl argues, this was a liberating project, to be aware of the individuality of a country or age, the release of the historical imagination in the effort to explore the past in its own right, from the inside.

Another of Ranke's strengths was his universalism, very different from later historicists like Treitschke who wished to place history in the service of Prussia and German unity. Ranke believed in the diversity of national cultures, making up the rich mosaic of European civilisation, each helping to work out God's plan.

Geyl argues that Ranke's inheritance is ambiguous. Ranke's notion of history as contemplation deprives people of that active participation in political life which occupies a central position in the political thought of Western Europe. All that Ranke can admit as the individual's contribution to the public cause is private activity and loyalty toward the State – a position that must have weakened resistance to those impressed by the later manifestations of German power. Yet how admirable, Geyl nevertheless concludes, are Ranke's 'serene matter-of-factness, that striving after comprehension, that openmindedness for historic phenomena other than those with which the writer himself felt in agreement' – qualities which are the 'complete opposite of the revolutionary fanaticism and doctrinairism of the men who half a century after his death threw Germany and the world into the catastrophe'.

Geyl's argument shows that the attitudes of the Cold Warriors and the end-of-ideology ideologues were not the natural or automatic or necessary, the right and inevitable, responses to the 'catastrophe'. Geyl ends his essay by praising Ranke for 'Comprehension, a disinterested understanding of what is alien to you ... the very breath of the civilization we are called to defend.' But, for those most enthusiastic about the Cold War, everything that Geyl does in these essays would appear to be abhorrent – his prizing of liberal virtues like intellectual inquiry, his notions of tolerance and of understanding the 'alien' and different, his spirit of 'compromise, humanity and peace', his warnings that the individual shouldn't be blindly subservient to state power, the very subservience that led to the competing totalitarians.

At this point, it may be useful to evoke the political context of the Cold War end-of-ideology metaphysical line we've been tracing, and my own attempt to examine the impact of this context in a paper I gave, at the 1970 Socialist Scholars Conference, on James McAuley.[5] During the 1950s this political aspect had of course both an international and Australian context. The Australian Association for Cultural Freedom, of which McAuley was a leading luminary, was part of the overall Congress for Cultural Freedom, that was based in Paris though its purse-strings (unknown to most of the participants) stretched back to CIA headquarters in the United States of America. It's strange that a body so dedicated to kicking a 'totalitarian' head whenever it might appear, turned out to be an attempted world-wide mobilisation of intellectuals dedicated to the promotion, defence, and service of American state power and interests in the post-war period.

As the British historian Hugh Trevor-Roper discovered, the Cold Warriors were attracted neither to Western liberalism (Pieter Geyl's 'positive' tradition) nor to disinterested intellectual activity. Trevor-Roper, along with Herbert Read and A. J. Ayer, went along to the initial meeting of the Congress for Cultural Freedom, provocatively held in Berlin in 1950. In his wry, witty report,[6] Trevor-Roper says that the British delegates had agreed to come on the assumption that the conference was organised for the purposes of intellectual discussion, not as a political 'demonstration'. But the latter it hectically turned out to be, and could only be, staged as it was in West Berlin before huge crowds. But the conference organisers hadn't presented it this way, and Trevor-Roper doubted that so many delegates would have turned up if it had been 'correctly advertised'.

What became clear to the startled eyes of the British delegates – in alliance with the Scandinavians and the French – was that the first allegiance of the organisers and key participants was to politics. In the panel discussion on 'Science and Totalitarianism', for example, Ayer began to speak to the announced subject.

To a disapproving audience he quoted John Stuart Mill and examined the philosophic justification of tolerance. The Greek chairman then explained that this was all irrelevant, since our enemies were too intolerant to be tolerated; and a German, declaring that 'in our times John Stuart Mill cannot help us', appealed for a rival dogmatism as a more useful weapon of war.

In spite of some attempts to return to an intellectual level, a political tone was thus early set and predominated for the remainder of the conference.

In Trevor-Roper's view, the American ex-communists like James Burnham and Professor Hook, and rootless European ex-communists like Arthur Koestler and Borkenau, starred in their intransigence, calls for political polarisation and narrowing of choices and alternatives, and intolerance. The British delegates, for example, objected to a particular sentence in the final manifesto: 'After professing the doctrine of toleration, the document added that those who believed totalitarian ideologies were to be "excluded from the Republic of the Spirit". All recognized in this phrase (ironically drafted by ex-communists) a justification of the American witch-hunt' – the hounding in the U.S. of radical writers and film-makers. Under pressure from the British delegates the sentence was finally withdrawn, 'Professor Hook and Mr Burnham protesting to the end'.

Trevor-Roper was particularly appalled by the behaviour of Herr Franz Borkenau, the Austrian writer.

Pouring out his German sentences with hysterical speed and gestures, he screamed that he was a convert from communism and proud of it; that past guilt must be atoned for; that the ex-communists alone understood communism and the means of resisting it; that communism meant and could only mean 'war and war and war and civil war and civil war and civil war' and that it must be destroyed at once by uncompromising frontal attack. Terrible though they were, neither the words nor the fanaticism of this speech were its most frightening feature. That was supplied by the German audience, whose applause on this occasion was different from any other applause throughout the congress: for it was hysterical. It was an echo from Hitler's Nuremberg.

After this speech the dramatic structure of the congress was revealed. On one side were the American and European ex-communists in alliance with the German nationalists in the audience ('anti-Russia, perhaps ex-nazi, and hysterical with a frontier-hysteria'). On the other in increasingly open opposition was the Atlantic bloc of the British and Scandinavian delegates with some French and Italians and others thrown in.

A slight pungent smell of British xenophobia is given off in Trevor-Roper's account. It was the British who had led the attack against those European and American ex-communist intransigents who had distinguished themselves by their non-English and non-Scandinavian hysteria and frenzy. Trevor-Roper concludes with a show of distaste, of liberal superiority, for ex-communists who'd initially swallowed communism – 'that obscurantist doctrinal rubbish whose residue can never be fully discharged from the system'.

Trevor-Roper also reports that at the congress Arthur Koestler delivered a long attack on England – an attack enthusiastically cheered on by the German audience – as parochial and isolationist. The English were refusing to see that the key issues of the time were that right and left are now meaningless terms, that the choice before us is communism or anti-communism, and that 'he who is not with us is against us'. Trevor-Roper didn't seem particularly disturbed or threatened by this performance, and the implication of his whole commentary appeared to be that the rock of English liberalism, with John Stuart Mill behind it, would be impregnable to such vulgar hysterical assaults.

As it turned out, it wasn't so impregnable. In *The Agony of the American Left* Christopher Lasch shows how the Congress for Cultural Freedom soon turned its attention to the stubborn isle. The British were to get the treatment via *Encounter*, which was established in 1953, and beside the CIA and American government operatives who helped run it, the journal was also to draw in British intellectuals like Stephen Spender and Frank Kermode.[7] The themes of Koestler's speech, that Trevor-Roper found so distasteful, were made its staple diet – part of what we recognise as a major meaning of 'end of ideology' theory in the 1950s. In the face of the need for a united front against bolshevism, conventional political distinctions had become irrelevant. Intellectual and political life in the free world should not be about being left or right, or socialist or pro-capitalist: everything should be subordinated to being anti-communist.

In Lasch's view, *Encounter*, for all its 'ultra-sophistication' of tone, and for all its claims to political realism, scepticism, and detachment – shown in the regular analyses of the deplorable state of affairs in Soviet Russia – was also remarkable for its 'unshakable faith in the good intentions of the American government'. In its very first issue Leslie Fiedler berated sentimentalists who believed the Rosenbergs, given the death sentence for alleged spying, to be conceivably innocent, and argued that their actions revealed the deplorable influence Stalinism had exercised for the last twenty

years over the mind of America. (It turned out later that the central
document which had been used to convict the Rosenbergs was a
crude forgery.) Fiedler thought it unbelievable that American
officials could be suspected of false accusations, and in a similar
defence of the United States, Lasch argues, *Encounter* would not
denounce the Bay of Pigs, the American coup in Guatemala, the
CIA's intervention in Iran, or its role in the creation of Diem in
Vietnam. 'The plight of the communist satellites wrung their
hearts; that of South Korea and South Vietnam left them
unmoved.'[8] *Encounter* intellectuals were placing their knowledge
in the service of American world power, the power – overt or con-
cealed – which has everywhere supported the global creation of
fascist and sub-fascist regimes.[9]

Lasch's argument is that the Congress for Cultural Freedom in
the early and middle 1950s represented an alliance between conservatives and liberals. But in the atmosphere of the extreme Cold
War pressures of the early 1950s the liberals in this sweet alliance
were largely on the defensive. Indeed, as Lasch shows, 'liberal intel-
lectualism' itself was a major target of Cold War attack. Borkenau
argued at the 1950 Berlin conference that totalitarianism grew
dialectically out of liberalism. With liberalism in decline in the
1920s and '30s, intellectuals looking for a 'ready-made doctrine of
salvation and a pre-fabricated paradise' (Borkenau's pleasant
words) turned to communism and Russia. Lasch argues that towards
the end of the 1950s after the discrediting of McCarthy and the
emergence of the desirability of detente, liberals in Cultural Freedom grew more confident and the dominance of the conservatives
began to fade.[10]

## The iceman cometh: James McAuley

In Australia, too, Cultural Freedom put itself on display, and in
1956 *Quadrant* was established, presumably as an antipodean com-
panion to *Encounter*. There is no space here to go into the Cold
War in the early 1950s in Australia,[11] nor into an analysis of
*Quadrant*. But let's briefly home in on James McAuley, whose institutional power as *Quadrant* editor and as a professor of English (in
Tasmania) was not at all negligible. McAuley's intellectual career

has something of the curve that we witnessed in the people who dominated in the parent Congress for Cultural Freedom, the ex-radicals from before World War II, atoning for their guilt with amazing levels of anti-communist hostility and anti-liberal intolerance.

McAuley, in the late 1930s,[12] as a young Sydney University sophisticate, was influenced by John Anderson – far more radical then than later – and was briefly close to communist positions; he was interested in jazz, and was part of a bohemian set that included A. D. Hope, Harold Stewart, and Oliver Somerville. His early poetry was in a direct line of descent from that of Christopher Brennan, emphasising the necessity of a symbolic realm that transcends mundane social and political life. Yet now, in the middle 1950s, a convert to catholicism, McAuley sounded like an Australian Borkenau in his fervent anti-liberalism. Perhaps not as extraordinary as the Borkenau in full flight that so stunned Trevor-Roper, but not so short of it either.

In his writings in *Quadrant* and in the essays collected together and published in 1959 as *The End of Modernity*, McAuley's social thought can be seen as insistently organicist, stressing organic connections between the human, the social, and the natural. He sees the last one hundred and eighty or so years as civilisation taking a mistaken path, turning away from the 'normal' state of society and the 'normal' state of man. Liberalism represents a state of individualistic pursuit of truth; it leads to uncertainty, lack of direction, and so ignores the natural certainty of the rationally-ordered universe. Liberalism breeds humanism, the belief in a merely human rationality, which must be inadequate. It must be inadequate since it is 'unnatural'. McAuley thus reverts to what is ultimately a medieval Aristotelianism for his social theory. The universe, and man's certain place in it, represents a divinely given rational order. In a 'normal' society man spontaneously recognises this rational order. Man is then both spontaneous and rational, and thus organic in himself, just as he is organically part of the larger social whole. Man *needs* such organic life, with its generalised certainty and direction; the organic, integrated personality will instinctively accept society's ordered values. Such values live by self-discipline, they are not imposed by authority.

McAuley's thought rests ultimately on an assertion that man has a single permanent nature, and the universe a permanent rationality; man and society have to fit themselves to these permanent natural features, or they become abnormal, unnatural and a prey to disorder. The assumption of a true human nature provided McAuley with an ethical language; men, for example, liberals who are merely humanist in their lives or intellectual methods, are characterised as 'morally deformed', that is, they are deforming their own basic true nature, which is guaranteed by grace. The liberal is deforming the 'natural law' of himself and of the universe.

McAuley's theory of what is 'natural' also provides him with an outline of history. The industrial age is seen in terms of an apocalyptic moment. Industrialism's associated ideologies of liberalism and materialism have led to a nihilist nothingness. In such a state, men again look for what is natural and normal: cooperation, uniformity, an ordered society. Hence various totalitarianisms, fascist and communist, arise to satisfy this need. But modern men, deformed by liberal experience, can no longer discriminate between the true and false in natural law. They find these totalitarianisms attractive, because of the order they *share* with the traditional totality. The totalitarian society, especially the communism of the 1950s, is thus really thrown up by liberalism's own human failure, and in answer to man's most fundamental need. Communism is the parody version of traditional society which is so seductive because it is so *like* traditional society in its pseudo-ideals of order and rationality. Hence to McAuley liberalism isn't a threat any longer in itself: it is rather the empty space into which normal traditional society should go, but which is in danger of being invaded by pseudo-tradition. In McAuley's own dramatic, paranoid, apocalyptic language:

Thus today, across the twilight Tom Tiddler's ground of shallow humanism, Tradition and Anti-tradition confront one another, each recognising its supreme antagonist . . . many of those who are sickened by the emptiness of liberalist humanism are deeply impressed, not distinguishing the counterfeit from the genuine ideal.[13]

McAuley sees modern history not as a period of defeat, but as a crucial apocalyptic moment, the moment in which traditional values can again step in and win.

The battle with pseudo-traditional communism is a perilous and exciting one, and the age, in its very emptiness, is ripe for the victory of tradition. At the same time, liberals must be vigorously campaigned against, because they allow the emptiness into which the communist alternative can step, and because they are too morally deformed to oppose totalitarianism. On the other hand totalitarianism (especially communism) is the powerful rival because of its pseudo-traditionalism. It must be desperately fought at all costs and wherever it appears; its vanguard proponents will be influential because of the weakness of liberals. Thus McAuley sees history as the arena of a crucial contest, with tradition on one side, and pseudo-traditional communism and, by weakness and default, liberalism on the other. Over the emptiness of liberalism, the proponents of tradition face the left-liberal alliance.

History is now presenting a vital opportunity for victory. In Australia such victory is more likely than in Europe, which is more ravaged by liberalism. As McAuley says, 'pure demonic evil is rare amongst us'. There is here a subdued version of a frontier myth: Australia is pristine and pure, undefiled by Europe's excesses and effete sophistication. Yet Australia preserves a significant part of the best of the European heritage, which McAuley sees in Burkean terms as 'the Common Law, the parliamentary method, humanitarian sentiment'.[14] These beliefs and institutions form a 'cultural matrix'. Allied to other past values of order, Australia can thus yet provide an approximate version of the ideal society. Australia, the pristine society, provides a unique historical opportunity, which can be grasped. As McAuley exclaims in the editorial to the first *Quadrant* of 1956, the journal which was to provide the body of social and political theory to facilitate this opportunity: 'In spite of all that can be said against our age, what a moment it is to be alive in! what an epoch for a magazine to emerge in!'

While apocalyptic, there is little of the more usual post-romantic pessimism about the present in McAuley's thinking, and the confidence he has in Australia and in the present historical moment carries over into his poetic theory.

McAuley insists on a presumed purity of literary tradition. Poetry is seen in organicist terms, but he dismisses romantic and post-romantic theories. He rejects the Coleridgean theory that the individual poet can by imagination shape reality for himself. He rejects expressionist poetry where the individual explores only the range of his own emotional life, without impersonalising his feelings. He rejects various kinds of vitalism, which exalt man's emotional life and energies as the primary reality. McAuley extends this last rejection to Australian kinds of vitalism, which are associated with values of strong emotion, honesty, directness of feeling, etc., values which, for example, are enshrined in the mateship tradition. For McAuley vital organic feelings must be incorporated into a rational contemplation of the divinely ordered world.

McAuley feels that romantic and post-romantic poetry is rightly about a loss of the 'old religion-centred way of life'. Yeats, Eliot, etc., rightly reject the 'naturalist-positivist outlook', and their work presents a powerful expression of the modern liberal plight. But they don't revert to traditional conceptions of the past: rather, modernists like them fall into the various traps of vitalism, which is irrational and anti-intellectual; into exalting themselves in prophetic stances, or into other kinds of subjectivism. Modernism confuses tradition with subjectivism and vitalism, rather than preserving tradition pure and whole.

At this point we can move on from McAuley's political arguments and statements of poetic theory to looking at his poems. The distress at 'subjectivism' and the revering of an impersonal tradition can be seen in the exhortations of 'An Art of Poetry', from *A Vision of Ceremony* (published in 1956), a poem dedicated to Vincent Buckley:

Scorn then to darken and contract
The landscape of the heart
By individual, arbitrary
And self-expressive art.

For McAuley the task of the poet is clear. The poet as an individual should submit to the religious order of the world, and should address himself to past literature's great 'themes', which he names as 'devotion, love, honour, courage and adventure'. The ordered nature of verse corresponds to the ordered nature of the universe: a strong form is thus a sacred and sacralising quality. In terms of form, traditional principles must also be re-instituted. The highest poetry is 'liturgical', presenting the range of man's inner spiritual states. Poetry also reflects the hierarchical order of society. As McAuley says, 'corresponding to the good breeding, courtesy, and refinement of the social ideal ... there is a poetic grace, courtesy and controlled vitality'. McAuley recognizes the aristocratic assumptions behind this ideal of urbanity, but openly approves of them. In 'A Letter to John Dryden', a programmatic poem written in 1953-4, he laments the modern lack of a highly educated upper-class audience who could appreciate 'well-bred' verse:

It seems (in Dryden's time) the serious poet could rely
Upon a well-instructed audience.

He is thus like a Leavisite in his self-conscious cultural élitism. The poet is to embody in his writing the finest social and spiritual ideals of the past and his role in the present society is to be an educative one.

What happened when McAuley tried this poetry was predictable, the more predictable because he considered it so easy again to write such verse. For McAuley, as the exultant tone of 'A Letter to John Dryden' shows, certainly thought it was going to be easy. He writes in this poem of T. S. Eliot:

Perhaps, you'd choose T. Eliot's mighty line,
To drift, and flutter, hesitate, opine,
Hint at a meaning, murmur that God knows,
And gently settle in a soup of prose.

McAuley is not only mocking Eliot's lack of ordered poetic form – the modernist poet's 'soup of prose'. In so doing he is joining in with Frank Kermode, as we saw in chapter two, in a desire to tame modernism, tone it down, and make it responsive to 'order'; McAuley is also anticipating Vincent Buckley's assault on modernism and its connexions with primitivism in the 1920s and '30s. McAuley is also scorning Eliot for thinking that the whole thing might be difficult: for feeling that there may be difficulties in defining what is 'religious' experience, in distinguishing religious experience from other experiences which look like it, in detecting the real from the hoped, and in relating religious experience to other kinds of experience.

The poems in *A Vision of Ceremony* are remarkably confident in asserting their achievement. The very brashness and pretentiousness of the book's title indicates this confidence from the start. But it is this confidence which reveals the poetry's failure. McAuley sees his poetic role as a socially and spiritually educative one. His poetry will exhibit the sense of organic culture, the feelings of spring-like rebirth, the aristocratic fineness, grace and urbanity, which will be the living example of tradition's success for Australian culture. His work will pave the way for a widespread cultural movement. But the danger of such an educative stance is that the poet will see *himself* as embodying these urbane and aristocratic values. The danger is that the cultural alternative will exist nowhere but in McAuley's poetic personality.

McAuley succumbs to this danger. He thought he could avoid personalism by eschewing any kind of prophetic stance, such as Ezra Pound adopted; but his attempt to hide himself in the aristocratic values of the poetry only reveals his self-consciousness in the attempt, and the extraordinary personal confidence and personal assertiveness that went into it. McAuley is utterly unlike English thinkers like Leavis, who see modern history as defeat for the old organic society and for organicist values. In McAuley there is no sense of apocalyptic defeat, no heavy sense of cultural pessimism. McAuley's confidence relates to his Australian situation. As the poem 'Nativity' shows, McAuley doesn't give in to any kind of determinism that organicism is historically done for. With a provincial brashness he feels its re-institution is eminently achievable. He continually writes poems in *A Vision of Ceremony* which *assert* the reality of religion-based and organicist values; but the transparency of the assertion reveals only McAuleys' confidence in himself as a cultural transmitter. The stress on his own poetic personality also has a political meaning: his urbanity was to be asserted against the unspiritual materialism of liberals and leftists. But again the self-consciousness of the urbanity reveals its thinness.

McAuley's sense of the European heritage is eclectic and external. His poetry doesn't flow naturally, but painfully in its heavy mental construction; it is intellectual in the most unsubtle ways. It is, finally, precisely what he hoped it wouldn't be: an 'arbitrary', 'individual', 'self-expressive' activity. In his prose and in 'A Letter

to John Dryden' there is a kind of giddy wonder in his discovery of
the European totality, and a heady excitement in the thought
of applying the totality to Australia. McAuley has no inward sense
of the European past, his grasping on to aristocratic values in *The
End of Modernity* is both brash and gross, and as only a provincial
eclectic could, he is excited at the completeness and totality of the
organicist system.

Perhaps we should view McAuley, however, as ultimately a victim of the 1950s. Its Cold War anti-communism allowed McAuley
a paranoid confidence in projecting himself into the centre of the
Australian historical moment. In the Australia of the 1950s
McAuley could believe in the victory of Burkean conservatism, of
medieval-Aristotelian concepts of liturgical poetry and of a concern for a past literature which emphasises themes of devotion,
love, honour, courage, and adventure. Incredible. Ridiculous. Yet
the Cold War in the 1950s, with the rightwing shift in politics and
the strength of the Catholic-DLP alliance, must have given the
McAuley of that time his confident feeling that there was a wave-
like historical movement in which communism and liberalism
would be submerged, while his own traditional values swept all
before them: he could feel utterly politically realistic and
hardheaded.

It couldn't last, and it didn't. During the 1960s McAuley's work
collapsed into desiccation, into the sense that the desired traditional values were more personal assertion than social hope. His
poetic theory, his sense of the European totality, his hopes for Australia as the new world, the new antipodean ideal Europe, all disin-
tegrated. The collapse coincided with the slackening of Cold War
attitudes, when the political and ideological polarisations, which
had been the basis of McAuley's buoyancy, began to dissolve.

*Captain Quiros* registered the change in McAuley's attitudes and
*élan*. The writing of the poem spans the two decades; it was begun
in the late 1950s and completed for publication in 1964. The poem
starts off extremely confidently, with McAuley employing an
impersonal narrative method and an 'architectonic' structure. But
the poem's aim, to find the 'new world' in the southern seas,
becomes the more illusory the closer the narrative approaches to
Australia. In the end Australia as the 'new world' society becomes

just an idea, 'Terra Australis', an unreal hope and conception. As the hope fades, the poetry's grand style becomes finally dispersed and desultory.

McAuley did not try this large 'impersonal' verse again. The collapse is expressed in *Surprises of the Sun* (1969). Unlike the title of the 1956 *A Vision of Ceremony*, the new title doesn't pretend to possession of an ordered universal vision. *Surprises of the Sun* opens with a group of autobiographical poems, followed by a number of rather desultory, dispirited lyrics. The autobiographical poems suggest a clear interest in Lowell. McAuley was now turning to a potentially personalist and egotistical form, presumably in order to confront himself with his own failure and to search in his past and in his family history for possible explanations. In the key autobiographical poem, 'Because', he writes:

It's my own judgement day that I draw near,
Descending in the past, without a clue,
Down to that central deadness: the despair
Older than any hope I ever knew.

Perhaps sensing the illusoriness and externality of his previous aims and theories, McAuley now starts from the beginning to find out the actual values that have been essential to his life, and to discover the reasons behind his present 'central deadness'. But the poems, unlike Lowell's, are not sustained nor particularised enough, because too many past attitudes of McAuley's from the 1950s remain, and because the explanation of his central deadness may lie not in his personal history, but in the literary tradition to which he rather waywardly belongs.

In his 1970 prose volume, *The Personal Element in Australian Poetry*, McAuley is obviously searching in Australian poetry for a justifying tradition of a personal style which is at the same time an assertion of rational moral control over experience. However, on the last page of the book he suddenly and hysterically lashes out at American 'black poetry',

with its verbal violence, its formlessness, its antinomian and antilogical frenzy ... and its secret winking inner light of wicked knowledge that 'out there' is neither freedom nor love but only one shelf of the vast hell of the egotists ...

McAuley hopes this kind of poetry will never emerge in Australia. But perhaps behind his hysterical rejection of it is the fear, both that the central fact of his own poetry is that there is no experience for him to assert rational control over, only the emptiness left by the defeat of his old values, his self now a prey to Manicheism and formlessness; and that 'out there' there may be no reassuring order in the universe.

Yet his poetry in the 1960s still retains a certain degree of confident assertion. He still wants his poetry to be urbane, since such urbanity indicates certain values of true civilisation which leftists lack. This political implication in the tone of his verse also infects his new personal style. Even in a Lowellesque autobiographical poem like 'Because', there is a slight ideological stiffness, a kind of assertion that to be so personally honest, and to be thus interested in inner analysis, are qualities which, again, the left notably lacks. He slightly ideologises his new capacity for personal analysis.

McAuley can be related to a particular tradition of Sydney writers, Brennan, Lindsay, Slessor, Hope, White – the tradition I describe in *Australian Cultural Elites*. These writers reject Australian society (and then society as such) because of the superior reality of European values, but at the same time they sense that they are not part of Europe's social texture or social history. They then opt for a 'third realm', a symbolic realm where European ideas, images, myths, symbols, prevail, but which doesn't have to depend on any actual society for its reality. The realm is conceived as natural, since society (modern and Australian) is not seen as answering to the ideal values of European history. The search is for a universal natural realm, and because they reject society, the writers in this tradition see themselves as having no political function, except perhaps one of cultural opposition. It would be useless to import in any prophetic or educative way the desired European values into Australian society, since there is no cultural basis in Australia for them, and in any case society is a contingent presence beside the permanencies of nature. In *Australian Cultural Elites* I describe this tradition as a 'provincial romantic idealism'. I would now think of it as a 'neocolonial romantic idealism' – the dilemma, as Terry Sturm has argued of Brennan's *Poems* (1913) and of Henry

Handel Richardson's *The Fortunes of Richard Mahony*, of not belonging to any society, only to a symbolic realm that may be illusory.[15]

McAuley is in this tradition in so far as he shares a Europeanising attitude. But McAuley diverges when he identifies a cultural base for his European ideas in Australia. McAuley's view is that Burkean institutions and organic society concepts carry over from the English 18th century and are crucially formative in the founding of Australian society. Hence institutions like the law, parliament, and the 'natural' conceptions of order and reason which they embody, form the organic 'cultural matrix' at the basis of Australian reality. These conceptions of order and reason would have been spontaneously accepted and lived out by the individuals in Australian society. Unfortunately, this cultural base has been hampered and over-laid by 'unnatural' 19th-century ideologies, like materialism, liberalism, and personalism. (McAuley's a great one for the -isms. Still, I once, long ago, in a review of a Leavis book in *Nation*, committed the folly of accusing the great and venerable critic of 'simplism' – a term which acquaintances forever after found irresistibly risible. But I could never follow McAuley in excesses like 'liberalist humanism'. For an -ist and -ism person, that's just going too far.)

McAuley's poetic and cultural project was bound to fail. He idealised the European past in the first place, and then took literally his own possession of Europe's ideal values (urbanity, grace, etc.), not sensing, as did other writers in this tradition, particularly Brennan, that these values belong to a European social history of which Australians have never been part. It was McAuley's Cold War brashness, and his intensity and certainty as a Catholic convert, which made him think he could so easily internalise a past European way of life, not just symbolic ideas of nature derived from Europe, and residing in the self, wherever it be.

McAuley's recoil to more personal, but still ordered poetic positions, only brought him closer to the problem at the heart of the literary tradition to which he belonged. The problem, on which Brennan's *Poems (1913)* is based, is that the 'natural' and universally conceived European essences such as McAuley wanted to possess, might only be the symbolic projection of his own, culturally isolated self, leaving him with a 'central deadness', like Brennan's 'hermit-heart'.

History moved past and beyond James McAuley, as for other Cold War conservatives, and certainly his obsessive anti-communism is not to be taken as representative of mainstream cultural life of the 1950s. Yet many of his emphases were influential on the less strident, more liberal ('liberalist'?) practitioners of Cold War end-of-ideology assumptions, in the later 1950s and into the '60s. In particular his assumption that life and being are fundamentally metaphysical, became a predominating theme in anti-radical nationalist literary criticism.[16] Influential New Critics like G. A. Wilkes – of whom more in the next chapter – and H. P. Heseltine would not have gone along with McAuley's propagandising for Catholic medieval values and so on, nor would they have defined 'metaphysical' in McAuley's particular terms and optimistic spirit. Rather, they agreed with a general Cold War lofty end-of-ideology view which looked down on the social and political as an unworthy human interest, and which paraded certain special interests – the metaphysical, the moral, the psychological, the introspective, the intellectual, the reflective, the contemplative – as the supreme location of interesting experience and, hence, of literature of quality.

# 4

# The Metaphysical Ascendancy

Brennan stands like a Colossus between the world of our first nationhood
-and the world of our modern endeavours.

> (Vincent Buckley, 'The Image of Man in Australian Poetry',
> *Essays in Poetry, Mainly Australian*, 1957).

Australian literary criticism and history has, like the eastern part
of the continent, been split by a Great Dividing Range. In the cultural history of the 1950s and '60s we can witness a drama of conflict and contestation similar to that we noticed earlier over the
nature and possibilities of romanticism, between radical critics and
historians like Raymond Williams and E. P. Thompson and Cold
War liberals like Frank Kermode. On the one side have run the radical nationalists – Nettie Palmer, Vance Palmer, A. A. Phillips, Russel Ward, Geoffrey Serle, Ian Turner, Stephen Murray-Smith. On
the other side of the great divide, and equally desirous to secure
and own the whole continent, fall the Australian New Critics and
Leavisites, G. A. Wilkes, Vincent Buckley, H. P. Heseltine, and, in
the 1970s and '80s, Leonie Kramer and Leon Cantrell.

This chapter will explore the relationship of knowledge and
power, the theme that Michel Foucault has made his own for the
study of ideas in institutional settings like psychiatry or punish-
ment. In Foucault's terms, the textcentric, formalist Leavisites and

New Critics constitute a 'regime of truth', a regime that in the main has successfully warded off the challenge of contextual approaches. In the 20th century, contextualism has lived on mainly in the form of the Freudian approach (rejected by the Leavisite and New Critical schools as reducing the text to psychoanalytic aspects of the author), the Marxist (rejected as reducing the autonomy of the text either to its relationship to the economic level or to the ideological), and, in Australia, the radical nationalist (rejected as reducing Australian literature to certain presumed distinctive characteristics of popular consciousness and the environment).

Intellectual arguments aren't 'won' or 'lost' in a purely intellectual sphere, by purely intellectual criteria and persuasiveness, and indeed the history of the conflict between the contextualists and formalists in the postwar period reveals the immense – if often invisible – importance of non-intellectual criteria in the history of ideas, especially the institutional power of the universities. Certainly we can notice particular knowledge/power convergences in the 1950s and '60s period: the period of the expansion of universities in Britain, Australia, and North America. For whatever we think of the relative merits of the contextualist and formalist approaches, in university departments of English it is the formalists who have achieved power and influence, who have set the parameters and tone for teaching in a department (and, hence, usually, in schools), the books on courses, the directions of postgraduate research . . . In this century, in English-speaking countries, it is text-centric formalism which has held the institutional power, and for this reason has become the orthodoxy, the ideologically dominant approach.

For one thing, the formalist project fits in nicely with the development of departments of English in this century, and particularly after World War II when university staff numbers grew enormously to cope with a mushrooming scholarship-supported student population. Departments of anything develop by marking off a particular area with a particular object (literature), with which it requires professional, specialised knowledge to deal (literary criticism as a distinct discipline). Formalism feeds on such professionalism and specialisation. Formalists tend to a highly exclusive distinction between the literary (what they like seeing in literature and language) and the non-literary (what they don't like others seeing). When this distinction is backed by power and the mystique of professionalism, the result is an attack on any notion of ideal plurality.

Formalism is very limited in its aims. It sets out to describe and evoke, rather than to explain. For the contextualists, the reverse is true: the text is to be seen in its relationship to something else, a preferred context, whatever it might be, that will help explicate a work's character. For the formalist, however, the only relations to be recognised are internal, how the various parts of a text function together. The only things outside the text that can legitimately be 'read' are suggested by the text's own use of codes and conventions. A particular text's codes and conventions will call into being other codes and conventions; its possible use of myths will refer to other myths. For the formalist, 'history' refers to the relationship between a text and all other texts – to 'inter-textuality' – and historical time is not the relationship of a text to a specific social history since all literary texts are seen as simultaneously present.

Consequently, contextualists and formalists differ in their approach to the question of disciplines and degree of specialisation. Contextualists, in their search for explanatory contexts, will be drawn to other disciplines – to cultural history or sociology or philosophy or the history of ideas or biography. Contextualists will be more likely to wish to blur any hard line drawn between criticism as a distinct discipline, and other fields. Often because of this contextualists will not see themselves primarily as critics. They are as likely to be historians or sociologists or biographers. Contextualists are more likely to try to be interdisciplinary, to desire to work with non-critics in a common attack on the problems of cultural analysis and explanation.

The formalists say that all these supposed explanatory contexts are just more and disguised versions of the author, who should be dismissed from view, should be 'dead' (the Intentional Fallacy). For the text exists not in the intentions of the author, or as a reflection of society, but in its creation by skilled, knowledgeable critics, establishing how it functions, and is similar to/different from other texts. For the formalists, the death of the author is the birth of the critic.

It follows that you have to have a high degree of specialised knowledge of the body of conventions, myths, references, allusions, of how these function in different texts. You turn your knowledge inward, away from other disciplines, and build up your own discipline as separate and distinct – as 'professional'. You then find yourself, after a short while, talking only to other critics. Intellectual interests narrow and narrow: critics become massively and embarrassingly ignorant of everything except their own inturned discipline.

Criticism begins to expand mightily under the steam of this intra-disciplinary logic. Instead of addressing historians or sociologists in a search for illuminating contexts, you tell other critics about how a poem or novel or play refers to this or that other poem, novel, play, how it uses this or that myth, how it has all sorts of allusions to previous works which enrich its own meaning. You set up and get going a proliferation of specialist critical journals. The age of criticism is on its way.

## The orthodoxy

In Australia the age of criticism began really revving up in the late 1950s and '60s, with the entry into departments of English of a new generation of highly trained professional critics. The new critics had youth, ambition, and sometimes energy on their side. They were usually trained in English literature, and they wished to apply the methods of analysis and techniques of scholarship learned from being students of such high literature to the study of the Australian field: a field, in effect, they were colonising with their Leavisite and New Critical confidence that they could possess texts, own them, handle them, know their inner reality, turn them inside out, 'read' them in a way that either non-critics like historians, or older non-textually-trained critics (such as in the main the radical nationalists), couldn't hope to do. As well they were highly trained in the analysis of poetry, and in the 'poetic' aspects of fiction (imagery, symbol, myth, irony) where contextual critics in general, from Marxist to radical nationalist, usually focussed on novels and short stories. Confident of their powers, aggressive in their use, they set

bout trying to reshape Australian literature in ways most amen-
ble to their own methods of analysis. They attempted to create
new 'Australian literature'.

The entry of this new generation of critics coincided in the 1950s
nd early '60s with a Cold War imperative, that social and political
nd ideological and utopian aspects of literature be dismissed as
relevant to the true nature of literature. Literature was to be seen
s moral and metaphysical only, and by a neat turn, only the ten-
ons and ambiguities of moral and metaphysical experience were
 be recognised as purely literary. This chapter will examine some
fluential essays by two of the new critics who rose to prominence
 these years and who were particularly enthusiastic about pursu-
g the all-round implications for Australian literature of this
etaphysical-centred view of the truly 'literary' – G. A. Wilkes in
ydney, and Vincent Buckley in Melbourne. And their essays in
rn proved highly influential for other and succeeding generations
f university-trained critics.

The ensuing generation of Leavisite and New Critics helped
rm an orthodoxy, instituting a metaphysical ascendancy that
eigns, if ever more shakily, to this day. By 'orthodoxy' I don't mean
at all these new critics felt and thought the same way, that their
ssays were like new-minted coins, shining out identity and same-
ess, that there are no discernible differences between Wilkes or
uckley or Heseltine or lots of other critics. On the contrary, it is
e very strength of an orthodoxy that it can combine difference,
ariety, even sharp conflict, with an underlying unity of assump-
ons.

An orthodoxy – what Foucault might call a 'discursive formation'
 grows and strengthens itself by the play of difference and dis-
greement within its borders. The contributors to an orthodoxy can
el like free subjects, unbound in consciousness, unconstrained by
ny thought that a conventional view is being 'forced' on them
om outside. Its very heterogeneity always keeps to the fore the
uestion: how can there be an orthodoxy which encompasses such
ifferent critical personalities (as, say, Wilkes, Buckley, Heseltine)?
Jo, there's not an orthodoxy, only a healthy state of critical affairs,
f growth of knowledge by proper scholarly disputation. How can
e be part of an orthodoxy if we disagree with each other so keenly

and often? We're freely choosing this kind of approach and vie
because it's so clearly persuasive, so right, true, and inevitable; it
so illuminating of so many neglected and unexplored aspects c
Australian literature. There's no orthodoxy, only healthy diversit
There's no 'formation' as Foucault's 'discursive formation' implie
only individual voices.

I've already recounted, in my story in the prologue of the haple
teenage Leavisite, the occasionally bitter differences betwee
Leavisites amongst themselves, and between the Melbourn
Leavisites like Sam Goldberg and Sydney New Critics like G. /
Wilkes in the Sydney English department in the middle 1960s. Nc
would I play down how strong and pervasive these difference
were. They relate to another historical narrative, a story I tried t
recount in *Australian Cultural Elites*, of frequent and persisting di
ferences between Sydney and Melbourne intellectual traditions t
do with how an intelligentsia should see itself and act, or not ac
in the larger society. In his book on *Scrutiny* Francis Mulher
argues that F. R. Leavis's journal possessed a 'militant, committec
interventionist cultural practice', the attempted if finally illusor
creation of 'an intellectual formation of a type virtually unknow
in and deeply alien to English bourgeois culture: an intelligentsi
in the classic sense of the term, a body of intellectuals dissociate
from every established social interest, pointed in its subordinatio
of amenity to principle, united only by its chosen cultural commi
ments'.[1] Certainly this type of committed, moralistic, judging an
proselytising intelligentsia – so congenial to Melbourne intellectua
traditions – proved alien to bourgeois culture at Sydney Universit
in the early and mid 1960s. But this intersecting narrative does nc
contradict our present story, that there was a convergence in criti
cism between Melbourne Leavisites and Sydney New Critics i
urging an exclusive moral and metaphysical focus.

Further, the stronger an orthodoxy is the more likely it is t
accommodate ideological and political differences in those wh
belong to it. For example, H. P. Heseltine was probably in thos
years in the social-democratic centre of the political spectrum
wrote happily in *Meanjin*, and admired *Meanjin*'s radical nationa
ist editor Clem Christesen. Leon Cantrell, as we shall soon see
could be noticed in the 1970s on the edges of the Communist Party

eing literary editor for a time of *Australian Left Review*. Yet all
ese critics, from Wilkes and Buckley to Heseltine and Cantrell,
ave produced texts that express and extend the range of the ortho-
oxy's basic premises.

1. In particular, they agreed that literature is primarily meta-
hysical, while possibly sharply differing over what is truly meta-
hysical, or which writers or works manifest metaphysical themes
nd in what ways.

2. They adopt and share a basic critical procedure, a methodo-
ogical operation to be surgically performed on all texts. They div-
le a text (and a writer's imagination) into a hierarchy of levels:
eep, profound metaphysical layers (the truly literary), as against
uperficial social or political or ideological or utopian layers (not
eally literary at all). The latter layers are but surface features, like
elatine on top of a pâté, tasted if you like, but not to be confused
with the strong, rich, subtle, European-style tastes below.

3. From this dissection a new kind of cultural history follows.
he literary spirit of a period or age is represented by literary
works that are either fully metaphysical in their own right, or by
hose true depths in texts once the non-metaphysical is scraped
way. (In some versions, this true literary spirit also represents the
entral human spirit of the period or age as well, its *Geist*.)

Armed with these critical assumptions and methodological pro-
edures, the new generation set about establishing a new 'regime
f truth'. For, in Foucault's terms, an orthodoxy, a discursive forma-
ion, is indeed productive of truth, of knowledge. But its desire for
ruth is at one with its desire for power over all other discourses,
ll other claims to knowledge of a chosen area. It both liberates
terature into new perspectives, and imprisons it anew. In these
erms, we can see the new generation producing enlightening
ccounts of Australian literature, revealing areas and aspects not
erceived by those within the fields of vision of other critical tra-
itions. In particular they wished to dismiss radical nationalist cul-
ural history, at the same time as making more sophisticated, or
odifying (sometimes drastically), the older metaphysical-centred
iews of Australian literature, like those squired by Norman Lind-
ay. The new generation, then, produced new knowledge, but only
o draw lines around it, to enclose it behind high walls.

Further, their desire for intellectual power was accompanied by actual institutional power, positions of power in universities in terms of teaching and setting of courses. Let's witness the desire for truth and intellectual power operating in some key texts by G. A. Wilkes, who became professor of Australian literature at Sydney University in the early 1960s (he was to succeed Sam Goldberg as professor of English literature, while professor Leonie Kramer was to take up the Australian chair), and Vincent Buckley (prominent in the early teaching of Australian literature at Melbourne University).

We can start by glancing at Wilkes's 'The Eighteen Nineties', an essay first published in a Sydney University arts journal in 1958 but later republished in the 1960s in much more accessible form. While the essay discusses 1890s literature, its implications could be easily perceived by later critics as covering Australian literature as a whole.

Wilkes' essay operates on what will become a very familiar move: it attacks the radical nationalist position for being too exclusive, for ignoring Australian literary works not amenable to notions of national sentiment and consciousness.

If we were to evaluate the nineties by strictly literary standards, then we should find that the mass of writers are men of minor talent, living through a poem or two in an anthology or a contribution to a collection of short stories; we should find that of the two major figures, Lawson and Furphy, Lawson is memorable not for the part of his work – his verse – that reflects the temper of the age, but for the part that transcends it, while Furphy's work is important not for its democratic temper or offensively Australian bias, but for its exploration of issues that are not local but universal in their reference. The political verse of Bernard O'Dowd is now mainly of clinical interest, Banjo Paterson is read by schoolboys. The best poetry written at the time, the poetry of Chris Brennan, is unrelated to social and political movements, as is the work of the most notable novelist to emerge, Henry Handel Richardson. The nationalistic, patriotic, radical tendencies in the writing of the period assure it a place in Australian social history, but its place in Australian literary history must remain in doubt so long as we continue to derive its identity as a period from features such as these.

Wilkes then implies that all such social and political concerns are pretty well hopeless for the production of literature ('Yet it remains true, I think, that literature inspired by national sentiment or by the zeal of the reformer is artistically the most insecure of all'). The final move of the argument now comes into view: we should recognise that the social and political are 'surface' realms, local and temporary, and therefore 'non-literary'. The metaphysical realm of existence, on the other hand, because its problems are more abiding and permanent than social and political problems are presumed to be, is somehow, by magical fiat, 'strictly literary'.

A related assumption in Wilkes' argument is that critics using social and political criteria are inevitably crude and unsophisticated: but critics using metaphysical criteria are thereby protected from such crudity, and are ever blessed with a subtle and complex sense of texts. Wilkes uses Furphy's *Such is Life* as his slippery stepping-stone for this argument ('no other book written in the nineties serves so well to show how far the valuation of a work by non-literary criteria may diverge from a strictly literary valuation'):

While the book may have a temper that is democratic and a bias that is offensively Australian, these are surface features, inessential to its permanent literary worth. The value set upon the novel by the social historian is largely irrelevant to its value as literature: *Such is Life* is memorable not as showing a stage in the evolution of the Australian democratic ideal, but as an exploration of the abiding problems of destiny and free-will, moral responsibility, and the operation of chance in the universal scheme – problems which have engaged writers not of Furphy's period only, but of all periods, and which are still in no imminent danger of solution.[3]

In a challenging review in *Southerly* of Grahame Johnston's 1962 collection, *Australian Literary Criticism*, in which Wilkes' essay appeared, W. M. Maidment, a longtime teacher in the department of English at Sydney University, took Wilkes' argument in this passage to task on pluralist grounds. 'One may ask', Maidment says about the general implications for criticism of Wilkes' argument on *Such is Life*, why interests of a metaphysician and moral philosopher are transferable as literary value criteria while those of a social historian are not; whether, if universals are manifest in particulars, a democratic response and an 'Australian' bias do not bear on problems of social relationship and organization as hoary and still unsolved as those Professor Wilkes mentions; and by what process of argument duration becomes value or proof of value.[4]

The New Critics have been ever eager to picture themselves in a happy pluralist posture, pointing out that the radical nationalist interpretation focuses only on a few people (Furphy-Paterson-Lawson), unjustifiably treats pre-1890s literature as a dark age, and leaves out 'romantic' and 'heroic' strains in Australian literature, as in the work of Patrick White, Thomas Keneally, A. D. Hope, Francis Webb, and R. D. FitzGerald, and in 19th-century predecessors like Kendall and Marcus Clarke.[5] Such recognition of Australian literary diversity has had its value in the past: but behind the pluralist gestures lies the tight grip of anti-radical-nationalist criticism on Australian literary history.

Wilkes says that an 'inflating process' has been at work using nationalist criteria to build the reputations of 1890s writers unworthy of high rank. But the Leavisites and New Critics themselves have enthusiastically engaged in building to giant-size the reputation of the figures they see as the metaphysicals in Australian literature – Brennan, Slessor, FitzGerald, Douglas Stewart, James McAuley, and in the novel Richardson, White, and Boyd. A kind of pulping process has gone on. Writers are harvested for a metaphysical essence; if they reveal this essence, as Furphy and Lawson are allowed to do, they may run up and join the canonical ranks of the metaphysicals, the Brennanites. If they don't so yield, they are discarded and thrown to the compost heap to feed the worms of literary failure, of impermanent interest. Further, critics like Wilkes, Buckley, Heseltine and Kramer can back up their views with solid institutional powers – as professors and senior members of English departments, commanding the respect and loyalty of their subjects and followers with more than intellectual means.

## Out in the cold: the process of exclusion

Students and teachers absorbing critical approaches and developing their skills in the 1960s and '70s in departments of English have been subject to a continuous process of institutional repression. We have in effect been excluded from knowledge of all Australian literature except for the Australian metaphysicals, or writers with a presumed major metaphysical aspect. The making of reputations and setting of canons can be seen most clearly in two handbooks for teaching that came out in the early sixties, Geoffrey Dutton's collection *The Literature of Australia*, and Grahame Johnston's *Australian Literary Criticism*, where the various Leavisites/New Critics combine and cooperate (in Johnston's collection Vincent Buckley scores a startling four chapters, and G. A. Wilkes three). For postgraduates and researchers and eager teachers the next steps unfolded as if of themselves: you start off by saying that all literary criticism hitherto in Australia has been dominated by the radical nationalist view which has tied us up to the post of (a narrow view of) Lawson and Furphy. We've got to shake ourselves free and explore writers ignored by the radical nationalists.

Now choose from one or more of Henry Kingsley, Marcus Clarke, Brennan, Shaw Neilson, Henry Handel Richardson, Fitz-Gerald, Slessor, Judith Wright, Douglas Stewart, James McAuley, A. D. Hope, Francis Webb; from expatriates like Christina Stead or Martin Boyd; and last but not . . . Patrick White.

Or, another step, but sideways, say: Writers like Furphy and Lawson have been misrepresented by the radical nationalists, for they really reveal noumenal metaphysical interests, for example the gloom thesis (the 1890s equals not optimism and brotherhood but alienation, loneliness, despair, doubt, suffering . . .).

Final step: a new aspect of Australian literature has been revealed.

Luckily for us, we can call here on some supporting evidence of how the orthodoxy became institutionalised. This is owing to the good offices of *Notes and Furphies* – the small but lively trade journal of ASAL, the fledgeling Association for the Study of Australian Literature – whose practitioners, by and large the younger brigade of Australian critics, or young in spirit, are helping to question the orthodoxy's textcentric, formalist, and metaphysical-only focus.

In the fifth issue of *Notes and Furphies* (October 1980) David Carter has described the establishment in 1959 of a course on Australian literature, the course being a formalisation, Carter notes, in weekly seminars, of the series of public lectures given by Vincent Buckley in the previous year. The list of texts for 1960, apart from a couple of poetry anthologies, prescribes the following:

Brennan, Christopher, poems as selected in class
FitzGerald, R. D., *Moonlight Acre*
Slessor, Kenneth, *Poems*
Wright, Judith, *The Moving Image*
Wright, Judith, *Woman to Man*
Hope, A. D., *The Wandering Islands*
McAuley, James, *Under Aldebaran*
Stewart, Douglas, *Four Plays*
Lawrence, D. H., *Kangaroo*
Lawson, Henry, *Collected Stories*
Furphy, Joseph, *Such is Life*
Richardson, H. H., *The Fortunes of Richard Mahony*
Herbert, Xavier, *Capricornia*
Prichard, K. S., *Working Bullocks*
White, Patrick, *The Tree of Man*
Boyd, Martin, *The Cardboard Crown*

The course, offered as one-third of third-year honours, continued until 1967, when it was combined with a few American texts, to become 'Australian and American Literature'. It wasn't until 1977 that pass students could catch sight of some Australian literature, as an optional extra to their usual fare. The reign of the anglocentric assumption in university departments of English – the division between the core courses focusing on English literature, with Australian, or other, literatures as marginal additions – is, however, another story altogether.[6]

Our point here is to note the institutional inclusion of certain texts, the systematic exclusion of extraordinary numbers of others. It may appear surprising that apparently non-metaphysical, even despised social-realist, texts like those of Xavier Herbert and Katharine Prichard are included. But, as we'll shortly see, in relation to *Capricornia*, the inessential social and ideological surface can often be bared to reveal a text's true metaphysical presence, authority and value.

Let's examine but one instance of the metaphysical orthodoxy's methods of exclusion and control. How much, in the common course of the teaching of and encouraging research in Australian literature, are writers set from the 1930s? Do we commonly have, as a coherent course, works from: Vance Palmer, Eleanor Dark, M. Barnard Eldershaw, Frank Dalby Davison, Leonard Mann, Kylie Tennant, Dymphna Cusack, Xavier Herbert, K. S. Prichard, Miles Franklin, Jean Devanny, Betty Roland? And what of the 1950s? Where are the courses on 1950s social realists which might include Alan Marshall, Judah Waten, Frank Hardy, Gavin Casey, S. F. Bannister, Eric Lambert, John Morrison, Dorothy Hewett? The worth of these writers remains to be investigated – but students should have been and should be given the opportunity to find out for themselves.

In 'The Eighteen Nineties' G. A. Wilkes draws attention to 'the limitation' the radical nationalist view has imposed on Australian writing and criticism, a claim repeated by his ex-student Leon Cantrell in his introduction to his 1977 anthology *The 1890s* – Wilkes and Cantrell standing rather in the relation of critical father and son.

FATHER:  The ballad verse of the nineties was good poetry of its kind, but if it leads to a demand that all poetry should be of that kind, literary development is arrested. It was well for the writers of the nineties to deal boldly with Australian material, but as the tradition has descended to their successors, novelists have come to believe that their main function is to celebrate the outback, as the only material left that is unequivocally 'Australian'. The fashions set in the nineties, I think it is true to say, help explain why so much modern Australian verse is concerned with transcripts of environment, why the novel of city life has been slow to establish itself, and why traditions of the less 'extrovert' kind, in both prose and verse, have so tardily won acceptance.[7]

SON:  This interpretation of the period [the nationalist view of the nineties] has been a potent force for conservatism in Australian literature and culture generally. During the early decades of this century the popular styles and themes of the nineties came to be regarded by many as the natural and appropriate norms for Australian writers and artists. For a period of some fifty years the local cultural scene was notoriously conservative and resisted departure from these earlier models.[8]

FATHER:   Yes, I said that twenty years ago.
SON:   Was it so long? Anyway, I thought what you said is so good that I'd say it again.
We've been so denied knowledge of the non-metaphysical aspects of Australian literature that we accept Wilkes and Cantrell's account of nationalist-influenced, post-1890s writing as true.

But is it? Are we dealing with hayseed no-hopers who merely slavishly followed their own blinkered view of the 1890s? If the ballad and other popular forms of the 1890s were the predominant literary models, why were writers in the first decades of the new century like Louis Esson, Vance Palmer, Katharine Susannah Prichard, and Betty Roland so attracted to drama? If the 1890s had many racist attitudes, can the same be said of Katharine Prichard in *Coonardoo*? Or does her interest in the validity of Aboriginal experience (however we qualify it) owe something to later and different influences: developments in early 20th-century anthropology more sympathetic to Aboriginal society; romantic organicist notions of Aboriginal community; the internationalism of the Communist Party? And as for literary conservatism, are the divisions between nationalist-influenced writers and their opponents all that clear? (We recall Patrick White's 1958 reference in his autobiographical essay 'The Prodigal Son' to 'dreary, dun-coloured realism', quoted with relish by Cantrell in his introduction.) How different is Prichard's interest in Aboriginal community from Patrick White's interest? In what sense does White's *Riders in the Chariot*, with its hysterical anti-urbanism, advance the Australian novel of city life? Don't romantic beliefs about natural feelings and the natural world establish a common bond between writers like Vance Palmer, Prichard, and Patrick White? Are writers like M. Barnard Eldershaw quite without the remotest experimental merit?

Jack Beasley's *Red Letter Days* (1979) reminds us that the Australian social realists of the 1950s and '60s formed a varied and rich tradition, in theatre and film as well as in the novel, and that this tradition involved stimulating – as well as often very rigid – aesthetic arguments about 'socialist realism', literature, and politics. Such arguments involved the obvious overseas influences of thinkers and practitioners like Engels, Lenin, Gorky, and Brecht – influences which were also not simple and direct, but themselves part of ongoing aesthetic disputes – as in the polemic about bourgeois realism, naturalism, and innovative, experimental realism that Brecht directed against Lukács.[9] Far from focusing on local content and the outback only, and ignoring city life, the first novel the Australasian Book Society published was *Crown Jewel*, Ralph de Boissiere's novel of West Indian life (now republished in England by Picador). Judah Waten's novels dramatise Jewish migrant experience in Australia; and many other novels explore urban working-class life. Wilkes says 'the novel of city life has been slow to establish itself' – perhaps Professor Wilkes thinks the Collingwood of *Power Without Glory*, for example, is a suburb of Bourke.

In Melbourne, in the 1950s, Vincent Buckley was promoting a similar critical enterprise. Remarkably, the overall argument of 'The Image of Man in Australian Poetry',[10] a key chapter in Buckley's 1957 *Essays in Poetry, Mainly Australian*, confidently concedes a great deal to the radical nationalist interpretation of Australian literary history that it sets out to oppose. It jumps onto the same terrain, but only to elbow its protagonist off. For a start, it accepts the well-known view of radical nationalist historiography that Australian literature can be perceived as going through successive stages of transplantation, adaptation, and cultural maturity.

Buckley accepts the basic historiographical premises and procedures of A. A. Phillips' account in *The Australian Tradition*: in particular, the evolutionist and historicist assumption that there is a central line of literary development – a basic entity called the Australian mind, a single spirit for each age. Following the radical nationalists and perhaps being even more enthusiastic than they, Buckley offers a lordly dismissal of Australian poetry in the 19th century, up to the 1890s: 'As so many critics have insisted', says Buckley, 'these poets were un-Australian in a crippling sense; they were aliens, with the imaginations of *émigrés*.' Into the rubbish bin of literary history go Barron Field, Michael Massey Robinson, Adam Lindsay Gordon, Harpur, Kendall, and 'even Victor Daley'. We have here but 'a poetry of the Anglicizers, the unassimilable, we might almost call them the poetically unemployable'.[11]

And Buckley goes on, as if he's intoning words from Vance Palmer or A. A. Phillips:

By the eighties of last century, the transplanted English approach was beginning to be replaced with something more vital, with a different view of man's endeavours and of the meaning which Australia confers on them.[12]

In the pre-1890s poetry, the faults of the émigré poetry came 'largely from the fact that Australia was not seen as in any sense a spiritual home'. In the 1890s, Australia happily became a 'spiritual home', but not in poets like Lawson or Victor Daley as we might expect the predictable logic of the argument thus far to reveal. (Daley appears to have a remarkably uncertain status in Buckley's argument: here our critic seems to have in mind Daley as 'Creeve Roe', the poet of social commentary, not the Daley of lyrical verse whose sensibility, Buckley feels, was 'soaked in the strictly ersatz mists of the Celtic Twilight'.)

Lawson and Daley were Australian democrats, though they also reveal a constant note of exile or alienation. They are 'poetically divided personalities', but they 'had a small range of emotions, embodied in a small and insufficiently resonant range of verse forms, tending to an uneasy cross between the ballad and the lyric; and their social and philosophical ideas were incomplete and crude'. What happens is that the optimism, melancholy, moral indignation, the joy and pathos, of Lawson and his ilk are 'bestowed on the external affairs of man', they apply only to the 'thwarting of man's social function'. Their ideas and feelings, though noble and genuine, are too circumscribed and 'exterior'. That's their real trouble: 'the relationship between objective and subjective within their work was too tenuous to ensure a poetic vision', a 'personal vision of man and nature'.

Who got the fit right? – Christopher Brennan. Brennan was no Angliciser, no émigré poet. Where Lawson is objective and exterior only, Brennan's view of 'man's plight' is metaphysical, that is to say 'subjective'. But it's also 'objective', relating man's inner struggles for wholeness to the society around it: Brennan's poetry 'gives a vision of every man's soul in its despair and exultation, gives a measure of man's aspiration to be not only free in society, but intact within himself'. Unlike the others, says Buckley, Brennan is fighting out the quarrel internally, 'as Yeats bade', so that Brennan's verse is the 'first and best emergence' in Australia of the depth and the universality of man's struggle with himself and with his destiny. 'For, more than most of the others, Brennan felt at home here – as much at home as he could feel anywhere; he could at least assume the presence of the land as the natural context for the working out of his personal yet typical struggle . . .' Contrary to popular critical opinion, argues Buckley, it is with Brennan that we get the first genuinely unselfconscious Australian poetry.

Brennan's poetry, particularly in *The Wanderer*, the concluding part of *Poems* (1913), is rhetorical, but Buckley likes such rhetoric with its 'Irish-sounding rhythms', and in any case it is still very personal:

deeply, desperately so; yet it is also representative of the human condition in a way, and to a depth, which makes Lawson's attempt at representative statement appear no more than the shallow striking of an average. It presents us with the image of man in metaphysical action, and not simply with the details of his day. It is, in other words, really a poetry centred on man and pregnant with his image.

A key procedure of radical nationalists like Russel Ward in *The Australian Legend* was to assert that the legendary values (egalitarianism, etc) they admired were 'typical' of and fundamental to the true Australian consciousness, if not of the 'average', exterior social life we see about us. Buckley is now using exactly the same distinction of typical (Brennan) as against average (Lawson) that the radical nationalists employed to exalt Lawson to the top of the 1890s tree of new and vigorous life. With the experience of the resurgence of feminism in the 1970s, it's clear how male-centred is the radical nationalist view of the representative Australian: but Buckley also follows them in this, throughout his essay as well as in its amazingly androcentric title[13] insistently reading the 'human portrayal' as male. The man, it seems, is our typical spiritual being, embodying Australia's representative interior/exterior, subjective/objective, personal/social struggles. As with the radical nationalists, throughout Buckley's essay 'man' and 'men' are words caressingly deployed.

In 'The Image of Man in Australian Poetry', we can see a process analogous to Hegel turning Marx on his head. Like Kermode in *Romantic Image*, Buckley begins his essay by stating that it is of the essence of poetry to be metaphysical, its 'central human concern': 'Poetry deals with man at a metaphysical level – but with man's metaphysical status reflected in his actual state, localised in his actual physical surroundings, embodied in his sensuous and spiritual reactions to his world . . . The complex of signs which we find in any really fine poem is a symbol of man's metaphysical state presented through whatever in fact is most real to him as a suffering and diurnal being.' What makes the 1890s a watershed in our poetry is not so much the creation of a social democratic spirit but that Brennan achieves this fusion of the inner symbolic with the outer and daily, and so looks forward to the really interesting and modern poetry of the 20th century in Australia, the mature metaphysical verse of poets like Slessor, FitzGerald, Douglas Stewart, Judith Wright, James McAuley, A. D. Hope, and Francis Webb. And of course these poets were to become, for the 1960s and '70s, a staple diet in university courses on Australian literature – the Triumph of the Brennanites.

What does Buckley mean by 'metaphysical'? In Buckley's historical scheme for 20th-century Australian literature, if all had gone well a straight line should have flowed from Brennan to the Brennanites, and Brennan's strengths were these: 'Brennan saw man in the perspectives of Greek tragic literature; and he evidently estimated his own life as a subject for poetry in the light both of that literature and of Christianity.'

But all didn't go well. The boulders in the way of this ideal evolutionary path were of two kinds: not only the exterior non-metaphysical 'nationalist' poetry that developed out of Lawson's verse, but also the anti-nationalist vitalists influenced by Norman Lindsay. Unfortunately, both kinds 'rely for the philosophical vitality of their poetry neither on Greek nobility nor on Christian'.[14]

It's in his *Quadrant* piece 'Utopianism and Vitalism', published at the end of the 1950s, that Buckley laments most sharply these retarding forces, not only on poetry now, but on our all-round literary development. This is a much crisper essay than the earlier one. Buckley argues against Phillips' notion in *The Australian Tradition* that there is a central tradition; rather, he perceives 'lines of influence', and the chief of these are a kind of 'utopian humanism or insistence on the soul's radical innocence, and a kind of vitalism, or insistence on releasing the basic powers of life'.[15]

In Buckley's view, it is the vitalist stream which, in its varying manifestations, has been the 'chief formative influence' on our literature, a vitalism inspired mainly by Nietzsche. At its most interesting, vitalism as a metaphysic of the will can be witnessed in Brennan, Henry Handel Richardson, and A. D. Hope. For theirs is a vitalism on a properly 'metaphysical level, or derived from a metaphysical preoccupation', although it hasn't very much to do with the day-to-day lives of ordinary people. This vitalism concerns the 'artist and his role'.

No, for vitalism as villainy, we have to trap Norman Lindsay in his mountain lair. Buckley throws everything he can think of at the old Sydney sage. Lindsay's vitalism is 'pseudo-Dionysian', and it 'is, of course, an anti-intellectual piece of nervous excitement which has very little claim to be discussed in terms of its ideas'.[16] This continues the assault of 'The Image of Man in Australian Poetry'. There Lindsay is the 'serpent in the garden' of the literary beginnings of Slessor and FitzGerald; a serpent which caught with its beady eye and tried to tempt to poetic death Douglas Stewart, Kenneth Mackenzie, Eve Langley, and even Judith Wright; and this 'serpent of vitalism', when uncoiled in the Lindsay group, and particularly in Hugh McCrae's poetry, gives us a view of man as no more than a sum of erotic incidents. Such vitalism is 'anti-tragic, anti-spiritual, and ultimately anti-human'. It has nothing to do with the 'nobility of stoicism' – an odd value to invoke in this context – and certainly nothing of the 'greater nobility of Christianity'. It is 'pagan'.[17]

But back to 'Utopianism and Vitalism'. To be metaphysical, then, is to be more than erotic; it's to incorporate the spiritual with the bodily, within the overall Greek and Christian philosophical and religious tradition. And this means another requirement: to be properly metaphysical is to be necessarily European, is to wish to domicile European spiritual dilemmas within Australia. Both Lindsayan vitalism and utopian humanism are at fault here. The serpent bites and sucks the spiritual out of metaphysical experience, leaving only the erotic and biological. 'Utopian humanism' reduces the European religious dimension to the merely primitive and animistic – the non-European, the non-Christian.

Vance Palmer's *The Legend of the Nineties* – a book which did much in the 1950s to focus attention and argument on the 1890s – shows us, says Buckley, that in the last quarter of the 19th century 'thinking Australians' were often motivated by the 'idea of a perfect, a perfectly new, a perfectly vital society', and we can see this idea expressed more or less well in writers of the time like Furphy (well) and O'Dowd (badly). They looked forward to a utopian future, as, later, does Mary Gilmore in her verse. But in much of the literature from the 1930s through to the 1950s, which nationalist critics usually call 'social realist', the idea of a utopian future doesn't hold much sway any more. After all, Buckley asks, who now believes in utopia, in the prophetic sense of Furphy and O'Dowd? 'No one. And since utopia as such has become impossible to believe in, many of our writers turn to the consideration of substitute-utopias.' Utopia, in any case, Buckley has already declared, while in part arising from a 19th-century belief in social evolution, is also the 'expression of a primitive or transferred religious aspiration to be washed clean, purified by the lustrations of history'.

Hearing this we recall the Anglo-American Cold War campaign waged against utopianism.[18] The utopian is for Buckley but a debased religious impulse, or merely 'primitive'. Humanism may have something going for it, but not utopianism.

Utopian-humanist writers like Vance Palmer, Leonard Mann, Kylie Tennant, Eve Langley, and Eleanor Dark now start placing their utopian visions in the past. They produce an 'inverted utopianism', an insistence on the 'self-contained, abiding life that can be lived by communities in touch with the earth'. Admirable in a way as this is, particularly in the case of Eleanor Dark, the best of these later period writers, the inevitable result is 'imaginative failure'. Dark's novels, for example, tend towards a preoccupation with the 'primal integrity of Australia as a place', a preoccupation not very far removed from the 'primitive animism' of the Jindyworobaks. This comes to a head in *The Timeless Land* (1941), for in this novel

> it is the roots themselves she tries to discover, the strength of the land itself, given imaginative life in the animistic attitudes of the aborigines. The restless search has ended in complacency, the complacency of an immersion in the primitive and the prehistorical.

Here is the 'failure' of the utopian humanist line of influence extending from Furphy and O'Dowd, ending in a 'nostalgic re-reading of pre-history, which puts utopia in the past and makes it inaccessible to the European consciousness'. Further, this is *not* 'social realism': rather such writers are working in the 'convention of the idyll'. It is Rousseauistic, a turning away from what most of us recognise as society.[19]

To be interested in the 'animistic attitudes of the aborigines' is to become immersed in the 'primitive and the pre-historical'. To explain this remarkable declaration we have to keep in mind Buckley's concern for the maturity of Australian life, a concern urgently voiced in 'The Image of Man in Australian Poetry'. And here Buckley, in relating literature to society, turns out to be just as reflectionist in his aesthetic theory as the literary nationalists he wishes to dislodge.

Near the beginning of 'The Image of Man . . .' Buckley asserted this truth: 'The tradition of Australian poetry, as of Australian society, has been an anti-intellectual one'. 'We' – Australians – are pragmatic etc., like our pioneers; we've never got over beginnings in which the life of the mind was a back number. The challenge overarching all is that we're a European society in Asia, in a distinctive physical environment with something of the 'primitive' about it. Stupidly, the nationalists respond to this challenge by trying to eliminate the European sensibility, as if 'white life' is alien to the land; while the vitalists come out with a fanciful romanticism which has no roots in any locality at all. Our best poets, however, following on from Brennan, have attempted to fuse the two traditions, and here is our best hope of maturity. This is the importance of Brennan and the Brennanites, of FitzGerald, Slessor, Judith Wright, James McAuley, Douglas Stewart, Francis Webb, Hope, an attempt to achieve a 'mutual adjustment of the objective and subjective worlds – the world of Australian landscape and manners with the world of European morality, and art, and spiritual values'. For, whether consciously or not, what these writers realise is that

European values can live in Australian forms; and if we seek further, we find that they are not in any exclusive sense European at all, but universal, and merely exemplified most finely in the cultures of Europe.

The prime issue is 'spiritual development' and the 'social and cultural manners which will express that development'. And spiritual development will be gained by poets whose task it is to search for the 'spiritual realities behind the social and historical ones', to speak of 'misery and joy' alike as spiritual things, having an intimate connection with our daily life, yet at the same time possessing an 'archetypal' quality 'fitting even into the dimensions of heaven and hell'.

Poets such as these are showing us the way, but progress is still a bit slow, compared to the profound and fine cultures of Europe. 'We are still to some extent lacking in thought, still lacking in fiery and decisive images of man, still scared of the final spiritual dimensions and of the interior experiments necessary to reveal them.' Still, 'we are on our way to being mature', Buckley reassures us, as long as we try to be more European, stoical, Christian, spiritual, and universal in our interests.[20] Writers should have, Buckley says in 'Utopianism and Vitalism' about Douglas Stewart and R. D. Fitz-Gerald, a 'calm acceptance of life'.[21]

Buckley's comment on Lindsay's manifesto about artists and society, Creative Effort (1924), is that it is full of the 'incoherent half-truth', of hysterical epigrams and dicta.[22] Yet Buckley is a difficult thinker to deal with for very much the same reason – these 1950s essays in particular are full of dicta, of arbitrary assertions and appropriations, writers roped together who shouldn't be. A strange sense hovers about them of the critic as an alien to the literature he's trying to guide, chide, and shape. For most of the literature he talks about is Sydney literature, and it's clear from his irritation with that serpent Norman Lindsay, so important an influence in Sydney literary traditions, that Buckley can't really comprehend its spirit, assumptions, stances, temper (except perhaps where he can extend an Irish tentacle, to curl around Daley or Brennan). It's metaphysical enough, particularly in Brennan and the Brennanites, to give hope and encouragement for Australia's literary future along approved lines; but it's a literature out of his own control, his strenuous prescriptive grasp.

In these 1950s essays, then, Buckley set himself, in the name of a Christianity opposed to utopianism and paganism, against what we noticed in chapter one as a prominent strand of 1920s, '30s, and '40s Australian culture – the aesthetic connexion (not confined to Australia, as these earlier writers and theorists were well aware) between modernism and primitivism. Buckley allowed the full weight of his Leavisite certainty to drop on the earlier period's interest in Aboriginal community as a critique of urban, industrial society.

Such an interest, he's saying, should not be. As a project it is utopian, and the Aborigines are 'primitive', and for Buckley evidently primitive meant primitive. Australian literature, as he urges in 'Utopianism and Vitalism', should accept Australia's Europe-derived culture, should basically accept the present contours of life – as Douglas Stewart and FitzGerald do. But this acceptance of what is has to be deepened by the introduction of a further European capacity for metaphysical experience, that is yet to become firmly rooted in Australia. Deepen the sensibility of people in this society, don't look for utopian (primitive/Aboriginal/prehistorical) alternatives to it.

Nevertheless, Buckley did permit himself to be tested by 1930s literature with an Aboriginal theme, in an essay on Xavier Herbert's *Capricornia* in *Meanjin* in 1960, later included in Grahame Johnston's *Australian Literary Criticism*. As we saw in the chapter on Anglo-American literary theory during the Cold War, with critics like Frank Kermode and Lionel Trilling, it's important for a criticism that's attempting to be hegemonic that its methods can be turned loose on all literature, not just literature that appears most congenial to its approach and interests. For its desire is that its approach be universal, not limited and partial. Such criticism will proceed by claiming that the features of a work it is revealing are its essential features.

W. M. Maidment points out in his review of Johnston's collection that Buckley's essay on *Capricornia* is a critical advance on 'Utopianism and Vitalism' in the same volume,[23] and it is certainly more persuasive, less assertive. A characteristic procedure is, nevertheless, employed. Buckley's eye is always casting about for a metaphysical dilemma, so we won't be surprised if he finds one in *Capricornia*.

Buckley begins by saying previous critics have misconceived the novel by saying it is simply about racial injustice in the Northern Territory, a novel devoted to the exposure of social wrongs. Buckley agrees that the social aspect is there, but there's more: *Capricornia* is 'not merely a social document. Its context is not only social, but metaphysical.' Herbert is concerned 'not only with the social injustice done to aborigines and half-castes, but with a cosmic injustice done to all men'. Indeed, we later find, the novel presents 'an anarchist view of the universe, and it is called forth by what seems to the author an anarchic universe'.

By the second page of his essay, Buckley – while granting that Herbert is 'centrally concerned with racial injustice' – says that the novel's creative energy comes from a source 'much deeper than any merely social indignation, however genuine and noble'. The metaphysical concern peeps from behind the explicit social concern, and is 'no less strongly held' and 'no less central or explicit'. These metaphysical interests are 'wider concerns', he goes on, until a few pages later he can claim that in *Capricornia* Herbert has created a 'disordered universe in which and about which he is really writing: that disorder which is his real preoccupation in that universe which is his real subject'. By now Buckley's argument is well launched: a metaphysical interest, which started off competing for attention with the social theme of racial injustice, has quickly become wider, deeper, and indeed is now the 'real subject'.

Buckley's standard operation on *Capricornia* – the dissection into a superficial social and profound metaphysical layers – is very similar to G. A. Wilkes' number on *Such is Life* in 'The Eighteen Nineties'. They also happen to discover pretty well the same metaphysical theme in both *Such is Life* and *Capricornia*. Where Wilkes espies in Furphy's novel a theme of chance and uncertainty in the universe, Buckley espies in *Capricornia* the irony which underlines all the other ironies, the non-human anomaly which gives a sardonic point to those proceeding from human stupidity or evil, that of chance, avoidable misunderstanding, the inevitable depreciation of the human fate. It is this underlying irony which is the real emotional impetus in the book; it is a rejection of any conception of purpose in the universe, a sort of inversion of the Christian idea of Divine Providence; men are fated to die by chance and misunderstanding.[24]

This compares closely with Wilkes's account of *Such is Life*, minus the explicit Christian terminology; and Buckley also differs in finding, as a good Leavisite should, a life-affirming comic energy in *Capricornia* (or at least for most of it), a quality which doesn't engage Wilkes's attention in *Such is Life*.

It is a remarkable tribute to the gathering strength of the metaphysical orthodoxy that its assumptions and procedures began to permeate the thinking of those who might be considered to be most at odds with it. We can conclude this chapter by glancing at a curious essay by A. A. Phillips, one of the radical nationalists whose stances G. A. Wilkes (implicitly) and Vincent Buckley (explicitly, in the 'Utopianism and Vitalism' essay) were contesting. Phillips is introducing the 1965 Angus and Robertson reprint of Barbara Baynton's *Bush Studies* (originally published in 1902).[25]

Phillips' problem is clear: how to accommodate to his view of the 1890s – as essentially optimistic, robust, and confident – Baynton's short stories, with their 'acrid' vision and 'angry disgust' with Australian rural life and in particular with the plight of rural women. Phillips recognises that Baynton's tone contrasts with the legendary view that the 1890s is distinguished by its celebration of the typical Australian, and that this 'undercurrent of revolt' can also be seen in the wryness and desolate scorn of Lawson's stories 'The Union Buries Its Dead' and 'A Day on a Selection'. A similar tendency is also present in Miles Franklin's *My Brilliant Career* and Norman Lindsay's *Redheap*: a 'revolt against self-confident Australianism'.

Phillips points to the importance in *Bush Studies* of certain symbolic themes – loneliness in a bush hut and being terrifyingly besieged, the fierce power of the maternal instinct, man's brutality to woman. Phillips then offers various explanations for these themes. They represent 'nightmare obsessions', and in writing these stories Baynton is 'driven by a need to free her own spirit' from such obsessions. The stories became a kind of highly personal exorcism, and here we feel, says Phillips, that 'we are moving in Freudian country, that the essential motive behind Barbara Baynton's writing is some need to free a burdened subconscious by symbolic expression'.

The legendary view isn't contradicted, then, because Baynton's protest against the experience of women in rural life is subjective, personal, obsessive. Further, the legendary view focuses on the 'initiative and independence' achieved by Australia's outback tribe: whereas Baynton, like Furphy in *Such is Life*, is satirising the 'peasant element' in Australian life, a 'survival' of feudal Europe. Here Phillips is arguing much as he does in 'The Democratic Theme' in *The Australian Tradition* (1958): the writers of the 1890s admire the outback workers and even the squatters – the true bush pioneers – but not the peasant-like selectors.[26]

Phillips allows, however, that the emphasis on terror in Baynton's stories partly arises from the 'sense of the crushing isolation of bush-life, particularly as it affects the bushwomen', a sense created also in Lawson's 'The Drover's Wife'. Further, the emphasis on terror can be related to 'a sense of spiritual darkness emanating from the land itself, a feeling of primeval cruelty . . .'

That sense of spiritual darkness emanating from the land itself touches Australian writing again and again; and almost always it comes from a deeper layer of the mind than the easy optimism, the simplicity of faith which are more constantly present. There is a sense in which Patrick White is more traditionally Australian than is generally supposed.

Phillips concludes by denying that he's contradicting himself, saying that Baynton's terror-impulse is subjective, yet also 'represents some mystic emanation from the Australian land'. This is no contradiction because her inner compulsions coincide with an element in the Australian life and environment she's interpreting.

'Barbara Baynton's Stories' is an interesting essay, more complex and troubled than the affirmations and fairly easy optimism, particularly about the 1890s, of 'The Democratic Theme'. Baynton's stress on brutality and cruelty forces Phillips into admitting that cultural periods have an 'untidy habit of contradicting themselves'. Yet the contradictions in his argument are really forced on Phillips by his own compulsive historicist obsession to find and define an essential spirit. How do we fit a sense of desolation and terror into the more usual radical nationalist view of 'the easy optimism, the simplicity of faith which are more constantly present'? The element can't be deemed merely personal, or explained away as merely about peasant survivals. It refers to another level of the Australian mind – 'a deeper layer of the mind', which Patrick White now creates for us.

Phillips, then, is coming very close to the dominant critical mode being established at this time by Leavisites and New Critics like Vincent Buckley, G. A. Wilkes, and H. P. Heseltine. A certain essential spirit – optimistic and robust – is swapped for another essential spirit, a sense of spiritual questioning or desolation or darkness or terror, which is then assumed to be 'deeper' and therefore the more truly essential. Phillips' essay wavers between, on the one hand, seeing this metaphysical concern as an 'undertone', and on the other agreeing that it is 'deeper' and so by implication the really representative element. It shows the growing strength and coming ascendancy of the Cold War end-of-ideology orthodoxy in Australian literary criticism that such a distinction could be made by A. A. Phillips, the optimistic radical nationalist of *The Australian Tradition*. And in focusing on the darker aspects of Baynton's stories, Phillips enters the territory of the gloom thesis, the subject of the next chapter.

# 5
# The Gloom Thesis

The gloom thesis is an important variant, a sub-genre, of the metaphysical orthodoxy. It was and is active in literary criticism and literary history – the figures we'll deal with are H. P. Heseltine and Leon Cantrell – and in the cultural history of one of Australia's most remarkable and controversial historians, Manning Clark. The contributors to the gloom thesis not only assert the centrality of certain metaphysical themes in Australian literature, but attempt to produce a new Australian literary and cultural history. In particular, they wish to contest what they see as the radical nationalist version of Australian cultural history as a story of egalitarianism, group loyalties, and social optimism – a spirit supposedly established in the vigorous days of the 1890s (Australia's adolescence) and built on ever since (our maturity as a nation in the 20th century). The gloom thesis would instead attempt to install a far less optimistic reading of the true Australian spirit as it is revealed in the true, the essential qualities of Australian literature.

## Manning Clark

Manning Clark was very important in helping to create the intellectual plausibility and power of this new cultural history, because as an historian he could contest the radical nationalist historians on their own ground. At the same time, as an alternative to radical nationalist literary history, he invoked a new spirit in Australian literature, which he wished to read back into Australian history and cultural history. The key text is Clark's 1956 essay, 'Re-writing Australian History'.[1]

Clark's argument in this essay breaks into a number of parts, not related very well, one bearing on the problem of neocolonialism and cultural history, another indicating Clark's feelings towards previous Australian historiography – including radical nationalist history – and a third drawing on an end-of-ideology thesis about the central place of a metaphysical perspective in the analysis of society and the writing of history.

In the first part of what turned out to be a very influential sketch of new ideas and emphases, Clark attacks the summary and patronising views on the true nature of Australians and Australian life by wandering British commentators. There's Froude in 1886 who said Australians are so immersed in money and practical things that the colony exhibits a severe lack of intellectual interests; Sir Arthur Conan Doyle in 1921 caning Australia for being spiritually dead; and D. H. Lawrence in 1922 knowing almost before he got here that Australians have no inner life, no inner self (set Lawrence down anywhere in the world and within seconds he knows its spirit). These commentaries add up to saying, Clark feels, that because of the indifference by Australians to things of the mind, there have been no arresting conflicts or contrasts in our history; it is a story of sameness and the middling view. Worse, this imperial British view has been accepted by Australian commentators and historians themselves, like Keith Hancock in *Australia* (1930).

With some sharpness and impatience Clark points instead to major ideological divisions, for example, between socialist atheism and religion, or the clash within religion in Australia between the Catholic and Protestant world views, with radically different ideas on questions of liberty, equality, democracy, education, the English or Irish inheritance. Here Clark is adopting a conflict-model of Australian society and history very close to Marxism.

Metropolitan cultural-imperialist attitudes, such as those of Froude and Lawrence, enforced in Australians a neocolonial dilemma, feelings of fear and uncertainty and doubt about the value of their own cultural efforts. But when Australian intellectuals return to the metropolitan cultural source, Britain or Europe, they feel alienated and excluded. The dilemma is dramatised by Henry Handel Richardson in the story of Richard Mahony, in his continual drive to go back and forth from Australia to Britain. The ground for Mahony's tragic madness and decline lay in his dual alienation from both Australian and British society and culture.

Clark's critique of neocolonialism and the cultural cringe adds his voice to the radical nationalist tradition of Nettie Palmer, Vance Palmer, Stephen Murray-Smith, Arthur Phillips, Geoffrey Serle, Ian Turner, Russel Ward. Yet there is also a crucial difference: whereas the radical nationalists defend Australia's cultural distinctiveness as its source of spiritual profundity, Clark defends Australia on the ground that it is the site, as much as any other, of human universality.

Clark does not believe such universality resides exclusively in European moral and metaphysical dilemmas, and in this sense his position can be distinguished from those poets and critics in the 1950s like Hope, McAuley, and Buckley who stress the centrality of European cultural experience. Clark differs from Vincent Buckley in particular here. In 'The Image of Man in Australian Poetry', Buckley accepts the stereotype that Australians are so pragmatic, so absorbed in the practical, pioneering tasks of creating a new society, that there's a flatness and lack of depth in their spiritual life. Buckley is a little worried that this is a cliché view, but still embraces it, while Clark rejects such a position precisely because it is a cliché and so blinds people to the achieved dramas, the 'great issues' and 'differences of principle' that mark our history. Following on from this, presumably Clark would not accept Buckley's grand Leavisite cultural-imperialism about the superiority of European culture. ('European values', said Buckley, in 'The Image of Man in Australian Poetry', 'can live in Australian forms; and if we seek further, we find that they are not in any exclusive sense European at all, but universal, and merely exemplified most finely in the cultures of Europe.') As Clark says, 'Europe is no longer the creative centre, the teacher of the world.' And asks: 'Is it not time for our historians to abandon their preoccupation with the causes and effects of the Australian Cultural Desert?'

Clark's rejection of cultural imperialism raises interesting questions of how we conceive and perceive the problem of nationalism in Australian cultural history, not only as it bears on the crucial testing period of the 1890s but as a continuing story. Like any culture formed in colonial and post-colonial conditions, Australian culture has been and is continuously subject to cultural imperialism from its English metropolitan source. But the only response to such imperialism, to the insistent (and often internalised) claim that the metropolitan culture is inevitably superior, is not necessarily the nationalist assertion of distinctiveness as a supreme and guiding value.

Rather, there might be a continuum of response, ranging from radical nationalism of this kind, to a feeling that the English themselves are limited or parochial, and that the standards by which a culture is to be judged and explored should be truly international and universal. In the 1890s period this internationalist and universalist response to the metropolitan assumption of cultural superiority can be seen in A. G. Stephens' criticism in the *Bulletin* and the *Bookfellow*, and in this sense Stephens anticipates Manning Clark's similar response to cultural imperialism.

Yet, given the Cold War context of his essay, Clark's opposition to cultural imperialism can be seen as a way of combating the radical nationalists on their chosen ground. Clark's essay redirects attention towards metaphysical themes that are claimed to be universal, but are in fact special, limited, and limiting.

A key purpose of 'Re-writing Australian History' is to run through various false 'comforters', the various historical interpretations that claim – as Macaulay claimed for British history – that Australian history is the story of political liberty and material progress. Just as Macaulay persuaded teachers that the 17th century should be studied as the decisive period in which British political institutions and the Protestant religion were moulded and set on their way, so Australian historians have directed attention to certain aspects of the 19th century as the basis for an optimistic reading of our history.

Clark, with some brusqueness, says such ideas must be laid to rest and that Macaulay's kind of history, taught throughout the English speaking world, won't do for Australia, with its Irish Catholic presence and tradition, a tradition in part arising from the early Irish convicts. This tradition meant that sections of the working class and the Labor Party were always closely associated with the Catholic Church in Australia. Further, such religious differences were important in two of the great events of the last one hundred years, the education controversy and the conscription crisis (as in Archbishop Mannix opposing Britain in World War I).

We have to lay aside the comforter that these same convict origins assured Australia of a good democratic kickoff in life. The convicts were not mostly good and respectable people forced into wrong by English economic developments like enclosure and by the savagery of the English criminal law: the great majority were 'professional criminals'.

In these convict days, nevertheless, we can indeed find the germs of some of the great themes in our history – 'the attitude to work', and the 'curious paradox of the warm embrace for members of the same group but a snarl for the rest of the world'. This latter attitude in particular went on to infect mateship and the ideal of 'brotherhood' in the 19th century, leading to xenophobia and support for the blessings of White Australia. As Clark says in his inimitable way: 'Instead of worshipping at the altar of mateship, we may find ourselves making expiation and atonement for such arrogance – for are we not that third and fourth generation on whom the sins of the fathers are to be visited?'

Another weakness of this Macaulay-like story of Australian history as liberal progress is to focus too much on particular periods and events like the Eureka rebellion of 1854 or the influence of Chartism, which supposedly made Australia a pioneer of democracy, the political and social laboratory of the world, with her experiments in equality of opportunity and material progress. First, Clark argues, this ignores the contribution of the period before the gold years of the early 1850s, for in this earlier time is the real germ of the belief in equality, and for good economic reasons: 'It was the labour shortage in country districts, rather than imported social and political ideals, which eroded the centuries-old belief in inequality.' Secondly, the focus on Eureka and the gold period

over-emphasises the degree of political democracy introduced after the gold rushes. Third, it concentrates attention on the political achievements in the period of gold and thus loses sight of two of the central facts of the period. This was the great period of the squatters – up to 1890. It was also the great period of bourgeois civilisation in our cities – the period in which cathedrals, town halls, universities, schools, banks and pastoral company buildings were put up as symbols of their faith.

Australia's past, rather than showing the achievements of radicals like the diggers at Eureka and of radical ideals throughout the society, reveals the economic power and political strength of the ruling class in the 19th century: the pastoralists and the urban bourgeoisie.

In this sense, Clark's analysis is rather like E. P. Thompson's correction to labour history's tendency to focus only on one class, in his famous preface to *The Making of the English Working Class* (1963). In Clark's view, we should look at the relationships between social groups, in terms which include different traditions of culture, of consciousness, ideology, beliefs, 'faith'. Such considerations should put paid to the simple view that in the 19th century it was the labour movement that was the cradle of progress, a view put by V. Gordon Childe and Brian Fitzpatrick, and in historians like Keith Hancock who have borrowed heavily from them. They would also put paid to the idea that the non-labour parties were the 'parties of resistance'; this is 'grossly unfair to the non-labour parties'.

Another fault Clark finds with the historians of optimism and progress is that they follow the ideas of poets who are shallow, indeed are 'small beer': poets like Bernard O'Dowd, Victor Daley (in his political verse), and Henry Lawson. Their ideas of mateship and brotherhood are like the costermongers of London sneering at everyone outside their own small circle as 'bloody aristocrats'; or like the ancient Jews who, wrote the prophet Isaiah, are harmonious within their own group but, when it comes to their neighbours, should dash their children to pieces before their eyes, spoil their houses and ravish their wives. Just so the Australian bushmen towards non-mates, non-brothers, non-whites.

These Australian notions of mateship were in fact the product of a special, isolated way of life – 'a mate was a bulwark against loneliness, a help in time of sickness and accident'. The trouble is that there was 'no attempt to make mateship universal in application – to extend it from the people they knew to all people'. Nor was there any attempt to find 'universal reasons for believing in it. You do not find them putting forward any metaphysical or religious reasons for their belief.'

Clark claims that turn-of-the-century poets were looking back nostalgically to obsolete historical conditions. The rural isolation of mateship was being destroyed by the coming of the railway, while the confident belief in material progress and in democracy can't be sustained into the 20th century. World war, revolution, and the revival of persecution means we should be responsive to a more pessimistic mood about history and human possibility, responsive to metaphysical dilemmas. We should look beyond the shallowly optimistic poets favoured by the radical nationalists, and turn to truly modern poets, to the poets of our generation, to Douglas Stewart, James McAuley, Kenneth Slessor. Poets such as these aren't concerned with the hope of a 'happiness founded on material well-being for all', but are concerned with 'much older' themes in the 'lot of mankind', themes of the permanence and close connection of 'agony' and 'joy' (Stewart), of the fear that democracy will not be the panacea but rather will sour and sicken 'every work of art and honour' (McAuley); while Slessor's *Five Bells*, with its concern for time and death, undermines the easy confidence about life of the nationalists.

Clark sees the universities as a bastion of the 'bankrupt liberal ideal'. Nor will the re-writing of Australian history come from the radicals of this generation, 'because they are either tethered to an erstwhile great but now excessively rigid creed, or they are frightened by the self-appointed inquisitors of our morals and political opinions', references presumably both to the rigidifying of Marxism into Stalinism, and to the persecutory attitudes of the Cold War. History will have to look to the 'creative writer', and such history will have to possess 'a point of view on the direction of society':

some great theme to lighten our darkness – that, for example, the era of bourgeois liberalism, of democracy, and belief in material progress is over, and that those who defend such a creed are the reactionaries of today. To be great as literature – the aim of all historians – it must be written by someone who has something to say about human nature, but, above all, it must be written by someone who has pondered deeply over the problems of life and death.

In response to the totalising approach of the historians of progress, we must have a new totality, a view – encompassing the whole of Australian life, urban and rural, working class and bourgeoisie – directed by metaphysical questions of what truly constitutes agony and joy, culture and mediocrity, 'life and death'.

## The trap of historicism

The final part of Clark's 'Re-writing Australian History' can be seen as anticipating and helping to forge a new and persuasive historicist perspective on Australia's past which is open to the same theoretical dangers and consequences as the historicism of the radical nationalists. Because the history of ideas has been neglected in Australia, there is a tendency to discuss historical arguments as if their theoretical premises are purely Australian, to be attacked or defended solely in the light of empirical evidence to do with Australian history. There is little sense that such arguments might be part of wider tendencies in the history of ideas, and that undeniable, important differences in empirical content might yet hide fundamental similarities in the philosophy of history. Numerous articles and books have sniped away on empirical grounds, for example, at Russel Ward, without ever discussing the theory of history that, as we saw in chapter one, he shares not only with other Australian writers like Vance Palmer or A. A. Phillips or Geoffrey Serle, but also with major movements in European historiography and social theory.

Clark has been so much promoted as a vigorous critic of left-Australianism that it might be useful to analyse his differences from and similarity to it, particularly in regard to Russel Ward's philosophy of history in *The Australian Legend*. To do so requires detaching Russel Ward from historians like Hancock, Fitzpatrick, and Gollan, with whom he is usually associated, and placing him firmly in the tradition of social thought and cultural history of Nettie Palmer and Vance Palmer. In an essay in *Quadrant* in 1978, for example, on 'Challenges to Australian Identity', Michael Roe argues that the Whig interpretation of history has been 'dominant' in Australia, and he associates this interpretation with names like W. K. Hancock, Brian Fitzpatrick, Russel Ward, and R. A. Gollan. The leading characteristics of Whiggism (what Clark has been referring to as Macaulay-like history) are its emphases upon the material, secular aspects of life, and a lack of concern for minorities and failures. To Roe's mind, one of the more remarkable consequences of the Whig concern for progress in Australian history has been the ignoring of 'mind, emotions, soul and creativity'.[2]

How far the Whig interpretation of history does in fact apply to historians like Hancock, Fitzpatrick, and Gollan I'm not certain. Roe's article is little more than a rehash, a fairly reverent updating, of the ideas of Manning Clark and, as we shall see later, of prominent 1960s new right intellectual Peter Coleman. Roe dutifully trots out the opinion that the Whig interpretation is the orthodoxy: 'the usually self-accepted picture of European man's experience and achievement in Australia' has been formed 'in a Whiggish mould, and by that token is genial, congratulatory, and optimistic'.

I think we have to stop lumping together radical nationalists like Russel Ward – concerned in *The Australian Legend* with an Australian non-urban distinctiveness – and labour historians like Robin Gollan in *Radical and Working Class Politics* (1960). How crude such a composite lump is can be witnessed in a masterly way in Roe's account. He argues, for example, that Australian Whiggery has had a strong Marxist tincture in figures like Fitzpatrick, Ward, and Gollan, and that these members of the old left were confident that Australia was peculiarly the product and property of the working man: 'For them, a Marxist elysium was the natural outcome of previous Australian experience.'

Do Fitzpatrick and Gollan really say this? Where on earth could one find such a position in *Radical and Working Class Politics*, or

Gollan's other major historical work? Is Gollan's tone really genial, congratulatory, and optimistic'?

Further, Roe argues that the Whig historians (though not Hancock in *Australia*) are not interested in 'ideas, art, religion', and that the sense of a 'pervading intellectual dimension' in Australian history is 'intrinsically non-Whig'. Does this, again, really apply to Gollan, who has written valuable essays tracing the influence on Australian radicalism and the labour movement of American utopian and anti-utopian ideas, in figures like Edward Bellamy and Ignatius Donnelly?[3]

Much more careful distinctions have to be made, then, between labour history and radical nationalism in Australian historiography. It might be that certain historians were at different times attracted to both, like Ian Turner. But the differences between the particular labour history assumptions of, say, Turner's *Industrial and Labour Politics* (1965), and the Ward-like radical nationalist assumptions of his introduction to *The Australian Dream* (1968) can be analysed as stemming from different intellectual traditions and philosophies of history.

Roe's claim that the Whig concern for progress in Australian history ignores 'mind, emotions, soul and creativity' also cannot apply to Russel Ward in *The Australian Legend*, nor to the romantic historicist school from which Ward emerges. *The Australian Legend* is an attempt to work out an argument about the conditions and importance of 'mind, emotions, soul and creativity' in Australian history – to reveal the guiding spirit or *Geist* of Australian society, a spirit that is to be perceived not in the observable, material conditions in which the life of the 'average' Australian consists, but in a vital spiritual core that is manifested in myth and legend. This is contrary to Roe's argument, because though the values Russel Ward stresses – egalitarianism, hospitality, mateship, independence, scepticism – are different from the forms of spirit discerned by Manning Clark in his historical writing, this does not mean that Ward is focusing on the material aspects of life. Rather, and rather obviously, Ward's writing suggests that it is consciousness, however defined and expressed, that is central to the historical process. The whole project of Australia's romantic historicist school – in particular Vance Palmer and A. A. Phillips and Geoffrey Serle in *From Deserts the Prophets Come* – is to suggest the kinds of 'mind emotions, soul and creativity' that they feel are appropriate for a society living in and with Australia's natural environment. Their consistent urging is that until a society possesses a unifying con sciousness it fails as a society: in Ward's words, it lacks 'cohesion balance and confidence'.

The Whig view of Australian history as the story of progress unity, and democracy has, argues Roe, come under considerable attack from both the right and the left in the last twenty years. Roe accords central place in this historiographical drama to Clark's 'Re writing Australian History', upholding it as the 'great manifesto of anti-Whiggery. Roe points to those parts of the essay where Clark attacks with some impatience and roughness the importance previously given to mateship and bush brotherhood, and the neglect of the cities in Australia's historical development. Such an attack would certainly have hit home against Vance Palmer's 1954 book *The Legend of the Nineties*, itself the culmination of views Palmer had held for decades and which had proved influential in the intellectual formation of *Meanjin* and later *Overland*. It could later apply to Ward's *The Australian Legend*, published in 1958, a couple of years after Clark's essay, since Ward's book can be seen as following, in terms of academic history, many of the directions prominent in Vance Palmer's thinking, particularly the historicist stress on a distinctive rural folk spirit, and a suspicion of the cities as the breeding ground of social division and cultural imperson- ality.

We can also see Manning Clark's essay, in his enthusiastic quoting from Slessor, Stewart, and McAuley, as helping to institute a new historicist paradigm, where the centre of Australian history and society is also taken up with certain qualities of consciousness – not egalitarianism and social optimism this time, but metaphys- ical despair, doubt, alienation, terror, and suffering. Clark's contro- versial book *In Search of Henry Lawson* (1978) can also be noticed as an expression of this paradigm, reading Australian history and in particular the period of the 1890s as the tragic drama of assertion and repression of metaphysical values.

Let's for the moment leave Manning Clark's 'Re-writing Aus-

ralian History'. That the first part of the essay comes very close
o a Marxist view of conflicting groups in society is not surprising,
given his Melbourne University background in the 1940s and the
strength of the Melbourne liberal and radical intellectual traditions. It must be a sign of the great attractiveness and per-
uasiveness of end-of-ideology in the 1950s, that Clark turns to
argely conservative Sydney literary traditions for new directions.
It is as if Clark is torn between his Melbourne inheritance and his
attraction towards a Sydney tradition which seems to speak to the
universal and eternal in life; and that Clark has thought deeply over
the differences between Sydney and Melbourne intellectual attitudes we know from his essay 'Faith' in Coleman's symposium *Aus-
ralian Civilization*. Looking back at 'Re-writing Australian History' now, its overall effect must have been contradictory: its first
part could influence an anti-neocolonial, anti-cultural cringe view
that Australia is a sufficient site of human and metaphysical drama;
its middle part attacking radical nationalist historiography drew
attention to the cities and perhaps encouraged the direction and
tone of urbanisation studies, but it also included sharp observations
that would please an anti-historicist marxist; and its latter part
stimulated a new historicist orthodoxy in cultural history.


## H. P. Heseltine

Manning Clark's inversion of supposed radical nationalist optimism
about Australian cultural history was enthusiastically followed by
a strand of New Criticism which tried to establish an overarching
pessimistic view of Australian historical and literary experience. As
an historian Manning Clark was particularly concerned to give
harsher, less optimistic readings of certain historical events and
attitudes that are held to be pivotal to the radical nationalist
account of Australian history – Eureka, and the gold period (what
of the continuing power of the squatters and of the bourgeoisie in
Australia's cities?), of mateship (it's really racism on the one hand,
and on the other a desperate defence against bush loneliness), egalitarianism and equality (they're really a result of the high demand
for labour). New Critics in sympathy with this anti-Whig historical

interpretation had to grapple with the pivotal place held by writers like Lawson and Furphy in radical nationalist accounts of Australian literary history – the view that Lawson and Furphy are profoundly representative of social optimism, brotherhood, egalitarianism, and so on. G. A. Wilkes in his essay on 'The Eighteen Nineties' questioned the radical nationalist view of Furphy. H. P. Heseltine, longtime member of the English department at the University of New South Wales, then Professor of English at James Cook University in Townsville, now Professor of English at Duntroon, attempted a few years after Clark's and Wilkes' essays to challenge the radical nationalist account of Lawson. Heseltine also wished to generalise from a revised view of Lawson to all Australian literary history, a project also pursued by Leon Cantrell a couple of decades later. In Foucault's terms, we can witness here the desire for new knowledge accompanying a desire for intellectual and institutional power over a whole historical field.

In his essay 'Saint Henry – Our Apostle of Mateship' in *Quadrant* in 1960-61, Heseltine follows the metaphysical orthodoxy's surgical procedure of dividing texts into social/political/ideological surface aspects, and profound underlying and essential metaphysical layers. He attempts to consign to the grave, and stamp on the covering earth, the figure that the radical nationalists had created: the Lawson of mateship, confident bush virtues, and radical social vision. For Heseltine the political side of Lawson's mind, 'the policy-making half', was superficial and uncreative compared to the half which controlled his 'real artistic talent'. The half of his mind that fortunately escaped this excision expressed truly profound feelings about the bush, for example, feelings of terror and a clinging to mateship because it was a last line of defence 'against an uninviting, even hostile frontier':

The Australian outback, as Lawson represents it, is unfriendly, frightening, aggressively anti-human . . . Lawson's most compelling response to the Australian landscape is one of horror.

Two decades later in 'Between Living and Dying: The Ground of Lawson's Art', an essay published in *Overland* (No. 88) in 1982, Heseltine wrote in support of Manning Clark's view in *In Search of Henry Lawson* of a 'divided and ambivalent' self. Lawson's best stories in the 1890s create human life as desolation, spiritual nullity, a kind of life-in-death state later also to be captured by T. S. Eliot in 'The Hollow Men'. This sense of spiritual paralysis is held in tension with a desire for rebirth, redemption, resurrection, a desire that is never really believed in the fiction of his best years (1892-1895). This tension between death and life, desolation and illusory hollow hope, energises Lawson's fiction, is indeed its foundation, its 'thematic groundtone', 'the very ground of his most important fiction', defines its 'canon', its 'inside narrative', 'the animating force behind nearly every significant story that Lawson wrote in the middle years of the 1890s'. It represents 'the deeper promptings of his imagination', Lawson's 'personal vision' for which he 'had to invent plots and characters, that it might enjoy a local habitation and a name'.

Here, then, is Lawson's best work, poised between nullity and forlorn hope, and hence ambiguous, ambivalent – a New Critic's dream. Yet, what a narrow field, what a small enclosed circle, of ambiguity and ambivalence this is, what a small number of concerns Lawson's texts have been reduced to! What a small prison house has Heseltine put such a varied, elusive, and fascinating figure into!

In an essay that appeared in *Meanjin* in 1962, Heseltine explicitly appropriated for Australian literature Lionel Trilling's notion of modern literature as 'terror':

The canon of our writing presents a façade of mateship, egalitarian democracy, landscape, nationalism, realistic toughness. But always behind the façade looms the fundamental concern of the Australian literary imagination. That concern ... is to acknowledge the terror at the basis of being, to explore its uses, and to build defences against its dangers. It is that concern which gives Australia's literary heritage its special force and distinction, which guarantees its continuing modernity.[4]

This remarkable piece of eloquence shows by the use of glib phrases like 'terror and its *uses*' that the metaphysical view of literature that Anglo-Australo-American literary theory was striving for during the 1950s (in Kermode, Trilling, as well as, as we've seen, in Wilkes and Buckley), had arrived and was now scaling the heights of orthodoxy, of easy statement, of the given, the *donnée*, natural truth. And it raises as well, in its simple inversion of 'radical nationalist' literary history, questions of historicism and the philosophy of history. We can explore these questions as they bear on Australian literary history, and at the same time comment on the tenacity and longevity of the gloom thesis, by staring at Leon Cantrell's contribution, having previously only glanced at it in chapter four.

## Leon Cantrell's 1890s

In 1977 Cantrell published in the University of Queensland Press Portable Australian Authors series his anthology *The 1890s*. In his introduction Cantrell explains that the 'principal aim' of the selection is to 'provide enough of the evidence for us to make our own judgments as to the nature and quality of the decade's writing'. Accordingly, Cantrell has included both representative minor works from the period, and drawn on its 'indubitable masterpieces'. As well, the editor has decided that it's clear to everyone, certainly too clear for any necessity of argument, what are the 'major concerns' of 1890s writers; he has 'isolated' these for us, so that we can notice 'a variety of approaches to similar themes: writing in Australia, city life, lyricism, politics and nationalism, the city versus the bush, and life up the country'.[5] Selections from the well-known and the lesser-known are then grouped about these themes as different sub-headings of the anthology: we can read the work of a variety of writers in the sure knowledge that it is undoubtedly either major or representative, and so we'll gain 'something of the wholeness of the period'. Before each section the editor places a little explanatory note, though none is intended to have the explosive force of the introduction itself.

*The 1890s* may well prove a useful book for teaching purposes, where students can dip into and taste a variety of offerings and decide for themselves on its major qualities. Yet as we read on in the introduction we notice that the seeming open-handedness quickly begins to stiffen and become peremptory in manner – we recognise yet another of Australian literary criticism's traffic police, directing and coercing the reader at every point. The bland, if merely impossible, pluralism of Cantrell's announced 'principal aim' conflicts with and is subverted by another, less selfless aim, which is to seek to show that the best writing of the period sustains a certain distinctive and unified spirit. 'My view of the 1890s sees a sense of alienation and loss as a principal literary hallmark', our editor tells us, and he says that the selection and arrangement of material for the anthology is designed to illustrate this principal hallmark.

The two aims conflict, and the second wins, and students will find in the anthology not an innocent offering of plurality and variety but yet another reinforcing of the dominant view of Australian literature and literary history, a view that has been practised by influential critics now for at least two decades, and which has been supported by the institutional power and the New Critical skills, professionalism, and sophistication of teachers in university English departments.

It is a signal feat of the new orthodoxy that it has managed to pass itself off, perhaps even to its own practitioners, as an almost daring counter-attack. Before telling us his own view of the spirit of the decade, Cantrell first sets up an anti-criticism which, valiantly, he's going to try and dislodge, and maybe, who knows, destroy for ever. Cantrell says that it was between the two wars that the 1890s acquired their legendary status as a golden era, the summation of a peculiarly and admirably Australian way of life. The writings of Lawson, Paterson, and Furphy were hailed as enshrining concepts of mateship, democracy and nationalism, and these forces were seen as receiving their basic stimulus from life in the bush. Such writers threw off the 'shackles of an imported vision', the English derivativeness which dominated before the 1890s, and established the 1890s as a time of social confidence and optimism. Literature in the 1890s was to be seen as embodying the political spirit and nationalist sentiment of the day; and it created for the nation a distinctiveness in terms of the ballad and short story, Australia's characteristic literary forms. Such a view, Cantrell argues, has left an unfortunate legacy for later literary practice and critical concepts. It has meant that the variety and diversity of 1890s writing has been underestimated; it has overstressed the local content of 1890s work; it has isolated the 1890s and obscured its continuities with literature before and after it, and in particular it has led to a neglect of pre-1890s writing as merely imported.

Cantrell discovers for our inspection 'two major assumptions which have not been spelt out and adequately discussed' in the continuing debate about the nature and importance of the 1890s. The first assumption he ferrets from its hole is that Australian life in the 1890s was significantly radicalised, promoting a vital period of democracy and national sentiment. Thus, writing in the iconoclastic spirit of Humphrey McQueen's *A New Britannia*, Cantrell challenges the 'common view' that in the 1890s the '*Bulletin* was a radical newspaper, espousing egalitarian views'. On the contrary, Cantrell finds, the *Bulletin* was like the labour parties of the day in its failure to 'support social and political restructuring in any other than a narrowly liberal-bourgeois sense'. The *Bulletin*'s 'principal political concern was for the preservation and furtherance of middle-class self-help and capital', and the *Bulletin*'s 'reputation as a radical, democratic weekly can only be understood in the context of our present undemocratic and un-radical society'.

Disqualifying the view that Australian life in the 1890s was in fact radical and egalitarian leads easily to Cantrell's attack on his second assumption. This is that 'Australian writing of the period can be regarded as a reflection of Australian life'. Lawson, for example, Cantrell argues, has been 'hailed' as the apostle of mateship and cited as the most representative of Australian writers because his work 'supposedly reveals the essential truths of our egalitarian, democratic tradition'. But Lawson was like so many other prominent writers – Steele Rudd, Barbara Baynton, Paterson, even Furphy in his living in Shepparton – who have been taken to represent outback values of mateship and equality: they were urban dwellers rather than fond inhabitants of the Never-Never. Cantrell sums up his feelings about this nationalist assumption:

The truth is that bush life is most frequently depicted in our literature of the 1890s as harsh and destructive of all but the basic urge to survive. Or, if Arcadian, as belonging to a bygone age, now lost. Egalitarian mateship is less common than loneliness and betrayal. Failure is more real than success.

Further, this is how the 1890s saw itself. The view that the decade is a golden age is the invention of later writers, of nostalgic chroniclers like George Taylor in his *Those Were The Days* (1918) and Arthur Jose in his *The Romantic Nineties* (1933). Their nostalgia was supported and given stringency by writers like H. M. Green, Nettie Palmer, Vance Palmer, and Russel Ward.

His anthology, Cantrell says, will show, on the other hand, 'how much of the best writing of the period recoils from those very features which the nationalist interpretation holds to be most characteristic and most affirmatively Australian: mateship, egalitarian democracy, the celebration of bush life'. These aren't the dominant notes at all in the thick knoll of Australian writing. The stories of Lawson, Baynton, Albert Dorrington, and Edward Dyson insist on the 'horrors of outback life, on the dehumanizing qualities of the frontier existence'. For writers dealing with urban material or philosophical themes, there was a binding thread of 'disillusionment' to be detected, as much in the way Lawson and William Lane respond to the urban landscape as 'bleak and inhuman' as in the tone of 'loss and resignation' in Brennan's work. Indeed, Cantrell here edges in an implied criticism of G. A. Wilkes, whom otherwise one might see as his critical father and mentor, when he notes that 'Brennan's affinities with other Australian writers of the 1890s have not been sufficiently drawn out'. We should see Brennan's 'images of loneliness, of deeply-felt alienation and despair' as akin to Baynton's *Bush Studies*, to 'The Union Buries Its Dead', and to parts of *Such Is Life*. This is the real 1890s, its harsh, living present, and any sense of a golden age by 1890s writers is reserved nostalgically for the past or hoped for as a future possibility.

In Cantrell's introduction the gloom thesis can be seen extending its creepers to grasp at the whole of Australian literary history. Cantrell cites the 1975 *Southerly* article by G. A. Wilkes, 'Going Over the Terrain in a Different Way', to show that the spirit of the 1890s, its sense of the future potential of Australia as opposed to the harshness of its present, appealed also to Harpur and Kendall. Developments in our writing in this century also accord with the spirit of the 1890s as shared and articulated by Brennan and Lawson, particularly in post-World War II figures like McAuley, A. D. Hope, and the author of *Voss*: 'The prevailing tone of the 1890s, an uneasy acceptance of a world which seems to offer more than it can give, is the major tradition of Australian writing.'

Marcus Clarke was among the Australian historicists upon whom the radical nationalists later drew. Remember how, staring at some pictures of Australian mountains, he declared that the 'dominant note of Australian scenery' is that 'which is the dominant note of Edgar Allan Poe's poetry – Weird Melancholy'. Clarke went on to talk of the Australian mountain forests being 'funereal, secret, stern. Their solitude is desolation. They seem to stifle, in their black gorges, a story of sullen despair.' Now Clarke's mountains have gained legs, and they have walked abroad and covered the whole continent with the same funereal gloom. Cantrell's anthology might henceforth be marked as a centenary celebration of Clarke's vision: the rich and varied landscape of Australian literature has been shrunk to one dominant scenery.

One of the curiosities of Cantrell's introduction is his belief that he stumbled upon and climbed these mountain forests all by himself. He talks of 'my contention' that the variety of Australian 1890s writing has been underestimated; he refers to 'my view of the 1890s' as involving a sense of alienation and loss as a principal literary hallmark; and he tells us with some breathlessness that the work of White, McAuley and Hope emphasises continuity with the view of the 1890s 'I have been advancing'. Maybe my glasses need new lenses, but isn't everyone familiar with the sight of influential figures in Australian intellectual life – not only in literary criticism, but notably also in historiography – bending over and drumming on the supposed coffin of radical nationalism, and for decades now? Remember Manning Clark's 'Re-writing Australian History' (1956)? Remember Heseltine on Lawson in *Quadrant* in 1960-61 and again in 1962 on 'Australia's Literary Heritage' in *Meanjin*? Even Cantrell's terminology rings eerie bells of similarity with Heseltine's choice of terms.

A disturbing and unsavoury feature of the polemic waged against the radical nationalist view of Australian literature is that rarely are the adversaries explicitly acknowledged – rarely are names named, or if they are, there is evident only a severe shortage of cited references, dates, page numbers, etc. It's difficult for readers to go back and check on the reality or not of the positions being pilloried. The anti-nationalist critics seem to be boxing with a ghost, which they can see but which we can't. But it is apparently a powerful ghost they're fighting, one which controls the citadels of Australian literary historiography, and stamps on the fingers of those who bravely try to storm its positions. Heseltine, for example, in the *Quadrant* piece, mounted a bold attack on the radical nationalist view of Lawson as celebrating mateship and bush society. This view, he says, runs as the 'received scripture', as the 'common reading of the Holy Writ'. But why can't he tell us who the high priests of this theology are? Similarly, G. A. Wilkes in his 1958 essay 'The Eighteen Nineties', in his own inimitable ghostly prose, also assaults the citadel of this ghostly yet powerful received criticism.

As we read Wilkes' 1958 piece we can also hear its phrases and terms echoing and resounding in Cantrell's 1977 introduction. Wilkes sets himself against the radical nationalist view that the literature of the decade reflects presumed social developments. 'The writing of this time (we are told) exhibits the awakening of an Australian national consciousness', says Wilkes; this view dismisses pre-1890s writing as 'the effete and derivative tradition of an earlier age'. It is true that many writers in the 1890s 'do make a vigorous use of Australian material', but two other things have to be kept in mind: 'the first, that this was not the *only* kind of writing that was being done in the nineties; and the second, that it may not have been the *best* writing that was being done'. And Wilkes goes on: 'The scope of literary activity in the nineties cannot be restricted to the literature of national sentiment.' [6] I like best in Wilkes' references to the nationalist view that magical little parenthesis, 'we are told'.

Cantrell too is obviously attracted to this stylish little touch as an adequate indentification of one's critical opponents: 'Writers and artists of the period learned to portray the country as it really is, we have been told'; and he urges us to 'look again at the literature, which, we have been told, enshrines the spirit of the decade'. Like Heseltine, Cantrell also commonly refers to 'a common view' – the vague and ghostly colossus that we've noticed before looming over and inhibiting the free action of tillers in the field of Australian literary history, like robber barons running rampage over poor powerless peasants.

We must ask openly – *which* is the colossus? *Who* forms the ruling orthodoxy in Australian criticism, the radical nationalists who apparently (we are told) present the 'common view', the received scripture, the Holy Writ – or their opponents? Who really are the influential people in Australian literary criticism? What *institutional* authority do they possess and exercise? Either more brave or more foolhardy than the rest, Cantrell does name a few names – Jose, Taylor, H. M. Green, and Nettie Palmer in views expressed between the wars, and Vance Palmer and Russel Ward in the 1950s; he also refers us to Ian Turner's *The Australian Dream* (1968). Cantrell would have made his list and the claim more plausible by adding Geoffrey Serle and A. A. Phillips; but Serle is, like the late Ian Turner, an historian, and Phillips was not English department based. Not one of all these people, and most of them are dead, is a practising English department critic. How can they, from the shades or from outside the university, or from university history departments, control the daily practice of Australian literary criticism?

In the 1975 *Southerly* article to which Cantrell refers approvingly, 'Going Over the Terrain in a Different Way: An Alternative View of Australian Literary History', G. A. Wilkes still goes on as if the radical nationalist view (again, about which we are 'told') remains dominant. Yet the counter-positions he gingerly edges forward as an 'alternative' are ones he had already programmatically sketched out in 1958; he has repeated its themes in numerous articles in *Southerly*, which he edits, and has had the opportunity of amplifying them at book length in *Australian Literature: A Conspectus*. You have to pause to wonder what Wilkes means when he says in 1975 that he's going over the terrain in a different way, unless he's referring to the way people lost in the Australian bush keep returning to the same spot. Many of the key anti-radical nationalist figures – Wilkes, Heseltine, Buckley – are professors wielding power over directions of undergraduate teaching and postgraduate research; and Mr Cantrell himself, complaining about the 'common view', was a senior lecturer in a university and chairman of its school of humanities, before becoming dean of arts at a college in Toowoomba.

It is critics such as these who represent the dominant orthodoxy, the Holy Writ of English department Aust. lit. crit. *They* are its high priests, enforcing a theology now at least twenty years old. And let's not be shy about the realities of university politics: because of the Anglocentrism of English departments, Australian literary criticism is a small field, a field in which critics must breathe more easily if they feel they can attack deceased writers from the 1920s or '30s, or freelancers like Nettie Palmer and Vance Palmer, or historians like Russel Ward, or that formidable parenthesis 'we are told', than professors in English departments who have control of appointments and promotions. Perhaps the real knife at the throat of Australian literary criticism is the particularly oppressive effect of the professorial system in a very small field of study.

So there it is. There's the poor figure of radical nationalism, bashed from pillar to post, tattered and torn, yet still paraded as the town bully. And there is the New Critical orthodoxy, ruling the roost but not crowing at all, and still apparently the tentative and younger challenger. The New Critics are like a cricket team which has just trounced the opposition, yet returns to the dressing room, dejected and glum, thinking it still hasn't won. How can we ever win, they sit there muttering. They feel like a club team that hasn't won a match for years, and their confidence has all but gone. Soon they'll become a laughing-stock, a walkover, and maybe they'll have to disband altogether, and then the 'common view' will have (we will be told) the centre all to itself, able to score at will. But we don't have to share these feelings of extreme modesty and ignominy: we're sitting on the hill, we can see the scoreboard, we can see who controls the selection of names for inclusion in university courses, and can work out the names actively repressed and silenced – almost all Australian writers outside of the major 'metaphysical' figures.

So that when Cantrell caps his exciting voyage into Australia's literary heritage by discovering that the 'prevailing tone of the 1890s' in Brennan and Lawson has affinities with that of James McAuley, A. D. Hope, and Patrick White, and that their work is the 'major tradition of Australian literature', we know we've been lucky visitors to this terrain before. We also realise that we're encountering here the language of monism, of exclusion, of ideological control – 'the prevailing tone', the 'major tradition of Australian writing' – and we're having to obey yet again the don't-argue beckoning finger of the critical traffic cop.

Behind the façade of Cantrell's regard for plurality and variety looms the fundamental concern of his critical imagination, a monistic view of Australian literature. At the beginning of his introduction our editor assures his readers of the width of the highway they can travel together; by its final page Cantrell has so far gone up a one-way road and changed gears and is exercising so heavy a right foot that he can justify various exclusions – like the Pacific writings of Louis Becke – on the grounds that they are 'removed from the spirit of the nineties I have attempted to capture'. Similarly, he has to exclude, he tells us sadly, the writings of 'Tasma', Praed and Ada Cambridge because 'the lives and books of all three writers were removed from the spirit of the decade which this anthology seeks to define. They belong to an earlier generation in our literature'.

Now, in his essay 'The Democratic Theme' A. A. Phillips tells us, as we saw in chapter one, that 'the spirit of a time somehow finds the voice which is suited to express it', and that Brennan didn't, unfortunately, suit the 1890s spirit:

One of the unluckiest accidents which can befall a writer is to be born into the period which does not suit him; and Christopher Brennan, for example, might well lament that his parents mated when they did.[7]

We're all sophisticated now; we smile at this – how silly to say only one sort of writer or writing suits a particular period, and not to acknowledge a period's diverse expressions and interests! Yet here we find sophisticated New Critic Mr Leon Cantrell – whose series of editions of this and that is manfully helping to supersede the yet still pervasive 'common view' of radical nationalists like A. A. Phillips – using almost exactly the same terminology and judgements.

The monistic design of Cantrell's selection goes very far to disqualifying it as a useful anthology. Yet even the evidence of Cantrell's own selection resists his monistic clutch and contradicts his historicist assertion that there is a unified spirit in the period and that this spirit can be hypostatised as 'alienation and loss'. In the section on City Life, for example, Cantrell includes a poem of Victor Daley, 'The Call of the City', which wittily rejects the idea of rural solitude:

> I know that hayseed in the hair
> Than grit and grime is healthier,
> And that the scent of gums is far
> More sweet than reek of pavement-tar.
> I know too that the breath of kine
> Is safer than the smell of wine;
> I know that here my days are free –
> But ah! the city calls to me

and in a refrain the poem lyrically celebrates living in Sydney:

> For when the hills are grey and night is falling,
>     And the winds sigh drearily,
> I hear the city calling, calling, calling,
>     With a voice like the great sea.

In the introductory note to this section Cantrell says that Lawson's 1888 'Faces in the Street' set the 'tone for the ensuing decade with its images of loneliness and misery', and he sees William Lane's depressing vision of urban squalor and unhappiness, the 'Saturday Night in Paddy's Market' chapter in *The Workingman's Paradise*, as written in the same prevailing spirit. But he has to dodge round, with a meaningless 'however', the fact of Victor Daley's affectionate poem on Sydney – just as Phillips tried to manoeuvre round the bulky presence of Christopher Brennan in his radical nationalist walk through the 1890s. In Cantrell's garden of misery the presence of such Daley poems is to be acknowledged only as an exception to the 1890s spirit – not as a growth of the period itself, but as seeds dropped on the ground which will take root and only really surface and spread in the future, as in Kenneth Slessor's 'similar fascination with the grimy beauty of our cities'. So, just as with the supposedly ever tendentious radical nationalists, some evidence is accepted as appropriate to the desired model of literary history, and other evidence is treated as exceptional, as untypical, as leftovers of the past or intimations of the future, not living expressions of the period's actual diversity and inevitable conflicting literary attitudes. Cantrell's critical broom, like that of his opponents, tries to sweep aside evidence of any drama of literary difference and opposition, of variety and contradiction. The literature of the 1890s has become the mournful monologue of the one composite historical actor.

In his haste to fumigate every corner of the decade with his own patented version of the gloom thesis, Cantrell destroys any chance the introduction has of contributing to a sociology and cultural history of the period's literature. Thus he dismisses as merely nostalgic George Taylor's *Those Were The Days* (1918) and Arthur Jose's *The Romantic Nineties* (1933). Nostalgic they may be, but they certainly aren't thereby useless: both books can provide extremely useful information, and hints and clues no less interesting because so often unwitting, about the attitudes of writers surrounding the *Bulletin*. In *The Romantic Nineties* Jose does celebrate the bohemianism of Sydney literary journalism, but he also makes it clear that it wasn't a uniform phenomenon. There was not one unified '*Bulletin* Bohemia': 'each *Bulletin* celebrity was rather the centre of his own clique, one clustering round Lawson [this was Brereton's, mainly], another round Victor Daley [this was the Dawn and Dusk Club], and so on'. Jose certainly does admire the 1890s as a kind of Elizabethan age of cultural vitality – 'Never since Elizabeth's days had a whole nation so unanimously clamoured for mind-food' – but he also suggests that the 'food-suppliers, congregated for a while in Sydney in a complex of mutual admiration societies, were at times a little above themselves'. In his loving descriptions of literary bohemian circles in the period Jose's reminiscences also clearly reveal how male-centred and exclusive were their cameraderie and friendships and intellectual exchanges. The Dawn and Dusk Club and other literary groups could include any number of mediocrities, nonentities and forgettables. Yet Jose in his chapter 'The Feminine Element' also tells the story of how Louise Mack was deliberately humiliated when she tried to have her work heard by, and to gain entry into, one of these male literary circles.[8] Such conscious rejection by men of letters may well point to one reason for some of the intensity and passion of feminist theorists and writers in the period, as with Louisa Lawson.

One little touch, when Jose admires Walter Jeffery, the then editor of the *Town and Country Journal*, as a true 'white man', reveals not only something of the extent of racist criteria and language in intellectual life of the 1890s, but its unshy persistence well into the next century. Again, Jose shows a slight Victorian moralistic stiffening when he reproves Lawson's prose (which he admires far above the verse) for its 'endeavor to be shocking, to insert unsavoury details' under the regrettable influence of the first Kipling stories.[9] Jose's suggestion that the 'influence of the young Kipling on Australian prose and verse in the Nineties' needs exploring is a good one, alerting us to the point that writers like Lawson were not simply recording reality but in part were responding to similar naturalistic literary impulses, attitudes and developments going on in contemporary English and European literature, for example, in England in the work of Kipling, Arthur Morrison and Henry Nevinson.[10]

In his introduction we found Cantrell making great play about how the spirit of the 1890s saw itself, spoke and felt surprised. So it's interesting to hear Jose stressing how highly Victor Daley was spoken of by the *Bulletin* literary circles Jose knew:

It is hard to express to this generation our feelings about Daley the poet. We watched for his acceptance by the London critics with complete assurance, and their neglect of him staggered us; it broke for ever the old, bad tradition that London's approval was worth something.[11]

The comment reveals the developing self-confidence of the literary community in the 1890s, a consciousness of achievement and an *anti-neocolonialism* – to be distinguished from radical nationalism – that rejected and resented any cultural-imperialist suggestion that, compared to the metropolitan, Australian literary products were necessarily inferior. In fact Jose's observations throughout his reminiscences of the élan and spirit of the male journalistic scene – and his feeling that this was a phenomenon of Sydney not Melbourne (Melbourne émigrés in Sydney included, Jose points out, Ashton, Streeton, Daley, Norman Lindsay, and Hugh McCrae) – is not just the product of a loony nostalgia but is supported by recent historical research. In his 1978 *Historical Studies* articles, Graeme Davison points to the strength of an emerging urban intelligentsia in Sydney in the 1880s and '90s, and argues that literary journalism, for newspapers, including radical labour movement papers, as well as for the *Bulletin*, enabled this intelligentsia to subsist and survive. In the depression of the early 1890s, which hit Melbourne much harder than Sydney, opportunities for work shrank and literary journalism became precarious: but overall in the period, literary journalism grew along with the growing urban reading public and the expanding urban communications network.[12]

Cantrell dismisses any suggestion of the 1890s as a golden age. Yet maybe Jose is right – it was a vital formative period for literary journalism, which gave financial support in Sydney for the existence of a self-confident urban intelligentsia; and perhaps we can observe in Daley's Sydney poems something of this confidence and sense of literary community and identification – an élan not of and for Australian society as a whole, but of a definable segment, a section of the professional middle class.

In his anthology Cantrell includes the Paddy's Market episode to show that utopians like William Lane didn't celebrate the squalid, distressing present but rather looked to a golden socialist future. Cantrell, however, neglects those chapters in *The Workingman's Paradise* which create a *Bulletin*-type radical intelligentsia of cartoonists, poets, artists, designers, and journalists. These chapters describe the Stratton circle, at their pleasant house on the north side of the harbour; the house is surrounded by a leafy garden, and the inner spirit of the household is shown as at one with the natural world of the harbour. Geisner, the idealised wandering revolutionary, tells the young bushman, Ned, that the 'most popular exponents of Socialism are nearly all press writers'.[13] The group consists of 'artist-souls', given to intense argument, yet warm and affectionate and often light-hearted in mood, and the aesthetic aspects of the house itself are celebrated. Wide-eyed Ned is informed that this is bohemia, and the novel in these sections can be seen as offering a glowing account of Sydney's early 1890s radical intellectual life. If Cantrell had stopped dipping only into his tin of black and had bothered to include one of these chapters, his gloomy picture of the 1890s might have exhibited some further large streaks of light.

Cantrell's introduction is also inadequate as critical theory. Nowhere does it show the slightest awareness of the importance of cultural and literary traditions, of the intervening agency of romanticism or naturalism, or different traditions of response to urban experience. It is knowledge of such traditions which could help explain the diverse literary expressions of the period. The English literary sociologist Peter Keating has argued for the existence of two major traditions concerning the city in 19th-century English prose writing, an 'industrial tradition' and an 'urban tradition'. The industrial tradition is located particularly in the novels of the 1840s and '50s (for example, *Mary Barton, North and South, Hard Times*, perhaps *Alton Locke*), which focus on the bitter historical conflict between capital and labour. This tradition also fed into much later 19th-century writing, as in that of George R. Sims, Andrew Mearns (*The Bitter Cry of Outcast London*) and Jack London (*The People of the Abyss*), which saw parts of London as an abyss of horrifying poverty and brutality that threatened the social order. The urban tradition, on the other hand, with its roots in an age-old tradition of London low-life scenes in English literature, and its relationship to Hogarth, is fascinated by the contrasts of city life, the presence of the bizarre and grotesque, the mystery of so many disparate types of humanity packed together. This tradition includes Pierce Egan's *Life in London* (1821), which looks forward to Mayhew and, most notably, Dickens' London novels. The urban tradition is often prompted by a concern for social injustice, but its primary aim is to explore social diversity not conflict and it does not share the tone of the industrial tradition, a uniform tone of seriousness.[14]

The contrasting traditions Keating identifies are also, I think, present and developed in 19th-century Australian literature. The tradition of seeing the urban landscape as the location of squalor and bitter class experience, equivalent to the 'industrial tradition', can certainly be witnessed in Lane's *The Workingman's Paradise*, and the evocation of 'Saturday Night in Paddy's Market' by Lane bears a remarkable similarity to a disgusted description of a Saturday night street market scene in working-class London in chapter eight of Kingsley's *Alton Locke*.[15] Yet both of these scenes, intended to typify working-class life in London and Sydney, can be contrasted to the chapter in Louis Stone's *Jonah* (1911) which almost enviously evokes the pleasurable shopping and eating of the Saturday night crowd at Paddy's Market.

These differences are not merely of perception, but of the way cultural traditions shape perception. A colonial 'urban tradition' might include stage adaptations of Pierce Egan's *Life in London*; the low-life journalism of Marcus Clarke and 'Julian Thomas' of *The Vagabond Papers*; and Fergus Hume's fine detective novel, *The Mystery of a Hansom Cab* (1887). It's a tradition which is evident in diverse aesthetic expressions and media, from theatre and popular entertainment to journalism and cartoons (Keating mentions Phil May as part of the London urban tradition), and it culminates, I think, in the early 20th century in Louis Stone's superb *Jonah*. It is true that a world-wide depression was developing in the 1880s and hit in the '90s; yet the depression alone won't account for the remarkable differences in perception of working-class life in Sydney between Lane and Stone in their chapters on Paddy's Market.

At the beginning of his introduction, before he's got into his monistic stride, Cantrell tells us that he has 'isolated the major concerns of writers to show a variety of approaches to similar themes'. Cantrell mentions these themes – writing in Australia, city life, lyricism, politics and nationalism, the city versus the bush, and life up the country – as if they're natural categories, God-given. They probably can make do as rough signposts; but they do not provide anything like a rich map of the 1890s landscape. The reference in Jose's *The Romantic Nineties* to someone being a true white man might have alerted our editor, if he'd read it for its value as a source-book of cultural history, to the strong and pervasive presence of racism in the decade. Yet such a theme is not recognised, which makes unfortunate the omission of figures like Louis Becke and Alex Montgomery, whose writings on the Pacific and southeast Asia could certainly reveal interesting insights into contemporary literary attitudes to colonialism and race. The exclusion of this kind of writing also makes Cantrell's selection rather parochial – over-emphasising, rather like the radical nationalists are held to do (we are told), local content.

Again, Jose's notes on the militant male-centredness of literary bohemian circles in the 1890s help us to suspect that our editor's themes don't necessarily represent the 'major concerns' of the period's writers. For example, Cantrell includes some pages of *My Brilliant Career* as part of his 'Up the Country' section. These pages

on the poverty and hardness of drought-stricken selector life might
serve Cantrell's theme, but they hardly represent the major concern of Miles Franklin's novel: a feminist exploration of the possibilities, or lack of possibilities, for an independent life for young
women in Australian rural society, selector and squatter, outside
of marriage, as in the following exchange between the young squatter, Harold, and Sybylla, to whom he offers the prospect of a con-
fining conventional marriage:

'... I have a frighful temper. Satan only knows what I will do in it yet.
Would you not be frightened of me?'
  'No fear,' I laughed: 'I would defy you.'
  'A tomtit might as well defy me,' he said with amusement.
  'Well, big as you are, a tomtit having such superior facilities for getting
about could easily defy you,' I replied.
  'Yes, unless it was caged,' he said.
  'But supposing you never got it caged,' I returned.
  'Syb, what do you mean?'
  'What could I mean?'
  'I don't know. There are always about four or five meanings in what
you say.'[16]

The passage, with its fascinating echoes of Ibsen, shows the vitality
in the period of writing on women's situation, attitudes, and
dilemmas, and Cantrell could well have constructed a thematic section with excerpts from *My Brilliant Career* as well as from Ada
Cambridge's *Unspoken Thoughts* (1887), Ethel Turner's *Seven
Little Australians*, Barbara Baynton's *Bush Studies*, and perhaps
from Louisa Lawson's writings. Another thematic section could
also have been organised around the theme of work, particularly
with the commercial and industrial development of the period;
parts of Lane's *The Workingman's Paradise*, as well as the factory
stories of Edward Dyson, are initial instances which spring to mind.
Lawson's stories could also be included.[17]

  We can finish this chapter by glancing again at Cantrell's bearing and role as a critical policeman, charged with enforcing Cold
War New Critical laws. In some ways it's strange that Cantrell
appears before us as so willing a member of the metaphysical orthodoxy. Mr Cantrell has been, after all, literary editor of the hardly

arch-conservative *Australian Left Review*, and the introduction itself at times shows a debunking, Humphrey McQueen type view of Australian radicalism, as when he chides the 1890s labour movement for being mildly reformist, not realising that 'real power is not to be found in the ballot box but through the control of property and profits'. It would seem that Cantrell has taken over a strand of New Critical orthodoxy, the gloom thesis stress on terror, alienation, doubt, suffering, and misery; and he sees this gloom as a kind of ideological superstructure, with, however, a rather uncertain relationship to the economic base, the world of 'property and profits'. This is interesting, and certainly a development on an idealist analysis, as in Buckley's or Heseltine's criticism, which focuses only on the presumed spirit of an age; and it shows the diversity of influences that have seeped into and coloured the small dam of our editor's critical attitudes. Yet we're still left with the touching puzzle, why does Cantrell think his view of the 1890s is original? The introduction is stamped 'Brisbane, March 1977'; surely Brisbane in March 1977 was not completely out of touch with Aust. lit. crit. developments of the last twenty years? Yet maybe we do have here an example of regional isolation. But before we lapse too far into sympathy, let's keep remembering that Cantrell's introduction and anthology will actively help, in university courses, the institutional repression of alternative views on, and knowledge of diverse areas of, Australian literature and cultural history.

# 6

# The New Right and the New Left in the Same Trap

In the last few chapters we have witnessed the mushrooming influence of the new metaphysical orthodoxy established in the 1950s and early '60s. An orthodoxy, we noticed, grows by permitting and incorporating the very heterogeneity that conceals its existence as an orthodoxy, a specific formation. Its assumptions spill over into the positions held by those who might be politically opposed to its conservative contributors (like James McAuley, or, in different ways, Vincent Buckley). It spawns variants and sub-genres, like the gloom thesis. It is influenced by and influences Australian historiography, in the figure of Manning Clark. And in turn Manning Clark's positions are appropriated in diverse and surprising ways, in the 1960s by the new right, in the 1970s by a strand of the new left, in the form of Humphrey McQueen. It is these appropriations of Clark that will concern us in this chapter.

## Manning Clark looks at Australian literature

In 'Re-writing Australian History'[1] Manning Clark becomes, it seems to me, a possibly unwitting precursor and perhaps prisoner of certain features of the intellectual right. This position arises from his feelings about the importance to historiography of literature and the imagination. An assumption of the Vance Palmer-Russel Ward radical nationalist tradition is that an admirable common culture inheres in the folk, in ballads and songs and yarns and legends. Ideally, intellectuals should reflect and express the best values of the folk, and so be organically tied to them; intellectuals and folk then form parts of the one community of spirit. In 'Rewriting Australian History' the reverse position is suggested. An assumption that surfaces in the latter part of Clark's essay is that it is an élite of writers, and in particular the poets, of an era or period who show the way in interpreting the character and experience of a society. But they have to be the right poets, the truly representative.

Clark's assumption is that the poetic imagination can see into the essentially human; in effect, it is not swayed by the historically incidental, the contingent, and the partisan. A further assumption seems to be that ideology is not ideology if it be metaphysical – that only the social and political are ideological, that to engage in ultimate religious questions concerning time and suffering and the meaning of life is to deal with humanity at a level that clearly transcends particular ideological considerations, contexts, constraints, formations. As if such history will be conceived from beyond history, in the eternal concerns of the creative imagination.

Which is naive indeed, a naivety that follows on from the romantic and Platonic assumption that the imagination creates and perceives human essences. For it means that whereas Clark will relate the work of certain poets like Victor Daley, Bernard O'Dowd, and Henry Lawson, held to have nationalist political interests, to contemporary ideologies, such a procedure will not be used for poets with explicit, declared metaphysical interests. They're apparently to be ever exempt from historical explanation. Such naivety is particularly dangerous for cultural historians – indeed, it undermines the very idea of cultural history.

Yet poets like Kenneth Slessor, Douglas Stewart, and James McAuley, on the contrary, only reveal how profoundly and intimately the aesthetic is affected by ideology. McAuley's views are ideological and political: they lead into the murky world of the Congress for Cultural Freedom, CIA funding and manipulation of intellectual life, and hard-line Cold War stances. Both Slessor and Douglas Stewart were influenced by Norman Lindsay, who had long opposed radical nationalism and upheld a consciously and defiantly élitist aesthetic. In Lindsay's view, the ordinary social world and ordinary people are death to the spirit. The creative few in a society should acknowledge each other as superior beings, and pursue not the passing shows of social action and political involvement, but the eternal verities of art and sexuality. There exists a higher and universal consciousness that artists should communicate with through the Image. But such communication is bound to be only momentary and fleeting, and then the creative spirit is plunged back into the ordinary world of time and division. Nevertheless, death will be a happy event, releasing the artist from bondage to the aberrations of this puny earth, and winging the artist's spirit off to the great consciousness in the sky. Meanwhile, the artist hides from the crowd in the inner city, relaxes in pubs, enjoys good food in restaurants – rather like the glorious Elizabethans of old – and writes verses extolling eternal verities like vitality and courage and heroism, as exhibited in poets, explorers, or their friends. Artists are hidden kings, and the pub/cafe/restaurant is their court.[2]

Lindsay, Slessor, and Stewart were members of a very powerful grouping in Sydney literary and journalistic life, and a sociology of literature in Australia could do worse than study its networks of influence and lines of power. Stewart was for a long time literary editor of the *Bulletin*, and was important in publishing; a friend of Slessor was R. G. Howarth, a member of the Sydney University English department and founding editor of *Southerly*, a journal which served the interests of these and subsequent Sydney writers, and which was resolutely anti-radical nationalist. Slessor himself was editor for a year of *Southerly*, and the journal overall helped to institute a New Critical-type view of Australian literature, that writers are important in so far as they express the moral and metaphysical rather than the social and political. If we trace this group's origins back into the 1920s, to the standing and influence of Norman Lindsay and the entry of *Vision* onto the cultural scene, we have a tradition that, well into the 1950s, was powerful in publishing, reviewing, mutual admiration and celebration, and institutional academic support. For decades, it was the Sydney literary establishment.

Nevertheless, in the new pressures of the Cold War, there was something outmoded about this particular Slessor-Stewart grouping, with Norman Lindsay on the mountain in the background: something defensive about their attitude to Australian (or any) society. They were an élite, pursuing art against society, the uncomprehending philistines; but they were also, as I argue in *Australian Cultural Elites*, pluralist, hoping to survive by being one social group (ideally, inner urban bohemian) amongst others; they didn't wish, as Melbourne intellectuals so often wished, to spread their values to the rest of society.

The new Cold War ideologues like McAuley and Vincent Buckley saw things differently. They wanted to go on the cultural offensive, and for McAuley *Quadrant* and the Australian Association for Cultural Freedom were to be his vehicles. In this sense, the shadow of Norman Lindsay weighed like a nightmare on the brains of the Cold Warriors. As we saw, Buckley in his 1958-9 *Quadrant* essay 'Utopianism and Vitalism' railed against Lindsay and his influence in *Southerly* and in the literary section of the *Bulletin*.[3] All the best Australian writers had to be seen as following on from Brennan, and Slessor, Stewart, and R. D. FitzGerald were to be enrolled in the pantheon – as long as they could be freed from their early worship of the magic mountain, the taint of Norman Lindsay's influence on them when young. For Lindsay's vitalism meant turning one's back on society, and the debasing of a true Brennanite metaphysicality into the merely physical, biological, erotic.

Norman Lindsay's kind of élite pluralism had to be pushed aside, and true (Christian) metaphysical literature proselytised throughout the intellectual community and established for teaching purposes in universities: just as Peter Coleman and Donald Horne wished to modify John Anderson's academic élitism and spread the values of the new right throughout society. In 1960 the Packer machine, Australian Consolidated Press, acquired the *Bulletin*, recruiting for editors in the '60s Horne, Coleman, and Peter Hastings; and in the same year Douglas Stewart, an old supporter of Norman Lindsay, left the *Bulletin* to go to Angus and Robertson publishers.

The new right was moving in, in some ways displacing the older literary establishment, in other ways trying to reform it to make it more active, agitational, propagandist – to improve its strike capability. If the persuasiveness and intellectual authority of the radical nationalists were to be effectively countered, the opposing metaphysical tradition had also to be refined and modernised. The metaphysical literary tradition had to be torn from its characteristic Sydney context. Its truths had to be generalised for Australian literary and cultural history as a whole, and in this generalising a sacrifice had to be made – the old man at Springwood. The wolf was to be made a lamb, and put on the rack; the serpent was to be skinned, dried, and hung as a warning of what not to be. Lindsay was to become a dead temptation, a forgotten embarrassment. Strangely enough, then, Norman Lindsay was in the end criticised most nastily, unpleasantly, and savagely not by the radical nationalists whom he life-long opposed, but by a fellow conservative.

I'm not trying to suggest that Buckley and Clark's views neatly coincided. If Buckley can be seen as trying to make Sydney writers Christian and stoical, Clark tends to embrace writers like Douglas Stewart and Slessor uncritically. He might possibly see Buckley's concern for stoicism, rather than Norman Lindsay-influenced vitalism and eroticism, as wowserish, and he'd be suspicious of too close an identification with Catholicism or any institutionalised religion. The point rather is that Clark was not recognising that the aesthetic and the 'metaphysical' are always embedded in ideological and political perspectives and conflicts. He couldn't so recognise, because he'd already predefined the metaphysical as beyond ideology.

## Peter Coleman and the new right

It might be thought, and the term 'ivory tower' suggests it often has been thought, that intellectuals in universities talk only to themselves: so that ideas of 'high' intellectuals like James McAuley or G. A. Wilkes or Vincent Buckley or H. P. Heseltine remain within a small circle of interest, influencing a tiny few about things rarefied and irrelevant. Not so. Many of the tendencies we have

been outlining in previous chapters as influenced by Cold War end-
of-ideology thinking spilled over into the more general intellectual
discourse of the Cold War period.

The spillover occurred firstly in the obvious area of university
teaching, helping to shape the assumptions and set the mood of a
generation of students. (I recall that when I got to Sydney University in 1963, religion and religious clubs like the Newman Society
seemed very strong, and also that in the next couple of years sophisticated students would walk around sporting 'Student Apathy
Group' badges.) The ideas of the high intellectuals also spilled over
into journalism, and in particular into the activities and energies
of the new right.

A note on terminology here. In *Australian Liberalism and
National Character* Tim Rowse refers to what I am calling the new
right as the new critics,[4] and acknowledges that he's following Warren Osmond's suggestion in his booklet on Sol Encel's sociological
concepts and context, *The Dilemma of an Australian Sociology*.
Here Osmond argues that cultural nationalism and 'what might
pretentiously be called New Criticism of the Menzies Era' are the
dominant frameworks in which Australian intellectuals related
themselves to their social environment. Osmond sees the main new
critics as Robin Boyd, Donald Horne, Peter Coleman, J. D. Pringle
(and later, Ronald Conway), and he includes as their literary allies
Patrick White, McAuley, and Hope.[5] Rowse widens this group to
include also Barry Humphries, Craig McGregor, Manning Clark (in
'Re-writing Australian History'), Leonie Kramer, Vincent Buckley,
and H. P. Heseltine.[6] That a rough grouping like this exists in recent
Australian cultural history I agree, but the use of the term 'new
critic' is an unfortunate confusion with its more established use in
literary criticism, particularly when thinking of the American New
Critics.

The term new right has therefore been preferred – indicating a
strident kind of radical conservatism – and by it I'm mainly referring to political commentators like Peter Coleman, Donald Horne,
and Peter Hastings. The new right took the ideas of high intellectuals like John Anderson in his Cold War phase, or James McAuley
or Vincent Buckley or Manning Clark, and tried to turn them into
the natural, ordinary, assured, and undeniable pronouncements and

currency of fortnightly and weekly journalism, in the *Observer* (1957-61), and then in the Packer *Bulletin* from 1961 on, the group having close links with McAuley's *Quadrant*.

The new right in the late 1950s and early and middle 1960s were in some ways very much like the new left in the late 1960s and 1970s: they were a group striving to put their views forward in a wide variety of ways, from books and journals to journalism; they wished to re-orient Australian intellectual life to radically new perspectives, which were held to encompass a total view of reality and history; they were full of energy, bustle, and fight. The difference is, of course, that the new right could attract and rely on vastly more institutional support and power – in the universities, from press barons like the Packer family – than the new left could ever draw on, even if they so wished.

As ideologues, seeking to restate the more exploratory positions of others as obvious truths, new right masterminds frequently became crudifiers, perhaps to the occasional embarrassment of the intellectuals they wished to enrol on their side in the battle against the declared enemies, in particular the left liberals and the radical nationalists. Such a process is revealed to its best advantage in Peter Coleman's introduction to the symposium he edited in the early 1960s, *Australian Civilization*.[7] We would have to call the intellectual style neobrutalist – all hard lines and harsh surfaces, and your opponents embedded in concrete walls. Coleman argues in his introduction, 'The New Australia', that the latter 1930s represent a decisive period of change in Australian history, the emergence of a modern Australia. Before this time, and especially towards the end of the 19th century, in Archibald's *Bulletin*, in Lawson's poems, and in the Labor Party, the 'Australianist' legend had too much sway and hold in actual Australian society. This legend was 'radical, populist, nationalist, racialist', and, according to Coleman, it somehow managed to enshrine a number of 'apparently incompatible attitudes', in particular 'naive humanism' and 'nihilism'.

Coleman is not (nor was Buckley, we recall) against humanism as such, for he later agrees with Max Harris about the neglected importance of the 'tradition of liberal gentlemen', these gentlemen being apparently, with their 'ideology of civility and humanism', the true builders of our nation. But 'naive humanism' invokes the dark shadow of utopianism; sure, 'naive humanism' contained a genuine democratic emotion, but in its Australianist version its chief expression, mateship, went along with the 'snarl of the collectivist bully', a snarl revealed in the bully-boy poet Henry Lawson.

The Australianist legend was also characterised by a 'nihilism' which isn't humanistic, but places a 'great value on frenzy, nervous energy, violence, vitality and robustness'. This brought together attitudes involved in anything from 'popular imperialism, commercial plundering, heroic balladry, to the cult of the bacchanal, the cult of sport, the singing of vindictive folk songs, or the preaching of bullying racialism'.

By what principle of handling and selection Coleman has thrown things into such a ragbag isn't made really clear – the 'cult of the bacchanal', for example, seems to recall Vincent Buckley's strictures on Norman Lindsay, who was anti-Australianist, although Buckley in his 'Utopianism and Vitalism' argues that 'utopian humanism' and 'vitalism' came together and became fused and confused in Australian literature, especially in the 1930s. But it looks as if Buckley's essay is being transcribed by Coleman at this point in his introductory effort: and, given our suspicion of the ideologue as crudifier, Buckley's 'utopianism' and 'vitalism' have become Coleman's 'naive humanism' and 'nihilism'.

The odd co-existence of humanism and nihilism, 'democracy and violence, the open smile and the broken bottle', is not, however, paradoxical, says Coleman. It's just what you'd expect from people in a new society, convicts and the like, or free settlers driven here by penury, ambition, or 'sheer discontent'; they didn't have a clue about the 'parent civilization' they'd been rejected by or had themselves scorned.

These outsiders and rejects helped form the 'democratic-nihilist complex' we know as Australianism, and Australianism was an 'anti-civilized movement'. It was an assault on the very 'institutional framework of civilization' itself, on the ideas of art, the state, church, university and so on. The trouble was such Australianists were either unwilling or unable 'to live the British or European way of life, with its conventions, pieties and hierarchy'. (Here we seem to be listening to James McAuley, to McAuley's Carlylean fantasy about Australia as a medieval paradise of organic Christian community regained.)

Still, there was a counter-tradition. For despite a 'hostile environment, critical and liberal minds survived and even flourished in the arts, the universities, law and Parliament', contributing to 'the Australian middle-class tradition' which, thank God and all the pieties and hierarchies, helped maintain our cultural life. As well there's the 'tradition of liberal gentlemen' Max Harris is so eager to tell of to anyone who'll listen. Liberalism here doesn't of course mean being left-liberal, or being weak towards radicalism or totalitarianism: it's something more akin to conservative-liberal.

Australianism played itself out in the 20th century, and by the late 1930s it was left to the 'liberals and sceptics who had kept civility and culture alive' to pick up the pieces of European civilisation in Australia and 'start again'. This is not to say the cavalry came. What an ill-chosen metaphor that would be. Coleman's upholders of English and European institutions of the arts, universities, church, law, and parliament were not tainted by 'violence' as a military metaphor might suggest. *They* were not 'coercive', as apparently the Australian radical tradition so decisively was. How could people who believed in the true English and European way of life with its 'conventions, pieties and hierarchy' ever go in for coercion, for political manipulation, discrimination, force, violence?

These good middle-class men were not historically racist – only the working class, the labour movement and radicals were. These good men also held themselves above 'vitality and robustness'; and certainly above frenzy, nervous energy, and the cult of the bacchanal. They were above all civil, and, it appears, good churchgoers.

In Coleman's view of Australian history, the middle class and middle-class activities in the church, arts, law, and parliament form a beneficent institutional complex. Coleman lets Manning Clark do the work for him at one stage by a long quotation from Clark's introduction to his *Select Documents, 1851-1900*, where the historian contradicts the 'progressivist assumptions' of the radical tradition by pointing out that at the end of the 19th century, the privileged group was not weak and tottering; its economic and political power had not been seriously threatened by Eureka and the radicalism of the 1890s.

It's hard to disagree with Clark's point. But we can be sceptical about what Coleman makes of it: the implied *admiration* of such ruling groups. We can ask of the ruling classes in Australian history, the privileged groups with the economic and political power: have they always been free of coercion and violence? What of the state and its coercive power? And what of other institutions in Australian society and history, like the army, police, intelligence organisations, prisons, asylums, repressive laws? What of their kind of institutional violence?

Coleman quotes another historian in support.

A. G. L. Shaw points out in his chapter that the Australian radical tradition always had a strong coercive element: in the 1930's this element was uppermost. The only answer to the problems of moral disorder, political revolution, totalitarianism, industrialization, foreign affairs, was more coercion.

Presumably this means that in the 1930s the coercive element was 'uppermost' in the Australian radical tradition – surely not in the society as a whole? Were any of Coleman's good middle-class people attracted to violence, force, coercion in the 1930s? Wasn't there indeed a flourishing of extreme rightwing thinking and organisation, including para-military conspiratorial organisation, in the 1930s? Also, in anticipation of 1975, Lang got dismissed in 1932. Who dismissed Lang and his elected government?[8]

Where did power lie in these years? Did it lie in the hands of a radical tradition trying to assist a working class clearly on the defensive, facing unemployment, eviction and hunger? Was it the radical tradition which tried to deny entry to the European anti-nazi Egon Kisch, which believed the elected government of Spain should not be supported in its fight against Franco, which admired Hitler, then provided military assistance to Franco's fascist forces, which tried to sell pig iron to an expansionist Japan? Who in the 1930s had the economic and political power to be coercive?

## The counter-revolution in Australian historiography

Following World War II came the counter-revolution. Coleman's introduction to *Australian Civilization* claims that the Australian legend also had its scholarly side in the work of historians like H. V. Evatt and especially Brian Fitzpatrick. But fortunately there was a counter-revolution in historiography against such people which corresponds, says Coleman, to the counter-revolution in poetry espied by J. D. Pringle in his *Australian Accent* (1958), in the reaction of A. D. Hope, James McAuley, and Harold Stewart to nationalism in Australian poetry. The counter-revolution opposed the 'radical-leftist interpretation' of Australian history by Fitzpatrick and his ilk which denied the 'contributions of the middle classes, the churches, the universities and non-radical reformist and liberal movements'.

This post-World War II counter-revolution has, says Coleman, been led by Manning Clark, who has done more than anyone else to 'release historians from the prison of the radical interpretation' (how coercive the radical historians are!) and has stimulated them to begin systematic study of neglected themes in our history, 'especially of religion', but also of free thought, education, culture, and business. Historians like Allan Martin, Peter Loveday, and Bruce Mansfield have weighed in to change our notions of political history, and political scientist Henry Mayer knocked on the head the idea that the Labor Party is the party of initiative, and the non-labour parties are the parties of resistance.

What's being demonstrated is the 'existence of a tradition of middle-class liberalism which did not and has not merged with Labor radicalism'. Of course, this work is still only incipient, in books-in-progress, monographs, articles, unpublished theses. But the ferment, Coleman excitedly reports, is real, and in ten or twenty years' time, when the material is collected, someone will completely re-write the whole of Australian history – 'and the counter-revolution will be achieved'. Meanwhile one really healthy sign is at hand: 'the very creation in Sydney of a *Journal of Religious History* in 1960 is symbolic of the strength of the new interests'.

Why the historians Coleman roped into his enclosure – as well

as others he names like Geoffrey Blainey and R. M. Crawford –
actually wanted to parade there being gawked at as the champion
squires of a rightwing reaction in the writing of Australian history
is not clear. In general they probably picture themselves as empiri-
cists and pluralists who are beyond ideological commitment either
to right or left. Certainly Henry Mayer later dissociated himself
from the connexion,[9] and it's difficult to see Manning Clark being
all that pleased by Coleman's portrait of his ideas. Indeed Clark
must surely have wondered if Coleman fully understood him. Certainly Coleman could gain some kind of warrant from Clark's statement that the latter 19th century was the great age of bourgeois
civilisation in our cities. But another of Clark's themes has been
a consistent attack on middle-class philistinism and wowserism –
the 'measurers' who, Clark says in a concluding comment to 'Re-
writing Australian History', deny the value of 'mystery' in life.

Yet Coleman, in providing this fairly rough-house kind of syn-
thesis, was helping, along with his new right colleagues in the *Bulletin*, to consolidate a new view in Australian historiography, that
could be spread abroad in social commentary and journalism.

The alleged counter-revolution in historiography was, as Tim
Rowse points out in *Australian Liberalism and National Character*,
part of the new right's general strategy towards the left: 'It was
one of their most adroit feats of rhetoric to succeed in characteriz-
ing their intellectual opposition as a left-liberal establishment.'[10]
This is precisely what Coleman does in his *Australian Civilization*
introduction. The radical tradition was the repository of the 'orthodox assumptions' about Australian history. This 'standard radical-
leftist interpretation' was given in 'nearly all textbooks', including
the *Cambridge History of the British Empire*, Vere Gordon Childe's
*How Labor Governs*, H. V. Evatt's *Australian Labour Leader*, and
Brian Fitzpatrick's *A Short History of the Australian Labour Movement* and *The Australian People, 1788-1945*. In this orthodoxy, Australian history is the story of progress, and the working class and
the labour movement – particularly in the 19th century – are the
chief initiators of such progress. This radical legend is like the Whig
legend in English history.

Again, Coleman is trying to stick close by Manning Clark's side
in making these claims. But how true is it to say historians like

Evatt, Childe, and Fitzpatrick represent the 'orthodox assumptions', the 'standard' view, in Australian historiography? What does this assertion mean in terms of the relationship between knowledge and power?

In *Australian Liberalism and National Character* Rowse himself, I think, wavers on this question. He points out that the ascription of orthodoxy is part of a strategy of the new right; but at other points he seems to believe in it himself. He writes of Manning Clark in 'Re-writing Australian History' as responding to the 'hegemony of the radical theme in Australian history' and that in the 1940s, in the work of Evatt and Fitzpatrick and Childe, and of Communist historians like E. W. Campbell and J. N. Rawling, 'this had been the historical orthodoxy'. (A little later Rowse writes that a 'certain literary canon emerged in the 1930s and 1940s' enshrining egalitarian values, and he refers to the 'left-Australianist literary orthodoxy of the 1940s and early '50s' – which in the 1950s went under to institutionally powerful critics like McAuley, Leonie Kramer, Vincent Buckley, A. D. Hope, Herbert Piper, and H. P. Heseltine.)[11]

As we've seen, the literary establishment in the 1930s and '40s was the Norman Lindsay-Slessor-Douglas Stewart-*Southerly* ensemble. This isn't to deny the importance of writers in a left-liberal or radical stream, particularly the strong presence of female writers in this period, demonstrated in Drusilla Modjeska's *Exiles at Home* (1981). But although they may have been contesting the persuasiveness and institutional power of the Lindsay-Slessor metaphysical school, they were unable to diminish it seriously, or to replace it.

But more generally: how can we believe, in the case particularly of Marxist historians like Fitzpatrick and Campbell, that they were the orthodoxy, the dominant force in Australian historiography? What sense does such a statement make? Has the bourgeoisie idly permitted leftwing intellectuals to take over the powerful teaching positions in universities, for example? Wasn't Fitzpatrick denied an academic history position all his life? Was Evatt an academic historian? Or E. W. Campbell, a communist?

We have, of course, to make a distinction, when talking of knowledge and power, between the felt moral authority of certain intellectual positions or kinds of literature, and actual institutional power. It could be argued that because the Whig interpretation of Australian history was persuasive, was powerfully and lucidly stated, then it must be the orthodoxy. But was it taught at universities? Was it well received and spread by journalists and social commentators? Who, indeed, in the 1940s, were the professors of history in our universities? If they encouraged any teaching of Australian history, what kinds of interpretation did they create, esteem, push as respectable and worthy of notice by students and postgraduates?

I'm not trying to argue that a certain (bourgeois) orthodoxy has all the power, and its radical or left opposition is always totally powerless. Rather, there will always be a conflict and contest of opposing views and interpretations. I simply have extreme doubts that a radical interpretation can ever have the institutional resources and backing to make itself the 'orthodoxy', the 'standard' view.

What of the 1950s and '60s, when Australian history teaching was quickly expanding in universities, and the conflict of views between historians was acute? Again, the run of institutional power was all the other way: Russel Ward was denied a position at the University of NSW in 1960, and had to be satisfied with the provinces; Robin Gollan was refused important teaching posts, and was confined until 1976 to a non-teaching research position. Certainly Geoffrey Serle is an academic historian, and so, late in his career, was Ian Turner. But how does this line-up compare in strength and senior academic and professorial muscle to Coleman's counter-revolutionaries, to Manning Clark, Allan Martin, Peter Loveday, Bruce Mansfield? And what of the other professors in Australian universities – have John M. Ward and Gordon Greenwood and Fred Alexander been famous for supporting the radical hegemony?

The counter-revolution in Australian historiography was precisely to establish a new historiographical dominance. Henceforth budding Australian historians were to see themselves in a daring role. They would break out from the stifling left-liberal Whig orthodoxy they were told was imprisoning them. They would explore new, neglected themes: the importance in Australian history of religion, business, liberalism untainted by radicalism, the middle class, the benevolent and beneficent institutional complex of the church, the law, and parliament. No one told them that such themes were becoming the new orthodoxy – which they were being taught! (It was, apparently, a smart thing to say by History honours students at Sydney University in the early and middle 1960s that 'what we need in Australian history now are more studies of conservatism'.)

Further, the counter-revolution effected a break with any view that the Australian working class, the labour movement, and radical ideas were indeed progressive. Rather, they were exclusionist, coercive, and racist. Coleman at one point refers to 'popular imperialism' as a nihilist aspect of the Australianist legend. The implication is that the Australianists, ensconced in the 1890s *Bulletin* and in the Labor Party, and presumably the working class generally, were mainly responsible for imperialist values. If we looked to British history as an analogous case, we would, following Coleman, have to say that the English labouring and working classes were primarily responsible for the racism which produced slavery and the Empire!

Whatever was questionable or horrific in Australian historical experience is, on this account, to be speedily sheeted home to the lower orders and the promoters of radical ideas, and to the latter-day historians who defended both.

## Humphrey McQueen and the new left

The new right's push for dominance in Australian intellectual life, and particularly in university disciplines, was at its height in the late 1950s and 1960s. The forces of the left, however, were also reforming and regrouping during this period, stimulated by the activity and new spirit of ex-Communist Party intellectuals, in journals like *Outlook* and *Arena*. The Cold War was on the wane, and an international revival of radicalism was occurring, in the marches organised by the Campaign for Nuclear Disarmament, and in the writings of new left figures like E. P. Thompson and Raymond Williams in Britain and C. Wright Mills in the United States. Ideology, which had been consigned to the rubbish-heap of history, an offshoot of totalitarianism and utopianism, was beginning to voice new interests and demands.

The new radicalism was given a great deal of direction and sharpness by the gathering protest against the Vietnam War. For it was the Vietnam War which proved so embarrassingly wrong Daniel Bell's pronouncement in *The End of Ideology* (1960) of the ending of ideological critique in modern societies. Instead there was an upsurge of the liberation movements (black, women's, gay), and a renewed focus on major exploitative features of industrial capitalism: the imperialist oppression of Third World societies, and at home, racism, sexism, pervasive hierarchy, and lack of participation in decision making. Such ideological questioning was soon to lead, especially in the 1970s, to an upsurge of likeminded intellectual critique and analysis and research, a challenge to existing interpretations of Australian society and history.

Yet the rising new left intellectual activity was not to be without its divisions and differences. An early example of such differences was a dispute about Australian historical interpretation between two young historians, Humphrey McQueen and Ann Curthoys.

In late 1970 Penguin published Humphrey McQueen's *A New Britannia*, and soon after it was reviewed in *The Old Mole*, a radical student newspaper, by an even younger historian, Ann Curthoys. McQueen was originally a student, then a schoolteacher, in Queensland, but he was to find a home in Canberra, initially as senior tutor in Manning Clark's history department at ANU, and Clark wrote the foreword for *A New Britannia*. McQueen's opponent in this contest, on the left, Curthoys, was at the time researching for her doctorate, broadly arguing for the close connection between racism and the dominant middle- and upper-class liberalism in Australian society in the 19th century. In her view, the historiographical point was not to ascribe blame to any one class for racism; the argument rather was that all classes were racist in ideology, and that which class, working or other, had the initiative at any one time in trying to pursue state action to enforce discrimination or exclusion was a matter for historical investigation.

*A New Britannia* was awaited with eagerness and a great deal of goodwill by the younger radical historians. Curthoys herself certainly hoped the best for the book. She saw it as a contribution to the radical intellectual culture being shaped by the Vietnam War protest movements – 'the horror of Vietnam has led to a questioning of Australia's place in, and vision of, the world'. The new left's concern for the importance of racism and imperial ideology in the present gave an edge to McQueen's assertion of the strength of these values in the working class in the 19th century; Curthoys granted that McQueen here had certainly made a point against previous labour historians for not sufficiently focusing on this aspect in the past.

But Curthoys also perceived serious weaknesses in *A New Britannia*. Her most damaging criticism was that McQueen didn't do what he said ought be done by a socialist historian – such an historian shouldn't retreat into the safe pastures of labour history, but must advance into the structure and history of the ruling class. *A New Britannia*, Curthoys argues, is devoted to describing the one class only, the labouring class and associated radical ideas, up to the end of the First World War. Against Russel Ward's view of the collectivist, mateship character of 19th-century Australia, possessed by a kind of natural socialist ethos, McQueen counterposes a view which stresses individual self-assertion. The working class was possessed by petit-bourgeois acquisitive ideals, the desire for upward mobility, and by nationalism and racism.

McQueen argues that this aggressively aspiring, competitive ideology of the lower classes was a triumph for bourgeois hegemony. But, says Curthoys, McQueen nowhere defines the 'bourgeois hegemony' by which the labouring classes are dominated. In general, Curthoys felt, the use by McQueen of the terms 'bourgeois' or 'middle class hegemony' were unilluminating if the general ideology of the middle class is never described, and that this lack was most damaging in the analysis of 19th-century racism. Curthoys recognised that the discussion of racism and nationalism is the most original part of *A New Britannia*, but his discussion of racist beliefs was debilitatingly vague, a vagueness which arose from his concern to establish the importance of racism rather than to explain its presence or to see why it was so universally held. Above all, the vagueness of McQueen's discussion of racism was caused by his ignoring the importance of racism in liberal thinking:

At times, McQueen comes close to the liberal historians. Many of the latter stress, and are most interested in, the racism of the working class, assuming that the middle class and pastoralist sections of the population were too educated to be so crudely racist. While McQueen, of course, doesn't say *this*, he does fail to make the analysis of the ideology of all sections of the population, including urban middle and landowning classes, which would be necessary to make racism in Australia comprehensible.[12]

About this time McQueen was obviously taking his tutorial role in life really seriously, not only presumably towards his students in Canberra, but towards the emergent Australian radicalism as a whole. He would be its instructor, guide, mentor, checking analyses for correct ideas. McQueen distributed a reply to Curthoys's *Old Mole* review, in roneo form, since *The Old Mole* wasn't to come out again for a while (I don't think it ever came out). It is a document to treasure. It certainly should astonish researchers who come across it in the future McQueen papers.

Australia's tutor in Marxism didn't, however, begin by trying to meet the main thrust of Curthoys' review – that *A New Britannia* suffers from an analysis of only one class, rather than of the relationships between classes. Rather, he decides to clarify certain confusions Curthoys has about the use of such terms as ideology and hegemony. McQueen said his own use of such a term as hegemony was ever clear and precise: any confusions about it were in the mind of Curthoys, not on the pages of his book. 'Far from being uncertain and clumsy my use of the word and the notion was at all times intentional and precise.' McQueen also is clear about the distinction between 'ideological dominance' and 'hegemony'. Hegemony, he says, he derives from Gramsci; but with ideology he has derived much from Lukács' notion of ' "false consciousness" (i.e. ideology)'.

So, ideology is false consciousness. 'Ideology is a false solution to the problems facing a class: racism, the desire for land, democracy are in this situation. Hegemony is the active acceptance of a lifestyle and world outlook: pianos, land hunger and the individualism consequent upon gold discoveries are examples.' Poor Curthoys, who cannot see such an amazingly clear distinction, was too dazzled perhaps by its luminous clarity, like the lights of a car at night, and wonders about its usefulness. She must be possessed by 'theoretical naivety' and can scarcely be, McQueen decides, a Marxist at all. 'For Marxist historians at least Curthoys has posed a non-problem.'

It was, however, Curthoys' paragraph on McQueen and the liberal historians which really worked wonders. He was enraged. The fell Curthoys, he says,

makes a shoddy attempt to lump me in with the liberal historians who revel in finding evidence of working-class sins. She is careful to avoid saying this outright and she explicitly denies that this is what I say, but even to raise the doubt is vile. If she wishes to attack liberals like Lipset she knows from my *Arena* article that I am happy to join her. But her slimy insinuations and innuendoes on this point are nothing less than contemptible. There is nothing to answer in this pseudo-allegation: it is simply necessary to expose it for the damnable malignancy that it is.

Given McQueen's observation of Curthoys' vileness, you'll notice that Curthoys didn't make a personal accusation against McQueen at all, a claim about his intentions or consciousness. She said his closeness to the liberal historians was 'unwitting', and that what she was really doing, in criticising *A New Britannia*, was discussing 'the consequences of McQueen's method'. That is, in the parlance of Althusserians, Curthoys was saying McQueen's approach and methodology were compatible with a certain problematic in Australian historiography – the conservative-liberal one.

And, given our explorations of Manning Clark's 1956 'Re-writing Australian History' and the stimulus it gave to Coleman's perception of a counter-revolution in Australian historiography, how true – and indeed, grossly understated – her insight is. For, we must decide, while the rhetoric of *A New Britannia* is loudly new left, its intellectual substance is very solidly new right.

It's certainly true that McQueen is not as absurd in his analyses as Peter Coleman, who in his introduction to *Australian Civilization* talks of 'popular imperialism' as if the Australian working class thought up the idea. McQueen claims that because Australia is a frontier of European capitalism in Asia, this has generated fears of the north and so made Australian nationalism essentially racist.

As Curthoys notes, however, such a suggestion that Australian racism is part of imperialism does not of itself explain racism.

In a later commentary in *Politics* in 1972 on the reviews of his book McQueen complained that almost no one who reviewed it saw what the book was about, a history of the Labor Party (in part, again, because of 'the abysmal level of Marxism in this country').[13] But as Curthoys observes in concluding her review, 'McQueen's book is dominated by the concern to debunk Ward's and others' idealisation of the Australian past.' Maybe not all reviewers are wrong all the time. It may have been McQueen's intention to write a revolutionary history that would undermine and disestablish bourgeois ideology and scholarship. But the main thrust of *A New Britannia* was to attack the labour historians, radical nationalists like Ward, and the so-called old left interpretation of 19th-century Australian history. In his first chapter McQueen singles out 'Russel Ward, Geoffrey Serle, Ian Turner, and to a lesser extent, Robin Gollan and the late Brian Fitzpatrick'. He was *continuing* a main thrust of the strategy of Manning Clark and subsequently of the new right, which says the radical interpretation is the dominant orthodoxy in Australian historiography and our first and obsessive duty is to smash it.

In certain respects McQueen follows Clark's 1956 essay and the introduction to *Select Documents* very closely. In chapter one of *A New Britannia* McQueen adopts Clark's view in 'Re-writing Australian History' that the convicts, rather than being pioneers of egalitarianism, were in fact 'professional thieves'. Here's McQueen:

The convicts were largely professional criminals who believed in nothing so much as individual enterprise. If the convicts did not establish a tradition of 'mateship' their acceptance of the acquisitive values of capitalism and their not infrequent successes nonetheless set the pattern for the free labourers who succeeded them.

This differs from Clark, who argued that the convicts set a pattern for mateship which was ingroupish and led to racialism. McQueen says, no, there was no mateship (and racism came from the workers, saturated with bourgeois hegemony in the context of Australia 'as a frontier of white capitalism'). But, fundamentally, McQueen takes Clark's point about the convicts as professional thieves and generalises it for the Australian 19th-century labouring classes up to World War I – the convicts 'set the pattern for the free labourers who succeeded them'.

In the introduction to his *Select Documents*, Clark argues that the radical interpretation idealises the achievements of the diggers at Eureka and their spiritual heirs at Barcaldine in Queensland in 1891; such idealisation ignores the maintenance of power by Australia's 'privileged group', and the racialism of the working class. Similarly, McQueen argues in chapter one of *A New Britannia* against the legendary view that there 'is an arch of Australian rebelliousness stretching from the convicts to the anti-conscription victories of 1916-17, buttressed at strategic points by the Eureka Stockade and the Barcaldine shearers'. Like Clark, he sees the bourgeois hegemony still well in control in Australian capitalist society, and such radicalism anyway is tainted by racism.

Who, then, was the intellectual persona we know as 'Humphrey McQueen'? Was he Manning Clark/ the new right with a new left mask? A counter-revolutionary in historiography with a revolutionary face?

What of this 'revolutionary' aspect itself? McQueen's Marxism was at this time remarkably eclectic. He looked variously to Gramsci and Lukács, as well as to Lenin and Mao; while in *The Old Mole* No. 5 he'd told readers of the importance of Louis Althusser's *For Marx*. What is most startling, perhaps, in this collection, is the disarming lack of dislike for Lukács' notion of 'false consciousness'. For such a notion complemented the Manning Clark/ new right kind of contempt for the Australian lower classes. In McQueen's Lukácsian view, the working class is imbued with false consciousness; and true consciousness must come to it from outside. In the 19th century the labouring classes were only too willing to embrace the bourgeois hegemony of acquisitiveness and so on; in the 20th century there's hope they'll accept true Marxist ideas, and in this they'll be guided by revolutionary historians, who cannot afford 'the luxury of historical misunderstanding'. The passivity of the working class – passive where not willing victims – makes it vital that the right kind of revolutionary theory, the right kind of truth is presented. Which perhaps partly explains why McQueen was so concerned in those years to claim that his Marxist understanding was *the* Marxist understanding, and that the historical understanding of others was not Marxist at all.

During the 1970s Humphrey McQueen went on to other and different things – his most important achievement, perhaps, being in the later 1970s to embrace a kind of Maoist nationalism, thus reversing his dislike of nationalism in *A New Britannia*. He's written on Australia's media monopolies and ventured into cultural history.[14] He seems to be influencing for the good some young historians, as in the journal *Bowyang*, to investigate Australian ruling class attitudes, organisation, culture, and power.

I'll conclude this section of my argument about the impact of Manning Clark and the new right on Australian historiography by pointing out again that their influence became so great that even an historian committed to an anti-liberal revolutionary history became a victim of the problematic they had established. Indeed, the 1970 Humphrey McQueen in the face of the Manning Clark/ new right historiography appears very much like *A New Britannia*'s version of the labouring classes in the 19th century: a willing victim of bourgeois ideological dominance.

And perhaps we should ponder the final lurking historiographical assumption in their work: an ancient conservative image of the labouring class in history as embodying the beast of the people, interested only in its animal desires (McQueen's acquisitiveness), ignorant (hence their racism and xenophobia – and 'barbarism', a term frequently employed by Clark), and needing to be curbed or moulded by superior knowledge (Coleman's benevolent middle-class institutions of law, church, and state, derived from Europe's hierarchical 'civilization'; McQueen's true Marxist consciousness as opposed to the working class 'false consciousness').

# 7

# New Criticism Grows Old:
# Leonie Kramer's Oxford History of
# Australian Literature[1]

When the brick-like *Oxford History of Australian Literature*, edited by Leonie Kramer, appeared in 1981, it experienced a reception of singularly little warmth, accused in the main of treating Australian literature in a cultural void. Why did a volume, supervised by the professor of Australian literature at Sydney University and drawing its contributors from the same department of English, meet with coolness, impatience, irritation, even contempt? How can this be explained?

Before we go on to this task, it should be mentioned that the *Oxford History* is really two books. The first encapsulates the critical approach, tone, and attitudes of Leonie Kramer in her rather perfunctory introduction and of Adrian Mitchell and Vivian Smith in their chapters on fiction and poetry: the book I'll focus on. The second book is a history of drama by Terry Sturm, displaying a very different – admirable – approach, which lies, unfortunately, between the same covers as the other one.

Like most of its reviewers I also found the first book – *Oxford History I* – of Kramer, Mitchell, and Smith irksome and dull, and feel it's a little demeaning even to grant it the importance of a serious study. But if *Oxford History I* has little intrinsic interest, it has a certain historical importance in highlighting the present state of literary criticism in Australia: of how the orthodoxy is trying to maintain itself, and why people are becoming more and more attracted to alternative approaches.

*Oxford History I* houses itself behind the institutional walls of the critical orthodoxy we've spent much of this book describing. Yet here is its initial problem: the orthodoxy is starting to age and wither: the walls of fortress criticism are beginning to crumble. Worse, it's beginning to *look* it. Despite all its institutional power, critics here, there, and everywhere – while retaining the necessity of detailed analyses of texts – are wanting to explore broader, more historical and contextual, approaches. Representing the orthodoxy, how can *Oxford History I* offer itself as presenting anything new to the world? How can it claim to be making a distinctive and needed contribution? After all, the main push for the metaphysical orthodoxy lies way back in essays like Vincent Buckley's 'The Image of Man in Australian Poetry' (1957) and 'Utopianism and Vitalism' (1958-59), in Wilkes's 'The Eighteen Nineties' (1958), in Heseltine's 'Saint Henry – Our Apostle of Mateship' (1960-61) and 'Australia's Literary Heritage' (1962). How can it be seen as rivetingly fresh in the 1980s?

The strategy to hand is the same that was employed by the pioneers of the metaphysical orthodoxy in the 1950s and '60s. This is to suggest that they – critics like Wilkes, Buckley, Heseltine – are not the orthodoxy at all. On the contrary: the orthodoxy is literary nationalism.

Somehow or other – mainly by saying it so loudly and so often – the view is sustained that the literary nationalists were, are, and always will be the critical orthodoxy in Australia, and the New Critics/Leavisites will always be admirable and daring for taking on such a powerful orthodoxy and pointing to serious qualifications, doubts, neglected areas, and new interpretations. What's never explained is: how can *they*, the metaphysical orthodox, who occupy the positions of power and influence in university teaching, *not* be the orthodoxy, the ascendant group?

This seems to be a fairly laughable, obviously spurious, strategy. But the faith of the orthodox in it is great. In 1958 G. A. Wilkes was arguing in this way against the literary nationalists – and still, in 1975, in 'Going Over the Terrain in a Different Way: An Alternative View of Australian Literary History' in *Southerly* and in his

*The Stockyard and the Croquet Lawn* (1981) uses the same tactic. And as we've seen, Leon Cantrell is another to be mightily impressed by the same evergreen strategy.

*Oxford History I*, then, inherits a by now old, arthritic orthodoxy, stiff in the joints. And Kramer, Mitchell, and Smith go through its moves and motions in a predictable, dutiful way. Why, in that case, should we be interested in what comes out?

In her introduction[2] Leonie Kramer criticises the literary nationalists for 'characteristic (and often repetitive) attitudes'. She tells us that criticism based on the legend of the 1890s is a form of cultural protectionism, and this can be 'prescriptive by laying down conditions in which literary values are less important than social attitudes'. To insist on the importance of Australianness, she says, 'at best introduces extra-literary considerations into criticism, at worst proposes a severely limited view of the possibilities of Australian literature'. Furthermore, literary nationalist historiography has insisted too much on Australian literature as a story of progress, of growth to maturity. Kramer, instead, argues that while her contributors might discuss the differences between literary periods, this is 'not to imply even a theory of development, let alone an achieved literary condition'.

Does Professor Kramer avoid these faults – these grievous faults that are usually sheeted home only to the literary nationalists? The introduction in fact mounts an obsessive and repetitive attack on assorted literary nationalists – Vance Palmer, Frank Wilmot, Rex Ingamells, and Judith Wright. Vance Palmer is a particular target, repeatedly returned to and given the skewer. The attack is so insistent as to become simple and obvious.

In her final paragraph Kramer declares that she and her contributors have tried to 'expose the critical assumptions upon which our judgments rest' – assumptions which, it doesn't take us long to see, issue forth from the New Critical/Leavisite orthodoxy of the last twenty years. But nowhere in her introduction is this body of work scrutinised. Where is the analysis of the critical principles underlying the work of Professor Wilkes, Professor Buckley, Professor Heseltine? Could it be that Professor Kramer feels their work is so slight and insignificant that it doesn't deserve our interest? The answer, probably, is no. To study the criticism of her contemporaries doesn't fit into the orthodoxy's strategy: which is to attack the literary nationalists as if *they*'re the orthodoxy.

Is there an element of cowardice in such a strategy? Kramer attacks Vance Palmer, Frank Wilmot, Rex Ingamells, and Judith Wright. None of her targets had or has any institutional power in Australian literary criticism. Why not make the effort to question those who had or have – her own contemporaries in university English departments? Why not assign *problematic* status to their critical writings, rather than only to the literary nationalists?

Kramer also offers, despite her disclaimer, a highly prescriptive progress model of Australian literary development, particularly for this century. Indeed, how can a criticism which declares itself to be one of value 'judgments' avoid being prescriptive? In her model, after the '90s of Lawson and Brennan sharing the honours, there's a trough until nearly WWII. The dun-coloured social realist fiction (yes, White's phrase is once more pressed into service) of Prichard, Xavier Herbert, Vance Palmer, and the like is not 'significant'. For: 'The revival begins in the late 1930s, with the first novels of Christina Stead and Patrick White. It continues into the 1940s and 1950s, with first volumes of poetry by R. D. FitzGerald, Judith Wright, James McAuley, Douglas Stewart, A. D. Hope and David Campbell, and takes a new direction with the flourishing of drama in the 1960s and 1970s.' If that's not a narrative of 20th-century progress, of literary development, what is?

## Curled lip criticism: the sins of repetition, restriction and prescription

It's strange that Kramer, so alert to prescriptiveness in the literary nationalists, should be so blind to it in the volume before her. For Adrian Mitchell's chapter in fact reveals, to use Kramer's own words, 'a severely limited view of the possibilities of Australian literature'. The social realists and the literary nationalists are Siberianised. 'The best Australian fiction has come', says Mitchell, 'from writers who are independent of that tradition'. Social realism descends from 'the nineties school', and is in fact false realism. Really (and here Mitchell is echoing Buckley's late 1950s essay 'Utopianism and Vitalism') it is sentimental, and, 'at its core, romantic'. Like Kramer (and Leon Cantrell in the introduction to *The 1890s*), Mitchell is drawn to throwing at the social realists and literary nationalists White's phrases from 'The Prodigal Son' (1958) about dun-coloured journalism and the Great Australian Emptiness. These attacks are so repetitive in Mitchell's chapter that they become (to use his own phrase) 'eventually distasteful': how to kick a body of writing when it's down, and then keep coming back and putting a few more in for good measure.

Mostly, Mitchell finds, Aust. lit. is obsessed with landscape realism, details of scenery, and bush life, and we should instead admire novels 'which break from the preoccupation with the distinctively Australian'. We shouldn't like Boldrewood, Paterson, Ethel Turner, or Mrs Aeneas Gunn, because they 'all alike endorse a sentimental core as the heart of their image of the real'. But even where it might be a novel of city life, like Louis Stone's *Jonah*, it can be seriously flawed. Stone's approach is 'mainly sentimental' and its realism 'only superficial', the example of this being that *Jonah*'s characters are 'presented in clear outline, but not substantially'. They are 'simplified, mere sketches of character', in the manner of the *Bulletin* – and the *Bulletin* receives precious little admiration in the pages of *Oxford History I*.

Mitchell is not opposed to realism at all as a fictional mode. But it has to be the right kind of realism to qualify for praise and placement on the steep, almost dizzy hierarchy of Australian fiction. Mitchell stresses again and again – with an unstoppable repetitiveness – the centrality of character in fiction, so that what quickly emerges in his chapter is a highly prescriptive demand for psychological realism. For Mitchell, the key entity of fiction is and should be study of the individual, the 'self', and in particular its 'inner life'. Mitchell's procedure is to ask of his authors: how much do they focus on the study of character, the individual, the inner life? In answering this question, his chapter becomes a narrative of progress for Australian literature. A charge sheet, scoring various credits and debits, is drawn up. The early memoirs, admirably, Mitchell starts off telling us, present 'the self as accountable', and so remain 'attractively individual'. In general, however, colonial fiction was far too dominated by various conventions like romance, adventure, melodrama.

It is Marcus Clarke and Henry Handel Richardson who get Australian fiction to proceed safely along the correct pathway. The strength of *His Natural Life* lies in Clarke's concern to look at what is happening to an individual. In Richardson's fiction 'naturalism devolves towards psychological impressionism, so that she may hint at the workings of the inner life'. She moves beyond naturalism in *Maurice Guest* because it cannot sufficiently display 'the truth of character'. In *The Fortunes of Richard Mahony* Richardson changes 'the usual practice of the Australian novel' by accomplishing a 'full and sustained analysis of character'; she studies the 'inner life of Richard Mahony'. Indeed, Richardson, Mitchell finds himself repeating, 'gave Australian fiction its first sustained analysis of character'.

Others in the 20th century can now build in sight of the landmark of her fiction – Stead, Boyd, White, Porter, Stow. But it is Martin Boyd who is the true hero of Mitchell's vision of the possibilities of Australian fiction. Here Mitchell offers some discriminations amongst the members of his Australian fictional élite, his great tradition. Boyd not only affirms the 'uniqueness of the individual', but watches also for the 'more profound significance of individual actions for evidence of the spiritual nature of man'. Boyd reaches to the 'more abiding truths, that transcend the individual and speak to all men. Individual actions sometimes acquire the significance of parables, aspects of the myth, touching the great prototypes of moral behaviour.' Boyd's 'real interests are the abiding and universal concerns lodged in the individual'; he attempts to unravel 'the essential self'.

Boyd is 'a much finer writer' than Christina Stead. The 'substance of Stead's fiction lies in her detailed presentation of her characters' inner perspectives', but Stead tends to be too ambitious and inclusive. Sometimes her 'fascination with the individuality of character competes with her interest in social theory'; there is a 'persistent melodramatic tendency'; she can be 'extravagant', and veer unevenly between the 'obsessive and the bizarre'. In *For Love Alone* this becomes a 'disjunction between inner and outer circumstance', between the 'novel of character' and 'the novel of ideas'. Our critic also prefers Boyd to Patrick White, because White tends to sacrifice the 'complete realization of character' to a symbolism bordering on allegory. The 'quest for a transcendent harmony, the reaching towards a vision of totality, competes with his sensitive understanding of character'. The danger in White is that 'character as archetype conflicts with character as individual and real', and here White's 'artistry' has its limitations.

Mitchell demurs at everything in fiction that detracts from the creation of character as 'individual and real'. This emphasis on character means a fairly enormous amount of Australian literature is excluded or diminished in value: romance, melodrama, adventure; social realism certainly, because it focuses on outer social conditions; fiction that is too extravagant or symbolic or allegorical. Fiction that doesn't satisfy the strict requirements of psychological realism gets the gimlet eye, even if ostensibly anti-social-realist, as with some of the new writing of the last decade. Mitchell's temperature doesn't rise when he glances at the work of Murray Bail, Peter Carey, Frank Moorhouse, and Michael Wilding, because they are 'more concerned with situation and meaning than with character'. The critic's eyelids droop over such irrelevant concerns.

Mitchell is trying to impose his own 'firm will' on Australian fiction: the tight, relentless, ungenerous will of the ideologue, the kind of will that can never sympathise and empathise with aims and desires different from its own. Australian fiction should be 'quiet' (a strange, obsessively recurring term), intelligent, temperate, cool, measured, tactful, controlled, still, deft, even, poised, steady, and, if witty, compact. The new ice age of criticism has come upon us; only cold-blooded creatures from now on need apply to survive. Australian literature will become so quiet no one will hear it.

Fiction should also be 'graceful', 'elegant', and 'gentle' (re Boyd). If writers don't conform to these highly sensitive qualities, then a reverse scale of value judgment is applied. White's insistent symbolism, for instance, particularly in a contemporary setting, is liable to become 'clumsy or distasteful'. In colonial times the pose of Savery's writing is 'eventually distasteful'. Rowcroft 'does not attempt to refine his perceptions', poor chap, and his main character is 'either sententious or droll, in that peculiarly distasteful but persistent (distasteful because persistent) facetious manner of much early 19th-century popular literature'. While Lawson rises above the 1890s muck by being delicate, sensitive, and subtle, 'the nineties school' of the *Bulletin* (its members going unnamed) tend toward farce or melodrama: 'their place in literary history is now to display the broadening of humour and coarsening of sensitivity that took place in the pages of the *Bulletin* (though to be fair, the *Bulletin* was also encouraging Victor Daley and Shaw Neilson)'. There's some dismay at the want of maturity shown by some writers. Norman Lindsay and Steele Rudd's fiction shares 'much the same adolescent humour'; Sybylla's sense of fun in *My Brilliant Career* is 'mere adolescent noisiness' and there is a 'touch of unpleasantness in her nature' that 'becomes tiresome'. *Such is Life*, too, can have its distasteful moments: 'Indeed, Furphy is so determined to be unsentimental that he goes too far, and Tom's comments on the unfortunate Ida are in distinctly poor taste.' Mitchell recoils from 'the unsubtle (even slightly distasteful) naming of characters' in *Capricornia*, and, with a touch of the gloom thesis, he finds that Herbert's humour, 'like so much Australian humour, carries violence at its core'.

Like much criticism influenced by the Leavisite tradition, Mitchell's comments slide quickly from a text to judgment of the sensibility – indeed the taste and manners – of the writer. We can notice this in his comments on the unfortunate 'Rowcroft's literary manners'; while Xavier Herbert's autobiography reveals 'coarseness and vulgarity'.

In the popular TV series *Prisoner*, Miss Bennett, the most repressed, repressive, and distasteful of the screws, known as Vinegar Tits by the inmates, always curls her lips into a contemptuous smile, or smile/smirk. She believes the prisoners are all animals, and there's no hope for them. You feel with the chapter on fiction that our critic also thinks most Australian writers are animals: rough, crude, coarse, distasteful, noisy. But special cells and privileges are provided for the 'quiet' trusties, the cool, controlled Boydites of Aust. lit. Mitchell has no notion of taking literature on its own terms: he doesn't respect variety, plurality, difference, of genres and modes; it doesn't disturb him that a great deal of Australian fiction doesn't even want to try to achieve psychological realism.

The assumption behind this unceasing flow of confident judgments on the sensibilities of writers – the assumption alike of

Kramer, Mitchell and Smith – is that critics themselves possess sensibilities so fine, intelligent and comprehensive that they can discriminate all the shades of feeling that make up the total human condition. The critic, in fact, is the true hero of *Oxford History I*: the arbiter of taste; judge, jury, and jailer; the scourge of literary bad manners. The critic's role in Aust. Lit. is to be dominant and domineering. The sensibility police have arrived, and set up a Katingal-like prison-house of criticism.

OFFICER MITCHELL: Officer Smith, are all the Australian writers in their cells? Have you seen to the poets?

OFFICER SMITH (Gulp): Yes, I think . . . I hope so.

OFFICER MITCHELL: (Hope he has. Not sure if Officer Smith is the right person for this job. A closet softie. A waverer.) Hold on. My God, can this be? I hear a noise. One of the prisoners is being extravagant or symbolic or not interested in character. How immediately distasteful. So adolescent. When will they grow up. BE QUIET DOWN THERE. Quiet quiet quiet quiet quiet quiet quiet quiet quiet quiet quiet. Better report this to Governor Kramer. She'll know what to do. Officer Smith, you run up and see the Governor. I'll keep watch here, and if there's any more noise they'll all be put in solitary. They'll know who their rulers are. The brutes. All I want is control and quiet. Is that too much to ask?

OFFICER SMITH: Governor Kramer, the writers are rioting! Well, making a noise.

GOVERNOR KRAMER: Oh dear. Always something. Why can't they obey instructions? I can't really deal with it in person, I'm afraid. I'm sure Officer Mitchell can handle any problem. And you, too, Smith, I can trust, can't I? I need men of tough, delicate sensibilities.

OFFICER SMITH: Yes, of course. (Gulp)

OFFICER MITCHELL (quietly determined): Where is he? Can't wait to get at their sensibilities and refine them.

*(Some years later. Two nurses are talking in a local loony bin.)* *(How coarse and vulgar.)*

1ST NURSE: Who's that nutter over there?

2ND NURSE: The one muttering to himself? They reckon he used to have a big future going for him. A university bloke.

1ST NURSE: What's he sit there muttering about all day?

2ND NURSE: He just keeps saying quiet, control, quiet, control, all the time. Over and over.

## The sins of the literary nationalists

We can now glance at Governor Kramer's other main charge against the literary nationalists, that by stressing Australianness they introduce 'extra-literary' considerations into criticism. Well, does *Oxford History I* also avoid these? And what are they, these fabulous, magical purely-literary considerations? For example, against the literary nationalists and social realists Officer Mitchell says that two of his trusties, Boyd and Stead, possess 'real social intelligence'. Why is this a purely literary consideration? Don't the nationalist critics believe that they perceive 'real social intelligence' in their versions of Lawson and Furphy? There might be a difference in values here, but where is the difference in critical procedure?

In her introduction Governor Kramer says that some of the writers she admires, particularly in the voyager tradition of poetry, 'demonstrate the persistent and deep interest in the positive aspects of Australian development' (No gloom thesis here! All is comforting.): 'The excitement and dangers of exploration, the qualities of character it demands and elicits, and the mystery of the impulse towards heroic endeavour are central preoccupations.' Yet, when the literary nationalists talk of the 'heroic endeavour' of the bush pioneers and the exploration of the natural world they inhabit, and evoke a legendary figure to indicate the 'qualities of character it demands and elicits', and say these amount to 'positive aspects of Australian development', such concerns are extra-literary and so dismissible. The orthodoxy, however, can praise Stewart's works and *Voss* in exactly these terms: 'Modern works based on themes of exploration and discovery re-create a past which might serve as grounds for belief in a future' (Introduction). Why can the orthodoxy come out with this kind of thing, and not the literary nationalists? Who legislates the one as revealing the literary, the other as leading into the wastelands of the extra-literary?[3]

Governor Kramer says social realists like Prichard and Herbert and Vance Palmer write about social groups rather than directing their attention to 'the quality of life and experience' and 'the exploration of character', thus leading to a 'sacrifice of artistry'. Boyd, on the other hand, is praised (as her critical son Mitchell praises him) because 'the centre of his fiction is character – the definition of individuality'. There might be clear differences of artistic method involved here, but why translate difference into an absolute distinction between the artistic and the non-artistic? Doesn't this sacrifice a wide-ranging, sympathetic criticism for an insistently moralistic and punitive drive to construct hierarchies?

Vivian Smith's chapter poses such methodological problems even more starkly. Indeed, we can feel rather sorry for Dr Smith. Leonie Kramer, one suspects, has bidden her contributors to take a high and lofty view of Aust. lit., and Smith's chapter duly opens with trumpets. Yes, he blares in the first couple of pages, it is 'important to keep perspective', to note that the history of Australian poetry is the 'history of accomplished minor poets, with a few outstanding figures', that Australian poetry 'has always been traditional and deeply derivative'. We always have to remember the 'derivativeness of Australian culture' in general and to keep in mind the 'burdens of a culture in perpetual difficulties'. After this, however, Smith's chapter settles down to a quiet hum. It offers the common view: the Australian poetic élite is composed of figures like Brennan, Neilson, Slessor, Wright, Douglas Stewart, Hope and Francis Webb.

But Smith doesn't merely set up his élite and sneer at everything else. On his third page he warns of the danger of being 'aridly dismissive', and in fact – to talk of sensibilities – he reveals a quite genial critical personality. As Dorothy Green observed in her review,[4] there is a disjunction in Smith between the head and the heart. He's generous towards figures like Gordon, O'Dowd, Mary Gilmore, even the Jindyworobaks. He still wants, however, to be prescriptive: to insist, in the manner of Vincent Buckley's 'The Image of Man in Australian Poetry' (1957), that Australian poetry should observe a 'middle ground' between 'mature use of the vernacular' and 'highbrow' verse. In these terms, he finds that Hugh McCrae 'lacks a sense of the pressures and necessities of everyday living'; and there's a similar kind of aridity in Baylebridge especially but also in FitzGerald and McAuley. So Smith wants a 'middle way', not really a plurality of different modes.

Early on, in talking of colonial verse, Smith asserts Kramer's and the orthodoxy's distinction between the 'historical, cultural, and sociological' interests of writers, and 'real aesthetic returns'. What is this 'real aesthetic' quality? Smith says of Harpur that he emphasises the landscape's picturesque, dramatic and more violent qualities, while 'later writers have concentrated on the arid monotonies of the Australian landscape, merging their sense of its social and cultural limitations with the sense of the repetitive sameness of the land'. Are these purely aesthetic considerations, or are they sociological and cultural? Smith also refers admiringly to 'Harpur's craggy, hard and austere will': do these refer to moral qualities, or to aesthetic criteria?

Smith admires in Gordon's verse 'moments of grace and relaxation' and also 'an unmistakeable energy' – again, these are moral values one might or might not prefer as admirable, but hardly propose themselves as intrinsically aesthetic. Apropos Gordon's energy, Dr Smith's colleague Officer Mitchell might conceivably dislike Gordon's verse because it is not still and quiet enough. Smith believes Gordon's verse captures an historical 'mood' in colonial times, the mood of social, economic, and political transition from the pastoral ascendancy. Can we conclude from this that Smith is a closet contextualist? – even a vulgar Marxist?

This concern for poetry as representational – the literary nationalist concern outlawed by Governor Kramer – becomes a guiding concern in Smith's chapter. O'Dowd retains interest in part because his verse 'touches on areas and perceptions that are still active and alive in the national consciousness': would a literary nationalist critic like A. A. Phillips have said anything different?! Smith doesn't like McCrae for reasons to which no nationalist would object, referring to his verse as part of a Celtic Twilight kind of 'highly aesthetic minor poetry' that misses out on 'the ragged vitality of life' – does this last phrase denote a purely literary quality? Smith admires Brennan and Neilson for their 'unshaken commitment to the values of art', a commitment which means they stand out from their contemporaries like 'oases in the desert'. He writes of Brennan that what accounts for the 'power' of *Poems*

(1913) is 'the agonising personal element, the passion and frustration, the spiritual restlessness and aspiration . . .' Here Smith is arguing that certain qualities of consciousness are responsible for the aesthetic 'power' of the verse: but why are they, more than any other qualities, strictly 'values of art'?

Smith also admires Brennan because he 'embodied metropolitan and cosmopolitan experience in his poems'. Similarly, he says of Slessor that in his 'best poems' he 'gives the sense of speaking from within a representative modern experience'. He writes of the title poem of Vincent Buckley's *The Golden Builders and Other Poems* that it 'conveys the sense of a representative modern consciousness': indeed, the 'achievement of the poem is in the way it recreates aspects of the experience of inner city life, particularly through its human inhabitants'.

These are heavily representational criteria indeed, with the aesthetic achievement of such poetry apparently dependent on its power to represent aspects of reality. Why is any of this different from literary nationalists, say, admiring someone or other for recreating 'aspects of the experience of (bush) life, particularly through its human inhabitants'? Why is a nationalist concern for representative experience extra-literary, while a concern for 'a representative modern consciousness' or a 'representative modern experience', or embodying 'metropolitan and cosmopolitan experience', are to be deemed purely literary values? Smith says that 'poetry is related to a sense of the truth of human experience and imaginative wholeness'. If this be so, who decides that some truths of human experience are more closely associated with the values of art than others?

Kramer permits throughout, including in her introduction, the use of sexist and racist terminology – at various points 'the individual', 'the Australian', 'the poet', 'the writer', and even 'the reader' are all 'he' and 'his'. Sometimes 'Aborigine' is given the courtesy of a capital A, sometimes not, even in the space of a single page, while no restraint is laid on Mitchell and Smith when, jarringly, they refer to 'the natives'. Mitchell also refers to 'the Aboriginal problem' – a highly sensitive, graceful, delicate, intelligent formulation indeed. Nor has Kramer queried Smith's opening statement that 'the first Australian poet' is Michael Massey Robinson: one might think that the first Australian poetry dated from some 40 000 years before (oral poetry, of course, but a little later Smith discusses popular European-Australian songs). As Dorothy Green points out, women fare badly throughout. Barbara Baynton gets half a par, Ada Cambridge not much more, *Seven Little Australians* not a whisper, Miles Franklin a violent slam, and Ada Cambridge's remarkable verse in *Unspoken Thoughts* no mention at all. Little things are indicative. In her introduction, discussing *The Aunt's Story*, Kramer talks of the novel as an allegory of 'the experience of the Australian making contact with the challenging civilizations far beyond his rural origins', and names the chief character as Theodore (not Theodora) Goodman!

We might finally wonder how much Professor Kramer enjoys Australian literature, or literature as such. Her introduction is covered with hard chips of a highly empiricist, rationalistic idiom, a reverence for facts, reality, and reason. She can blithely refer to the 'facts about landscape' or 'the facts of colonial life', or 'the facts of the past and present'; against nationalist critical theory she urges that 'reason would suggest . . .'; she writes critically of Judith Wright that in her attitudes to 'aboriginal man' and Australian history 'legend is . . . substituted for reality'. It would appear, then, that literature is finally a species of legend and myth, not reality, facts, reason. Is there here, beside the strangely naive attitude towards history as 'facts', a distrust of the imagination for not being factual? What *does* Professor Kramer find interesting about Australian literature? She doesn't like the literary nationalists and social realists – they're too obvious, simple, uncomplex. But when she writes approvingly of her heroes, she comes out with the dead phrases we saw before like 'The excitement and dangers of exploration, the qualities of character it demands and elicits, and the mystery of the impulse towards heroic endeavour are central preoccupations'. If that's all there is to the supposed best of Australian literature, we might well wonder why anyone should take any interest in it. Finally, on a lighter note, the editor should perhaps have tried to restrain Dr Smith's enthusiasm at one point when, in referring to Douglas Stewart's interest in verse patterns, he finds that Stewart is concerned with 'total effect, more than the fondled details of its saying'.

## Oxford History II

We shouldn't, nevertheless, end this analysis on a note of ridicule. *Oxford History II*, the chapter by Terry Sturm on Australian drama, is all that *Oxford History I* isn't. If the former seems to emerge from a highly judgmental form of Leavisism, Sturm's criticism can probably be related to Raymond Williams and so-called left-Leavisism: attentive to the texts, but situating them in a variety of contexts, historical and institutional. Drama is treated as having definite conditions of production and reception. Sturm evokes the excitement and fascination of colonial theatre, with its melodrama, burlesque, farce, pantomime, fantasy, magic, operetta, musical comedy, nautical plays, and the way it celebrates theatrical conventions themselves as images of British identity and ideals.

The 1900-1960 period, he feels, is characterised by a form of realism that stresses tragedy, conveyed through a focus on personal relationships. After 1960 drama has returned to a spirit of comedy; it still has a strongly naturalistic component, but it also often takes up 19th-century forms of popular entertainment, burlesque, pantomime, farce, and so on, although without the happy endings of colonial melodrama, reassuring that now all will be well. Unlike the approach of *Oxford History I* Sturm's method is to analyse and explain, rather than to judge and dismiss. He doesn't sniff at colonial theatre because it's sentimental and doesn't attempt (say) psychological realism – the last thing it wanted to do! He doesn't pronounce that the moral and metaphysical are privileged aesthetic themes; he doesn't aridly dismiss social realism, doesn't assume it will be inherently inferior to other forms; he can praise some recent Melbourne radical theatre for dramatising 'ideological forces'. The result is that Sturm's chapter *explains* so much more about culture.

Sturm's chapter is especially important for its anti-élitism. For Sturm, unlike Kramer, Mitchell, and Smith, does not assume the superiority of so-called high literature, whose only purpose in life is to be judged by critics. Sturm has a very keen sense of how culture is created for particular audiences, and of how particular audiences in turn participate in the creation of cultural meanings. For this reason his essay is highly suggestive for the study of popular culture in Australia. As he points out, there are clear continuities between 19th- and 20th-century popular forms, in the way film, radio, and television directly inherit and develop earlier theatrical genres and conventions as part of their staple entertainment fare.[5] Such 19th-century theatrical elements are both American and British in origin, and, Sturm's chapter allows us to see, much of the distinctiveness of Australian popular culture emerges from the transformation and blending of these dual influences.

## It's crisis time

The metaphysical orthodoxy is in crisis. That it is a clear conclusion we can draw from the hostile reception to Professor Leonie Kramer's *Oxford History of Australian Literature*, or to the virtual non-reception of Professor G. A. Wilkes's assault on the 1980s, *The Stockyard and the Croquet Lawn*; it sank like a stone. Many of the relatively younger members of the critical profession are dissatisfied with the assumptions of the orthodoxy – that only metaphysical themes are 'literary'.

There is a further liberating effect: an awareness of regionality in Australian literature. One of the achievements of the orthodoxy in its prime in the late 1950s and '60s was to create a hierarchy of Australian writing which was centred in Sydney and Melbourne (mainly Sydney poets plus Patrick White, plus Melbourne or Melbourne-derived novelists like Henry Handel Richardson). In effect, the writers favoured by the metaphysical orthodoxy were to be perceived and saluted as constituting Australian literature as such – as the only literature worthy off attention, emulation, and study. Much of the initial impetus for this Sydney/Melbourne appropriation of Australian literature came in the 1940s and '50s in the work of denigration by literary figures like James McAuley and A. D. Hope of what had been prominent movements emanating from elsewhere – in particular, *Angry Penguins* and the Jindyworobaks, associated with or stimulated by Adelaide literary figures.

The virtual crushing of these movements and expressions (in the Ern Malley affair, in Hope's caning of the Jindyworobaks as the boy scout school of Australian poets) cleared the ground for the critics of the metaphysical orthodoxy to in effect hail Hope and McAuley, and poets and writers conceived to be like them (for aren't they the true successors of Christopher Brennan?) as the real achievement of Australian literature. In the last few years, however, studies suggesting the continuing value and importance of the regional literatures previously despised (like the Jindyworobaks) or largely ignored (like the literature of Western Australia) have begun to appear. Here again, then, the orthodoxy is losing its once tight grip on what 'Australian literature' should be taken to mean and how it should be approached.

# 8
# A New Formalism?

Our principle is the study of literature as a specific category of phenomena. It goes without saying that no other principle can stand beside it, for instance, that literature should be studied as a psychological or biographical document, as the emanation of the soul of the poet or that literature is a 'reflection of life' etc.

(Boris Eykhenbaum, Russian Formalist, 1924[1])

To give a text an Author is to impose a limit on that text, to furnish it with a final signified, to close the writing. Such a conception suits [previous] criticism very well, the latter then allotting itself the important task of discovering the Author (or its hypostases: society, history, psyché, liberty) beneath the work: when the Author has been found, the text is 'explained' – victory to the critic.

(Roland Barthes, French Formalist, 1968[2])

The notions that plurality and ambiguity can be seen as virtues, not vices of literature, and that a deliberately invoked tension between meanings can reveal a good deal about the nature of language, are perhaps not unfamiliar to English or American students of the subject who have been exposed to the ideas of Richards, Empson, Leavis and others. But Barthes' 'outlaw' status confirms that they have tended to order these things differently in France.

(Terence Hawkes, *Structuralism and Semiotics*, 1977[3])

In our beginning is our end. The crisis faced by the orthodoxy in Australian university departments of English is in many ways part of an international crisis in the teaching of literature. What happens when an orthodoxy, once so dominant and even liberatory for criticism, comes to be perceived, by younger critics and students, as narrow, exclusive, and debilitating? Certainly the upholders of this orthodoxy, the professors and senior staff, will still hold their institutional positions and power. But what happens when they possess only institutional power and lack wider intellectual authority? What happens when a new critical generation looks like becoming attracted to alternative approaches and methods?

New Criticism as a teaching practice in Anglo-Australo-American universities was forged in the Cold War, and particularly in the plausible rejection of utopianism as relevant to what literature is and should be. This dominant teaching mode in departments of English had, however, to withstand more and more radical challenges as the Cold War faded, and new ideological movements and forces grew in the 1960s and '70s, in particular the revival of utopianism in the counter-culture, the new energy of Marxism and the challenge of structuralism and semiology. Approaches like Marxism, structuralism, and semiology threatened the very existence of departments of English as an isolated and self-sufficient discipline. Structuralism and semiology suggested that literature was not a special, privileged realm, that a literary text was a system of signs just like advertisements, film, television programmes, detective novels. They challenged the assumption of 'high' literature as the basis of exclusive study: all culture was a system of signs, of language, and so should be regarded as of equal interest. In this way, 'high' literature was threatened with dethronement in the name of broad, wideranging cultural studies. Marxism, particularly of Althusser and Althusserians influenced by structuralism, also challenged the formalism of English departments, the focus on texts and the minimising of illuminating contexts, by suggesting that literary texts always operated within modes of ideological production: literature had to be related to a society's dominant ideologies, and if you argued that literature was essentially moral and metaphysical, then in fact you were trying to pass off ideological considerations (of class, sex, race) embedded in moral and metaphysical themes as if they belong not to society but to the universal order of things.

In recent years the colonels of the literary critical profession have tried to restore a formalist emphasis on texts (or 'textuality') as beyond ideology and history – by appropriating certain themes from semiology and its associated linguistic theory. Here we can think of the 'deconstructionists', in particular the Yale deconstructions discussed by Frank Lentricchia in his *After the New Criticism* (1980), who have followers in Australian English departments like Howard Felperin, Professor of English at Melbourne University.[4]

What are these kinds of deconstructionists trying to do? Well, what do the practitioners in any field usually do when their usual methods are failing and being rejected? We can draw a neat analogy with the comics world here. In an essay in *The Comics Journal* Peter Sanderson notes the same phenomenon of withering, decay, and lack of appeal in many comic books as we've been witnessing in New Criticism.

Many of today's leading superhero series suffer from their own longevity. After 20 years of stories, it is amazing that *Spider-Man* retains any vitality at all. Long-lived series best maintain their creative strength if after a certain point they undergo revisions that both return them to their roots and send them off in brand new directions . . . On becoming editor of *Batman* in the early 1960s, Julius Schwartz . . . revitalised an utterly moribund series by ridding it of all the junk it had accumulated over more than twenty years: Batwoman, Bathound, Bat-Mite, the ludicrous pseudo-science fiction plots, and even most of the costumed villains for a while. Batman was once again basically a detective in a comparatively realistic world. After *Batman* once again grew stale in the aftermath of the 'camp' wave of the later 1960s, the series underwent another revision that brought it even closer to its conceptual basis. The grim atmosphere of the *Batman* stories of 1939 and 1940 returned, and Batman became *the* Batman once again, the obsessed hunter of murderous criminals. With each change, the series' writing and graphic style also took on more sophistication and more contemporary feel.[5]

'Long-lived series best maintain their creative strength if after a certain point they undergo revisions that both return them to their roots and send them off in brand new directions' – exactly what these deconstructionists are trying to do! When in doubt, go back to first principles, shed all the now unpopular accretions and accumulations of the years, and take off again. Or try to.

The deconstructionists are attempting to regain dominance for formalist criticism by returning to the common source of New Criticism (and Leavisism) in late 19th-century symbolist, and early 20th-century modernist, literature and theories of language: T. S. Eliot's impersonal theory of poetic creation, in his essay 'Tradition and the Individual Talent', discussed in chapter two; Russian formalist theories; and the structural linguistics of Ferdinand de Saussure. In this, the deconstructionists have mainly followed French semiologists like Roland Barthes and philosophers of language like Jacques Derrida. We can notice the process of going back to New Critical first principles by observing some key developments in influential texts by Roland Barthes.

Barthes ranged widely in his intellectual career, from publications like *Mythologies* (1957) where he examines events in popular culture like wrestling, to more formal treatises like *Elements of Semiology* (1964) which show Barthes' debt to Saussurean linguistics. In his early work, particularly in *Mythologies*, he was interested in the relationship of signs or signifying systems to ideology, or fragments of ideology. In later work, however, as in the essay 'The Death of the Author' (1968) and in S/Z (1970), Barthes moved away from this kind of combined text-context approach to one centred more on relating the nature of literature primarily to the nature and operations of language. I'll begin by glancing at 'The Death of the Author' – which establishes the don'ts of his later approach – before being sucked unresistingly into the web of S/Z, his long essay on the Balzac short story *Sarrasine*. For it is in S/Z that Barthes allows the new positives of his criticism full play.

## The death of the author

In 'The Death of the Author' Roland Barthes takes a long view of Western history for the last 500 years, and decides to throw out most of it between the middle ages and recent developments in language theory and modernist literary practice. The notion that the author is all-important, the supreme object of critical scrutiny, is a result of the break-up of the middle ages, and can be ascribed to large tags like English empiricism, French rationalism, and the personal faith emphasised in the reformation. In this movement of history the fact of the individual was swept to the fore. The result in specific cultural terms is that criticism will busy itself for the most part in suggesting, for example, that Baudelaire's work represents the failure of Baudelaire the man, or that we should analyse Van Gogh's art primarily in terms of his madness, or Tchaikovsky's music in terms of his psychological guilt about his homosexuality.

The explanation of a work is sought in the man or woman who produced it, in their character or circumstances or 'genius'. This was never so in medieval or traditional societies, where the notion reigns that a narrative is performed, but this narrative belongs to the collective voice of the community or of a section of the community. The notion of an individual author is, therefore, a relatively recent one in history, and if so, can possibly be reversed. At any rate, that's what late 19th- and 20th-century writers, greats like Mallarmé, Valéry, and Proust, and in movements like surrealism, have attempted to do. Mallarmé is particularly important in being the first to set this historical task, for later writers as for criticism. The famous leader of the symbolist poets (who also heavily influenced our own Christopher Brennan in the 1890s) saw that in a literary text it is the 'language' of that text that speaks, acts, performs, and not the author: to write, says Mallarmé (according to Barthes), is to go through a 'prerequisite impersonality'. Thus Mallarmé's whole poetics consists in suppressing the author, the 'me', the subject and person, the biographical writer, in the interests of the writing itself.

Further, modern linguistics of the Saussurean kind celebrated in Barthes' 1964 *Elements of Semiology* assures us that when people speak, the sentence – and the 'I' of the sentence – becomes part of cultural codes (conventions) of speech, which can be analysed independently of the individual biographical authors of the speech-act. The sentence joins the world of language, and the 'I' of the sentence is constructed by codes, of varying and differing cultural meanings.

In the old bad way the relation of author to his text was conceived as like father to child; the author exists before the book, thinks, 'suffers', lives for it, and then gives it birth out of his personal experience. But the modernist post-Mallarmé writer, on the contrary, sees writing as a 'neutral, composite, oblique space' where the author's identity is lost in the new utterance – rather like T. S. Eliot's poet's mind which, like platinum, remains 'inert, neutral, and unchanged'.

In Barthes' terms, the modern writer's power is not to express an 'original' personality, to express 'passions, humours, feelings, impressions', but to 'mix writings, to counter the ones with the others, in such a way as never to rest on any of them'. Eliot talked of the newness of art as being the way feelings, emotions, and literary experiences are combined in new and unexpected ways; and Barthes similarly feels that a text is a space in which a 'variety of writings, none of them original, blend and clash', for the text is a 'tissue of quotations drawn from the innumerable centres of culture'.

. . . a text is made of multiple writings, drawn from many cultures and entering into mutual relations of dialogue, parody, contestation, but there is one place where this multiplicity is focused and that place is the reader, not . . . the author. The reader is the space on which all the quotations that make up a writing are inscribed without any of them being lost; a text's unity lies not in its origin but in its destination.

If the author no longer counts in analysis, then only the reader, the critic, does: Barthes in effect is recommending the same explosion of text-centred criticism that we have witnessed in Anglo-American-Australian criticism this century. Where the New Critics, following Eliot, have talked of the Intentional Fallacy, Barthes adopts the flashy phrase, the author is dead, but the meaning is so similar it doesn't signify (as characters in Jane Austen's novels say). Where New Critics talked of the Imitative Fallacy, Barthes says that writing refers not to reality but to codes, and that writing is not 'an operation of recording, notation, representation, "depiction" ', but rather a space referring always to other writings. The Barthes critic will 'disentangle' the way a text speaks to, parodies, contests, other writing: so too the New Critic – in a swarm of thou-

sands and thousands of articles in the professional critical journals
– shows how this or that work alludes to or parodies or refers to
other writing. The Barthes critic sees that a new conception of time
follows on from the irrelevance of the author for criticism, for the
text is not referable back to the specific time of the authors – not
to their 'society, history, psyche, liberty' – but to all other literary
texts from whenever which are simultaneously present (drawn on,
alluded to, played with) in the codes of this text: as in Eliot and
New Criticism, literature is part of an ahistorical present.

The Barthes critic will refuse to ascribe a single, 'ultimate' meaning to a text, and will emphasise that the 'space of writing is to be
ranged over' for its 'multiplicity' – just as the New Critics have
always stressed that there should be 'a play of mind' by the critic
across the multiple meanings of a poem, never granting ultimate
priority to any one. Barthes says that his kind of criticism is an anti-
theological activity, truly revolutionary since to refuse to fix meaning is, in the end, to refuse God and his hypostases – 'reason, science, law'. The New Critics say that the ideal critic, like the ideal
modernist text, explores dilemmas and ambiguities (as in the
unresolvable dilemma of reason and intuition), embodied in a
drama of symbols. Criticism should finally never rest on anything
except the act itself of exploring, so that it is a far more subtle
activity than the rationalism of science could ever comprehend.
Barthes says that texts are 'intransitive', they don't act directly on
reality, and they perform no other function than that of the 'very
practice of the symbol itself': a text is part of language, and so does
no more than contribute to the endless play of codes that language
is.

One of the more irritating verbal ticks of people influenced by
or interested in French structuralism and semiotics is the use of the
word 'scandalous': the scandalous force of this or that proposition
for our ordinary notions. What's amusing about Barthes' 'The
Death of the Author' is how unscandalous it is. How strange it is
to observe someone in 1968 being so bold and iconoclastic as to
say that, despite Flaubert, Mallarmé, Valéry, Proust and the sur-
realists, 'the sway of the Author remains powerful' . . . 'The *author*
still reigns in histories of literature' . . . 'We are now beginning to
let ourselves be fooled no longer . . . it is necessary to overthrow

the myth . . .' For decades now New Critics have had their Intentional Fallacy and their Imitative Fallacy, but only now has French history proclaimed M. Barthes the one to pronounce the equivalent negative rules, the Author Fallacy and the Reality Fallacy.

We also shouldn't be surprised that New Criticism and Barthes' precepts are so comparable. After all, when Russian formalism was rediscovered and re-presented to the English-speaking world, most notably by Victor Erlich in his *Russian Formalism* (1955), its similarity to New Criticism was held to be of great interest. The reason for this could well be that in the 1940s and '50s New Criticism still appeared new and exciting; its institutionalisation in English departments hadn't yet become all-pervasive, and it seemed closely related to new philosophic developments about the importance of symbols in language and perception of meaning in the world.[6] To stress the similarities of Russian formalism and New Criticism was itself part of an ideological attempt to clear the way for the inevitable march of 20th-century intellectual developments that saw form and structure as more important than historical origins and causes.

What, then, is *new* about Barthes' approach? Why has it attracted formalist critics? And in terms of what happens to comics, having returned to the roots of New Criticism, in what new directions do the deconstructionists wish to go? How do the deconstructionists wish to relate to modernism, with which New Criticism was so closely associated?

As we noted in chapter two, the great modernists like Eliot, Pound, Leavis, were concerned by what they saw as the crisis of the new century – the way 'culture' was now opposed to 'civilisation' (the industrial world, the commercial ethic, utilitarian philosophy, the spirit of rationalism). The rationalism needed by industrial society had built on the renaissance notion of the individual as self sufficient, logical, making all necessary decisions in life, the creator of his/her own knowledge and destiny; the result was rationalism gone mad, leading to an impoverishment of natural feeling, emotion, intuition, and organic contact with the natural world. The modern individual was a sick soul, split between dualities like mind and body, thought and feeling, consciousness and unconsciousness, imagination and rationality, reason and intuition,

intellect and instinct; and this process could be seen in the literature of the last few centuries. The modernists wished to see the
human made whole again, as had been the case in 'organic' pre-
industrial or non-industrial communities; and they saw literature
as a key means of attempting, in symbol, myth, metaphor, image
– in non-rational aesthetic modes – to harmonise the dualities that
tear asunder the life of the spirit in the modern world. For if such
harmony and wholeness couldn't be achieved, cultural disaster
would surely follow. The historical theory underlying modernism
was apocalyptic, conceived in the mood we recognise in famous
texts like *The Waste Land*.

I've argued in this book that the metaphysical ascendancy in the
Cold War years of the 1950s and '60s, in Anglo-American criticism
as in Australian, attempted to get away from this apocalyptic historical theory, with its critique of modern industrial society. Yet
the Cold War critics were still encased in a language bequeathed
to them by the modernists and thence by the early New Critics and
Leavisites: a language that was entwined with the urgent need for
'wholeness' of 'self', and unity with nature, where the literary work
was seen as exploring dualities in the hope (however remote or
illusory or momentary) of reconciling them. The exploration of
dualities made the literary work ambiguous, ambivalent, paradoxical, ironic; but the hope of wholeness lay in the power of the
imagination to try to reconcile and synthesise opposing qualities.
New Criticism has, then, traditionally possessed two potentially
conflicting tendencies: the interest in ambiguity, and the concern
for wholeness.

What Barthes has done, followed by the deconstructionists, is to
jettison the modernist interest in 'unity' and 'wholeness' – a
wholeness sometimes looked for in the 'unified vision' of the author.
For in this way modernist critics like the New Critics had smuggled
in again the Intentional Fallacy (the *author*'s vision) and the Imitative Fallacy (knowledge of the dilemmas and dualities that divide
the individual and deny to him or her harmony with the world).
Barthes in 'The Death of the Author' restated as strongly as possible
the need once again to cast off these fallacies. He urges criticism
to return to the (New Critical) first principle of interest in the act

itself of exploration of literary language, exploring dualities, ambiguities, ambivalences, paradoxes, ironies.

Barthes and the deconstructionists have, then, gone back to the roots of modernism, only in order to reverse its values. For the modernists, the metaphysical search for wholeness was related to a pessimistic, often near despairing, view of the course of modern history. Such pessimism doesn't hold for the Barthes of 'The Death of the Author' and the deconstructionists: on the contrary.

If division and fragmentation and discontinuities were seen by the modernists as sources of disaster, anguish, fear, alienation, bewilderment, for Barthes and the deconstructionists such fragmentation and division are sources of pleasure and indeed joy. The deconstructionists are now saying, in effect, division and fragmentation should be celebrated, not feared, just as Nietzsche said we should not seek for total theories of society, but should leap with Dionysian pleasure into the realm of uncertainty and dilemma, for there is no other realm. We should celebrate what the modernists deplored. And we shouldn't look for a unified self, because none such exists or can exist.

As Frank Lentricchia argues, the later career of Barthes recalls a certain strand in the theories of language of Jacques Derrida, the 'post-structuralist' French philosopher. Here language, following Saussure, is perceived as an infinite play of difference (where a thing is defined by what it is not, rather than by any positive qualities – you only know something because it's different from something else; language has no 'positive terms'; everything has traces of everything else.) The deconstructionists, using Derrida (and Saussure) for their own formalist purposes, wish to view literature not as a product of an author or of a time (society, history), but as part of language. They want to release literature from author and society/history into language as the infinite play of difference; and they wish to stress 'play', the creative act itself of the ideal critic as s/he explores ambiguity, multiple meanings, without ever feeling any need to search for wholeness or harmony because such a search would mean curtailing some meanings and allusions in a text as you (the non-deconstructionist) search for a false unity and totality, or moment of unity.

Instead of the anguish, then, of an Eliot, Pound, or Yeats, we have a new historical stress on criticism as play, pleasure, joy. Criticism becomes affirmation, of the vitality and restless, untameable energy of language, whose differences are unbounded. This might strike us as a new metaphysics, where language itself has become the ground of being, the one true source of life. A rather reassuring view of the world. And since each critic searches and plays with the literary meanings of texts as s/he wants and finds the meanings s/he wishes, the enterprise is joyfully individualistic and indeed solipsistic.

Since the critic, in post-structuralist theory, is, like anyone, made up of a crowd of selves – constructed by diverse and contradictory discourses – then there is no accountability for such criticism. It's not produced by any one 'self' or 'I', that 'self' or 'I' belongs to language anyway. 'I' am traversed by 'selves' (discourses) that express 'me'.

Nevertheless, the individualism of deconstructionists is especially worthy of notice. One of its major signs is the unwillingness of deconstructionists to be called deconstructionists, and their suspicion of each other's claims to be true deconstructionists. In this way they nicely exhibit ideological strands (individualism, competitiveness, freedom from any ties) congenial to their position as members of the professional middle class. Nothing could be more cosy. The older idea of the literary intellectual as detached from society, possibly hostile to it, given to radical (socialist or conservative) critiques, part of an intelligentsia pursuing cooperative intellectual activity, is now replaced by purely individual performances. Gone is the idea of collaborative critical effort: instead we have a competition to see who can out-'deconstruct' other critics by laying open a text to as much ambiguity as possible. Individualism, competitiveness, solipsism, play, masturbatory pleasure, the celebration of language – is here the future of criticism?

What does this new criticism look like? We can do no better than examine Barthes' most notorious work. And what I think we will observe is a kind of happy New Criticism, dancing about on the page, all pleased with itself, discovering this and that ambiguous meaning. We can also see why Barthes' later work is so useful to attempts to restore a new formalist, anti-historical criticism just as

New Criticism itself is looking worn and faded and slack and open to attack.

## Roland Barthes' S/Z

S/Z was published in Paris, France, in 1970,[7] and is a book-length study of an 1830 Balzac short story, *Sarrasine*.

*Sarrasine* concerns a party at the home of a very rich family, the Lantys, in a nouveau riche part of Paris; at this sumptuous party the narrator, himself a guest, tells a fellow-guest and friend about the true identity and history of an old Lanty relative wandering about the rooms. This old man is really the source of the Lanty fortune, for he used long ago to be a soprano, celebrated throughout Europe, and thereby become rich. He was, however, based in papal Rome (he's an ex-street urchin) and there lies the rub, for in papal Rome only males could be singers, and so to gain the honour of becoming a soprano, dressed on stage like a beautiful woman, one had to lose one's reproductive powers. Meanwhile a peculiarly stupid young Frenchman, a sculptor, Sarrasine, goes to Rome to study his art, goes to the theatre, sees the Lanty relative, then young, and with the stage-name La Zambinella, thinks he's a she, falls head over, tries to make love to her as they quaintly used to say, and finally finds to his horror what to everyone else in Rome was as common knowledge as breathing, that she's a he. The abduction which yields this revelation, however, is interrupted by the entry of some hired assassins of the cardinal who is protecting (nudge nudge) the singer. Sarrasine gets stabbed, while La Zambinella, the castrato, lives on, stashes it away, and finishes his life wandering round his relatives' houses like death warmed up giving the shivers to their guests.

That's the simple narrative surface, but of course Barthes finds all sorts of meanings below the surface: how he does shows the supposed distinctiveness of his method.

Barthes introduces us at the beginning of S/Z to his notions of the 'readerly' text and corresponding critic, and the 'writerly' text and corresponding critic.[8] The implications of Barthes' terms very much recall Sorel's distinction of producers and consumers, itself taken up so enthusiastically by John Anderson and the Sydney free-thought tradition – the élite few who are active, enterprising, productive in life, as against those who merely receive, consume, accept reality.

There are, then, two kinds of readers of literature. The 'readerly' reader is s/he who is inert before the text, who follows and stays with its surface narrative course from beginning to end of the story, who thinks a story about a besotted sculptor and a singing eunuch is a story about a sculptor and a eunuch: who doesn't actually engage with the text's more hidden, symbolic meanings, meanings which have to be worked for, discovered, recreated and released.

This is the task and the pleasure of the readerly critic's binary opposite, the writerly critic, 'to make the reader no longer a consumer, but a producer of the text'. These are Barthes' ideal critics, for they are like writers themselves: they follow (as does Eliot's preferred critic) the ideal practice of writing, of literature, itself, which is finally to follow the vast activity and operations of human language from time immemorial.

Let us first posit the image of a triumphant plural, unimpoverished by any constraint of representation (of imitation). In this ideal text, the networks are many and interact, without any one of them being able to surpass the rest; this text is a galaxy of signifiers, not a structure of signifieds; it has no beginning; it is reversible; we gain access to it by several entrances, none of which can be authoritatively declared to be the main one; the codes it mobilizes extend *as far as the eye can reach*, they are indeterminable (meaning here is never subject to a principle of determination, unless by throwing dice); the systems of meaning can take over this absolutely plural text, but their number is never closed, based as it is on the infinity of language.

In these works, there 'cannot be a narrative structure, a grammar, or a logic'; and 'nothing exists outside the text'. Such texts don't try even in the least to represent or imitate any outside so-called reality; rather they endlessly 'play' with 'multiple' codes of meaning. They are 'multivalent', since the 'integrally plural text' can never be assigned one single meaning, can never be summed up by 'some singular system' like a pervading ideology, and can never be adequately discussed by simply classifying it in terms of genre as this or that historical mode or style. The ideal text lays itself open to the infinite play of codes, which is language.

The élite family of ideal plural texts, however, is still a small and close-knit one, composed largely of figures like Proust and the fairly recent French 'new novelists', with honourable ancestors in Flaubert, Fourier, and Sade. The reverse of the plural texts are the readerly or classic texts, which unfortunately 'make up the enormous mass of our literature'. There is still, nevertheless, hope left for readerly texts: they are never totally bereft of plural meanings, since every text, however designed to be classic, leaves its author for dead and enters the world of texts which refer to other texts, and codes which refer to other codes.

Here indeed the Barthes writerly critic is very much like Eliot's New-Critic-to-be in 'Tradition and the Individual Talent'. Eliot said the critic takes a text, sees how it relates to and ceaselessly refers to other texts in the moving 'tradition' of all texts, and to do this has to know the 'mind of Europe', the repository of literary codes. Barthes says likewise. The critic restores a text, not to its 'individuality', but to its 'function' as part of an overall 'typology of texts'; and the critic, the I which approaches a text, is 'already itself a plurality of other texts, of codes which are infinite'.

Barthes' criticism evaluates by nosing out and measuring how much ideal plurality washes around in the space of the text. For with readerly texts we are dealing with 'incompletely' or 'moderately' or 'modestly' plural systems of meaning, which possess but 'partial reversibility'.

Now, what does Barthes mean by 'partial reversibility'?

Well, to move into a classic text like Balzac's *Sarrasine* the writerly critic steps below the level of the surface narrative of events and characters' actions to find a 'textual network' that, 'on its symbolic level, is reversible', because on this level meanings and suggestions are created which allow you to perceive them all over the text – you can move backwards and forwards finding these, forgetting about the narrative surface which wants to rush you headlong from puzzling beginning about the identity of an old person to the exciting denouement and end of Sarrasine and his infatuation.

We can take a simple example of this, which seems greatly to excite Barthes by its discovery, though it would be merely common or garden produce to a New Critic. One way of approaching Sarrasine as a character is *not* to see him as the narrative surface beckons us to do – French naif in wicked Rome – but as a general symbol of the realist artist, and so of realism as an historical project and fallacy. A realist artist like Sarrasine will consider that there is always some kind of absolute truth or reality that can be reached (and so imitated, represented) if you pare objects down enough, if you uncover their denotative essence. Consequently we find the sculptor, when as a child he was at church, 'whittling the pews' as early attempts at carving, or at school he might be kneading breadcrumbs into shapes. This childhood and adolescent activity prefigures, anticipates, the way he tries in Rome to carve a statue of La Zambinella, and the final way he tries to undress 'her', to see the true 'essence' of femininity (as he fondly imagines) beneath her beguiling appearance.

This, I take it – having been trained in the similar procedure of Leavisism/New Criticism – is what Barthes means by 'reversible'. When later in the story you read of Sarrasine sculpting or trying to undress La Zambinella in a kneading or whittling way, you think back to these earlier symbolic suggestions (symbolic because they suggest more than mere literal whittling; they connote, rather than denote). So you are moving backwards and forwards through the text, seeing all these things, all the time.

A major point looms for Barthes in Sarrasine's impulse to uncover and then represent the 'illusory' essence of La Zambinella.

This impulse, which leads Sarrasine, the realistic artist, and the [old-style] critic to turn over the model, the statue, the canvas, or the text, in order to examine its back, its interior, leads to a failure – to Failure – of which *Sarrasine* is in a way the emblem . . . *beneath* La Zambinella (and therefore inside her statue) there is the *nothingness* of castration, of which Sarrasine will die . . .

The nothingness at the heart of the castrato is the nothingness at the heart of realist literature and aesthetics. Barthes italicises this discovery: '*the novelistic real is not operable*', for the realistic discourse is in fact a pretence: 'it pretends to believe in the prior existence of a referent (a reality) that it must register, copy, communicate'. Further, recent semiology backs this up about the failure of realism, for it contests the supposed hierarchy of denotation and connotation, where connotation is a secondary realm of codes, suggestions, and allusions, and denotation refers to primary, original meanings, to truth and objectivity. Not so, says such semiology, denotation is really only a myth, an illusion that there is an objective reality rather than ceaseless codes and connotations about reality. Denotation, indeed, 'is ultimately no more than the *last* of the connotations'.

Sarrasine's clutching at nothingness reminds us that realism also commits another sin, which, apparently, no one before M. Barthes has exposed and excommunicated. This is to do with the theory of character in fiction. If we have a realistic view of character, then we would think in terms of Sarrasine as a kind of real person, with 'a life off the page'. Fallacy, fallacy.

We occasionally speak of Sarrasine as though he existed, as though he had a future, an unconscious, a soul; however, what we are talking about is his *figure* (an impersonal network of symbols combined under the proper name 'Sarrasine'), not his *person* . . .

Sarrasine – like the other characters – is not some jerk you'd meet in the street, with a real life and future (if he hadn't had his ribs tickled by an assassin's stiletto) outside the text. Sarrasine is a character because he has a 'symbolic purpose', which is to reveal the failure of realism. Similarly the beautiful, mature Madame de Lanty's 'symbolic role is clear', to create a castrating figure. Her husband, however, the Count de Lanty, a banker, is a dried up old prune; his 'function is symbolic' too, to indicate being castrated, and so to help 'fill out the paradigm *castrating/castrated*'.

Further, we would be committing a grave error to suppose that the narrator of the story is either objective, or disinterested, or stands for Balzac, the author. For the narrator, says Barthes, is a character like the other characters. 'Such is discourse: if it creates characters, it is not to make them play among themselves before us but to play with them, to obtain from them a complicity which assures the uninterrupted exchange of the codes: the characters are types of discourse and, conversely, the discourse is a character like the others'.

The text 'plays' with its characters, placing them in symbolic roles, functions, patterns; and the story, the discourse, is a character, because it acts for itself, preventing Sarrasine, for example, from knowing too early things about Zambinella's identity which would have finished off the suspense and mystery of the narrative too quickly. Indeed, says Barthes, 'the discourse, and not one or another of its characters, is the only *positive* hero of the story'.

This is, of course, commonplace stale stuff to Anglo-Australo-American Leavisism and New Criticism. In 1933 L. C. Knights, an associate of F. R. Leavis, wrote *How Many Children Had Lady Macbeth?*, an essay famous in the English-speaking critical world as an attack on the Shakespearean critic A. C. Bradley. Knights' point was that older criticism of Shakespeare was tied to a biographical approach to the characters, as if they lived off and after the page, as if one could speculate how many children a character like Lady Macbeth had in the quieter moments of her life. Rather, we should say that her character is not a free personality, but exists only to embody a certain patterning of values. These values – as for all the characters – are to be discovered in the tragedy's poetic language, they are created by the dense interplay and tension of opposing and conflicting symbols. A character, says Knights and Leavisism/New Criticism for ever after, exists in and for the text's play of meanings and values. T. S. Eliot in 'Tradition and the Individual Talent' takes the practice of poetry as the basis for the critic's activity, and Knights is really extending Eliot's point to drama: a Shakespearean play is like a very long poem, and the critic investigates the characters in terms of the play's structure of images, metaphors, and symbols.

In similar terms New Critics have transferred criteria suitable to poetry to fiction, where a story or novel is seen as a structure of dramatic tensions between various values embodied in different characters, values to be investigated in terms of strands of images, metaphors, symbols.

This New Critical approach to fiction works best with so-called 'poetic novels', like those of D. H. Lawrence and Patrick White. Lawrence, indeed, said long ago, like Barthes is now breathlessly telling us, trust the tale not the teller, the text, not the author, and he also had a famous theory of character whereby the novelist was interested not in the surface aspects of a character's personality –

what they'd look like in the street – but in their deep sensibility, their instincts, natural passions, sexuality, and so on, which could only really be created in terms of poetic (symbolic) language.

New Critics, however, certainly did not stop at the modern 'poetic novel', but began – just like M. Barthes in his work-out on arch-realist Balzac – to interest themselves in reinterpreting in their own terms earlier 'realist' fiction. Again, just like M. Barthes, they refused to take realist fiction as in fact realistic, as merely transcribing social reality. They looked for patterns of tensions in imagery and symbols below the narrative surface of realistic texts. Thus works like Dickens's *Bleak House* could be reinterpreted as strongly interested in metaphysical themes, of darkness, despair, hopelessness – and this for Dickens – Charles Dickens, previously thought to be a social realist writing about the comedy and quaintness of London street life.

And in Australia – Australia mind you, hick as hick, to which civilisation in the form of semiotics has only been carried by the enlightened few in the last few years – in Australia New Critics have for decades now been busy reinterpreting its erstwhile social realists like Henry Lawson and Joseph Furphy. During and since the 1940s, for example, various Sydney University English dept. critics or products like Oliver (though in a slightly wobbly way), Mitchell and Wilkes (all to become professors), made it a critical commonplace that 'Tom Collins', the nominal author and narrator of Furphy's *Such is Life*, is not to be taken as representing Furphy the author himself. Collins is a bit of a fool, half the time he doesn't know what's going on about him even while he's sure he does know, he gives false information, he misdirects: in short, he sees far less than the text itself does, so that for most of the time the text is playing with its own narrator. Further, critics such as these warned against accepting the narrative surface of *Such is Life*, that it is a realistic portrayal of the Riverina social spirit and mores in the latter part of the 19th century, and said that the novel concerns itself with various moral and metaphysical dilemmas like free will and determinism.

Yet more: a recent and very interesting paper by Julian Croft at the 1979 conference of the Association for the Study of Australian Literature extended all this by arguing that *Such is Life* consciously plays around with literary conventions in ways very similar to what happens in Laurence Sterne's *Tristram Shandy*: a favourite novel of the Russian formalists precisely because it is held to draw attention to its own literariness, the way it knowingly constructs itself out of conventions (codes), a novel which has been seen as a very early precursor of modernist marvels in the same line, the works of Proust and Joyce and the French 'new novels'. So, semiologists/semioticians, here's a surprise for you, *Australia* has its own *Tristram Shandy*, its own formalist's delight, its own fully operating auto-referential text! Get to it! Funny though, that the New Critics have got there before you – by decades.

We can say that Barthes' project in S/Z has a dual inheritance, a debt to Saussure, Russian formalism, structuralism; and an identification with the history of modernism. In terms of the structuralist tradition, we would expect Barthes' approach to be scientific and neopositivist. Such a criticism will set out to describe the workings, the devices, the machinery, the how it is done, of the text, of *Sarrasine*. New Critics like to sport with 'themes', which lie below the narrative surface and do the real work of structuring the text. Barthes tells us first to designate 'lexias', arbitrary units of reading in which lie 'the units of meaning (the connotations)'. For example, 'Femininity (connoted) is a signifier which will occur in several places in the text; it is a shifting element which can combine with other similar elements to create characters, ambiances, shapes, and symbols.' Other connotations perceived in the various lexias include not only castrating/castrated and femininity/masculinity, but passive/active, death/life, cold/warmth. 'The lexia thus lays the groundwork, in introductory form, for a vast symbolic structure' of 'antithesis'; and antithesis, the clash of two 'irreducible' 'plenitudes' or 'opposites', produces a delightful field of ambiguity and 'equivocation'. Barthes even finds in one musical voice of the text 'a preciously ambiguous value' – ah, how well loved he must be by New Critics after such acknowledgement of their own stock-in-trade! – ambiguity-hunting.

The Barthes critics, out with their hounds, have to sniff out each connotation as the 'starting point of a code', the 'articulation of a voice which is woven into the text', and the five main codes that somehow put themselves in the way of the hunt as appropriate for running down a readerly text like *Sarrasine* are the Voice of Empirics (the proairetisms), the Voice of the Person (the semes), the Voice of Science (the cultural codes), the Voice of Truth (the hermeneutisms), the Voice of Symbol.

The 'five codes, the five voices' intersect to form a 'network' or 'grid' through which the text passes and becomes whatever it is. Now – I've spied a contradiction – Barthes tells us all in good faith that we can enter the house of the text through any door or window of any of these codes, which have no necessary order of importance or hierarchy. As Barthes intones: '. . . we shall refrain from structuring the symbolic grouping; this is the place for multivalence and for reversibility; the main task is always to demonstrate that this field can be entered from any number of points'. Indeed, says Barthes, 'to choose, to decide on a hierarchy of codes, on a predetermination of messages, is *impertinent*, since it overwhelms the articulation of the writing by a single voice' (don't blame me for such leadfooted italicising, it's Barthes).

Is Barthes himself altogether free, however, of such gross *impertinence*, such limiting of *plural* interest in the text? Barthes quickly tells us that of the five codes which 'endow the text with a kind of plural quality' – Barthes' repetitiveness will soon earn its own commentary – the hermeneutic and the proairetic codes limit plurality, while 'only three establish permutable, reversible connections, outside the constraint of time (the semic, cultural, and symbolic codes)'.

But keep ploughing on and you find Barthes deciding that in a readerly text like *Sarrasine* the cultural codes are also limiting, indeed are 'nauseating'. They're but a boring mixture of received ideas, an army of stereotypes, and they are what is most outmoded about Balzac; they reveal overall that such readerly literature is replete literature, subject to the bourgeois educational system and bourgeois ideology.

So we're left, then, with the 'symbolic' and the 'semic' (character as symbolic) codes as of any great interest in classic realist discourse – codes which, we've seen, are New Criticism regurgitated. The New Critics were and are primarily concerned with the nature of literary language itself. And, historically, it's an interest they shared with the Russian formalists. Barthes, too, is interested in sinking literature into the sea of language.

With language, meanings are never closed, all is plurality to infinity. The ideal plural text is so interesting because it is like language itself: 'In modern texts, the voices are so treated that any reference is impossible: the discourse, or better, the language, speaks: nothing more.' In the ideal text the 'thematics' are 'infinite', and so respect the 'enduring character of language'.

*Sarrasine*, nevertheless, is plural enough to include some of the endless ambiguities and play of codes of language. When Sarrasine finally realises that Zambinella is a castrato, he reassures the singer by crying that if she were either a man or a woman he'd kill her with the sword he's drawn. But you are 'nothing', he tells the relieved castrato. Aha, comments Barthes, Sarrasine can't kill Zambinella because the castrato is 'beyond life or death, *outside all* classification: how to kill what is not classified?' For it is the 'very existence of difference which generates life and meaning; the ultimate horror is not death but that the classification of death and life should be broken off'. The castrato is outside classification and so 'outside nature'.

So, language is being, is classification, is the endless play of binary opposites (life and death, masculine and feminine etc.) which generate 'life and meaning', the dramas, tragedy, and horrors of existence. As Barthes reports in 'The Death of the Author', Greek tragedy has an ambiguous nature, because its texts are 'woven from words with double meanings that each character understands unilaterally (this perpetual misunderstanding is exactly the "tragic").'[9]

The plural text understands this infinity and plurality of language itself most clearly, and tries to return its writing to language as much as possible, without grammar, logic, realist narrative and other impertinent impediments:

In fact, the meaning of a text can be nothing but the plurality of its systems, its infinite (circular) 'transcribability': one system transcribes another, but reciprocally as well: with regard to the text, there is no 'primary', 'natural', 'national', 'mother' critical language: from the outset, as it is created, the text is multilingual; there is no entrance language or exit language for the textual dictionary, since it is not the dictionary's (closed) definitional power that the text possesses, but its infinite structure.

'Circular': the text moves ideally towards being circular, beginning from and returning to language.[10] In *Structuralism and Semiotics* Terence Hawkes admits to a passing fear that Barthes in this regard is coming up with no more than a tautology, in that the raw material of the writer thereby becomes the end product of his writing.[11]

I think language for Barthes performs something of the same role as the endless play of metaphysical dualities/opposites can perform for New Criticism: it is the metaphysical ground of being.

Even Terence Hawkes[12] knows that Barthes commits a blatant sleight-of-hand in disliking the so-called cultural or reference codes of *Sarrasine* – 'even though', admits Barthes, 'all codes are cultural'. Certainly in *S/Z* Barthes shows only the most token interest in the 'cultural' meanings of *Sarrasine*, for example, 'REF. Ethnic Psychology', the plays of meaning concerning Mediterranean passion or worldliness or the like. These are usually merely given the pretentious notation, REF. Ethnic Psychology, and then Barthes passes on to his real interest, the language of *Sarrasine*. For, despite *Sarrasine*'s being caught up in the constraining hermeneutic realist narrative code, the story, finally, can be seen – like the 'plural text', like Proust or the new novelists – as about itself, as auto-referential: 'Ultimately, the narrative has no *object*: the narrative concerns only itself: *the narrative tells itself.*' And in being about itself and not about any reality or referents outside the text, *Sarrasine* 'reacts on language and demystifies, ravages the innocence of its utterance'. *Sarrasine* reveals the fascinating operations of language itself.

Why does Barthes come out with self-admitted sleight-of-hand, separating language off from the cultural codes? Why is he forced into such an intellectual crudity? And has such crudity political implications? New Criticism was forged in the 1920 and '30s not only as a movement away from 19th-century approaches which collapsed the text into historical and cultural contexts; it was also in tension with the strength of Marxist approaches at the time, which stressed the social determinants of literature, how society shapes the text. The Marxist approaches of the time may have been crude, economist and deterministic, and the New Critics had a lot going for them in insisting on the autonomy of the text, its inner realities; but the New Critical stress on the metaphysical content of these inner realities was also a way of combating any 19th-century and contemporary Marxist call for literature to have a social purpose, to help change ideological formations and so history.

Some of the modernist writers and critics, the later Eliot, F. R. Leavis, Yeats, Pound, also believed that literature – while its autonomy had to be respected – could have a social purpose, a kind of radical conservative one in restoring to society and culture the finest values (however defined) of the past. But New Criticism, as we saw in previous chapters, as it developed and took hold as an academic discipline and became triumphant as a practice in the lovely 1950s, eschewed this social purpose aspect of its modernist ancestors – or was embarrassed by it in so far as it still vigorously existed amongst the Leavisites. For a triumphant 1950s New Criticism, literary study was a contemplative act, an act superior to the sordid political and social worlds of the present, dwelling on metaphysical dilemmas that didn't need historical and cultural explanations because they are universally human.

Similarly, we can perceive a silent struggle in Barthes' text: he is not only fighting a long-delayed action against older reductivist biographical and historicist approaches to literature, he is also moving criticism and the study of culture away from its main radical exponents in France in the 1960s, the Althusserian Marxists. For the Althusserians, literature was to be seen as relatively autonomous: it was a structure in itself, but it also had various deformations, 'silences' and 'absences', which revealed the 'relative' shaping or determination of the text by its historical context – by ideology.

Barthes' whole effort in S/Z is to oppose any such notion of the 'relative autonomy' of the text, and that is why he denies what he knows, that all language – the symbolic images and rhetorical operations he so dwells on – is cultural, as Saussure had said. Barthes says no, language is so 'plural' that it can't be tied down to any ideological specificity and so historical explanation, because language's origins are lost in the mists of human time; and because language is so plural in its meanings, it can't be seen as determined by any shaping force – for example, by ideology.

At first when you read S/Z what's so puzzling is the incredible and almost hysterical repetitiveness of the text: almost every page, almost every sentence if he can swing it, Barthes hammers away, be plural be plural be plural, plurality is marvellous, the ideal text is plural, the readerly text can be plural, connotations are plural – language is plural. You get sick of the sight of 'plural' on the page.

His repetitiveness about 'plurality' is a terse insistence against any kind of Marxist approach which sees the text as even partially or relatively determined by history.[13] By insisting that literature belongs to language, which can be held to be universal, Barthes can discover that a text requires no social, cultural, and historical explanation. Its most interesting – plural – meanings are referable back to the wash of language, a bottomless pool of symbols and rhetorical figures and binary opposites – to an area as mystically and metaphysically conceived as the symbolic nature of literature and language as conceived by the New Critics. In these terms, the historical and cultural and social can be dismissed as merely superficial, local, temporary aspects of a text – Barthes' basic operation in S/Z – and the dualities and opposites that are universally human are its profound and abiding structures.

Politically, then, S/Z is safe, as contemplative of the universal and eternal as New Criticism, and so appropriate for university departments to become an institutional force. This, of course, is not the image such a trend in structuralism and semiotics has of itself, Barthes referring to his critical approach as 'truly revolutionary' ('truly revolutionary', says Little Sir Echo Hawkes).[14] And certainly Barthes' semiology seems determinedly anti-bourgeois, because by showing the play of codes, connotations, signifiers, in the world, it undermines the attempts of the bourgeoisie to present its notions of reality as natural; because he rejects almost all of Western history: in particular, the Aristotelian theory of art as an imitation of reality and the classical rules of criticism this theory supported; and because he rejects the bourgeois-individualist theory of the text as merely expressing the author.

Hawkes reports that Barthes in *L'Empire des Signes* (1970) assigns to Japanese culture an ideal status, as a way of life in which signifiers have a higher status than signifieds.[15] But western civilisation, while so much of it can be dismissed as promoting 'closure', is not all hopeless. Barthes applauds the middle ages and Dante, for example, for knowing 'the linguistic nature of the world' and that 'passion comes from books', for knowing that 'truth' is a matter of assigned and conflicting meanings.[16] Further, Barthes applauds of course the modernists and their precursors – Flaubert, Mallarmé, Proust, Genet – for allowing their texts to be as open as language itself.

The association with modernism certainly gives glamour to Barthes' enterprise, just as it does to New Criticism. But does it make it *necessarily* 'truly revolutionary'? Radical certainly, but radical doesn't always mean revolutionary, it can just as likely mean radical-conservative. Pound, Eliot, Yeats, Lawrence, all rejected 'bourgeois' civilisation, the individualism that has apparently reigned since the renaissance and the reformation, yet all were to various degrees in the interwar period attracted to fascist ideas and ideologies because they appeared to revive hopes of establishing a new organic community above the individual. Eliot and Pound looked to the middle ages for a time when art and society were unified, when alienation was not, when the individual could feel fulfilled in a larger whole, and Pound, like Barthes, looked also to Asia, in Pound's case to mandarin China, admiring the ideogram as an open-ended linguistic and aesthetic form. Pound went on to radical feats like broadcasting for Mussolini in fascist Italy. Leavis, too, admired pre- (or non-) industrial organic community, and became remarkably politically conservative, while the origins of American New Criticism were in a conservative southern agrarianism. I'm not of course arguing that Barthes is a conservative thinker like these particular modernists: only that an association with modernism is no guarantee of admirable values.

To be interested in an aesthetic of symbols and myths that create the ambiguities and paradoxes of metaphysical dilemmas is certainly to be clearly in one sense anti-bourgeois. New Criticism appears superior in its concerns to the sordid materialist (in its popular sense) social and political concerns of the capitalist society around it. But it also leads to the kind of massive narrowing that I outlined in earlier chapters, the turning of literature into its own (metaphysical) image, the exclusion of all other interests.

Similarly, I think/predict, we can see Barthes' semiology in S/Z as helping to create a revived formalist criticism that will ignore the cultural, social, political, and ideological meanings of literature as time-bound and of the narrative surface, and will promote a kind of universal myth criticism – literature reveals the grand oppositions and dualities of life as embodied in language – reminiscent of Northrop Frye.

How safe can you get!

One other disagreeable thing. In 'From Work to Text' in *Image-Music-Text* Barthes proposes a 'hedonistic aesthetics', where the critic who responds in a full way to the open plurality of the text will experience *jouissance*, something more than pleasure – joy, delight, bliss, including sexual bliss.[17] The Barthes critic will penetrate in a sexual way through the surface veil of the text to its real life, via the text's 'several entrances'.

Again, I'm not convinced that this is altogether a breathtakingly new idea. New Criticism also plays with sexual images in its notions of the critic's activity: as with Barthes, the text only lives in the critic as reader, and the critic is to feel open to, receptive of, the text's meanings; at the same time, the critic will penetrate the text to uncover these meanings.

Barthes' sexual imagery seems far more brutal, nevertheless, than that of New Criticism. Barthes says the narrative surface has to be 'broken'.[18] He artlessly and italicisingly tells us that the work of the commentary 'consists precisely in *manhandling* the text, *interrupting* it'; more quaintly, he will 'ravage' the 'innocence' of the text. The Barthes critic, then, turns out to be a kind of macho rapist.

Rape involves not pleasure, but power, so I'm mystified to find Barthes saying near the end of S/Z, near the end of his hysterical, repetitive propaganda tract for a fake 'plurality', that he has had 'some pleasure in describing' *Sarrasine*'s 'symbolic field'. Having turned as much of *Sarrasine* into as writerly and plural a text as he can, Barthes presumably has been experiencing *jouissance* most of the time in S/Z. But I can't see it – I can't see any wit in the writing, any lightness of touch, any humour, that makes S/Z enjoyable to read and that might have made it enjoyable to write. It strikes me as a dry scholastic work, more befitting a medieval monk than an interesting modern critic; it's full of scholastic retailings of this or that connotation or symbolic connection, and this and that rhetorical figure ('prosopography', 'catachresis'). It's gymnastic, and full of big words, but its movement is everywhere so slow-motion and laboured. It's overall pretentious and full of itself, and the only humour it gives off is in its being so ridiculously solemn.

But Barthes does exercise a brutal, violent – in its repetitiveness and insistence – power over *Sarrasine*, because, like the rapist warning all women in society that they shouldn't desire freedom, Barthes wants to show all critics of culture that there is only one way of approaching texts. His way. For like most self-proclaimers of pluralism and libertarianism, Barthes is not pluralist at all: the whole mode of S/Z is at once to proclaim, look, go into the text wherever you like and find as many meanings as you can in the clash of codes: at the same time, he says only the symbolic and linguistic codes are interesting, forget about the rest, never attempt social/ideological explanations of culture. Ignore, that is, all history. Ignore context. Exclude. Censor.

There's something imperialistic about Barthes' project, the desire to lay claim to certain territory, in this case, cultural analysis. Perhaps Barthes' claims to hegemony, the only right way, are an extreme answer to God Althusser's and the Althusserians' previous extreme claims to knowledge of truth, science, and social laws, and that literature's ultimate meaning is its explanation by ideology.

In some of its manifestations the Althusserian project certainly denies plurality, displaying an extreme and unpleasant functionalism: all things and everyone in society function as part of state ideological apparatuses. It is useless having desire, wishing for liberation; there can be no way out of the system. In these terms Michel Foucault's heterogeneity of discourses and Barthes' pluralism are a healthy response: if only, in Barthes' case, his plurality was actually a plurality, not a strict and smothering hierarchy.

If Althusserianism was in many respects bad, mad, and wrong, this particular trend of semiology to extreme formalism is not pretty either – nor, I think, is it necessary to structuralism and semiology that it should run to such formalism. Compare the French anthropologist Claude Levi-Strauss' analysis of the Asdiwal myth with Barthes' of *Sarrasine*. Levi-Strauss takes the story, explores its internal relations, and then shows that the main meanings of the story run directly counter to the official values of the community; that the myth reveals, that is, profound conflicts within the society. He also contrasts this version of the Asdiwal myth with another version in a nearby community, and shows that the differences between the two versions can be related to differences in social organisation and environment: the result is a fascinating study of both inner meaning and explanatory context.[19]

In contrast, how little does Barthes do! If he were examining the Asdiwal myth, he would have taken the myth of one community, and, like Levi-Strauss, explored its internal relations, but more elaborately: he would have shown that this Asdiwal story constantly refers to other myths held by the same community, so that there is a constant play of codes in the story, and then he would have ended up saying, triumphantly, look it shows how all culture shows the ceaseless play of codes, just like language. But everything else that Levi-Strauss did Barthes couldn't have done, because his movement is away from specific societies with specific histories, to the ever more generalised universals of language. In so doing, Barthes can't explain anything, he can only, as he says himself in S/Z, 'describe'. Barthes of course would think that no limitation at all, but, comparing him to his fellow structuralist Levi-Strauss, we can see what loss there is.

Barthes, we may happily conclude, doesn't tell us anything about the why of texts, only a limited how, puffed out to look like an all.

# 9
# Conclusion

In this book I have argued for an approach to cultural studies that tries to overcome the deep split between text and context. A text has to be studied in and for itself as well as in its context. Both are equally necessary moments of analysis. Neither should be reduced to the other. *In a Critical Condition* argues that when cultural study is centred only on the text, is formalist, it represses important aspects of literature, film, communication; and when a rigidly contextual approach makes the text disappear into a context it neglects important aspects of cultural phenomena. The two have always to be combined in analysis, held in a difficult balance.

A text cannot be studied as a self-sufficient entity – we can't be satisfied with merely studying its internal relations or its relationships exclusively to other texts. Ideally, we have to examine a text's conditions of production and consumption (or reception) as well as its specific internal reality. If we took film as our example, this kind of broad-ranging critique would be clearly (one would think) necessary. To study (say) Hollywood films, we would have to go into the institutional structure and constraints of Hollywood studios, the power of producers, financial-market pressures, freedom allowed to the directors, attitudes to scriptwriters, the state and development of film technology. We would examine, that is, whether a certain studio (Warners, say, in the 1930s) was producing a distinctive kind of product, and why this was so. Were studios like Warners laying down policies and guidelines (or an unspoken 'atmosphere') about the kinds of audience they hoped to reach – in terms of class, gender, ethnic community, sub-culture, age, political consciousness – and how did this affect the way films were constructed? Were only some themes permitted, and others silenced, censored and self-censored?

Then there are the texts themselves. How much did the films in their specific internal reality live out or resist these conditions of production? Do they belong to a recognisable genre – western or gangster movie or musical or whatever – and so join a history of filmic conventions and codes (which themselves probably derive from 19th-century theatre, vaudeville, melodrama, musicals, and so on)? Are these genre conventions reshaped, discarded, transformed, and if so, how and why? Is it because of a relationship to ideological situations, dilemmas, anxieties: for example, is there a shift in Hollywood gangster movies away from realist conventions in the 1930s stressing the effect of the social environment on the individual, to new conventions in the 1950s which focus on the psychopathology of everyday individual gangster life (as in the movie starring James Cagney sitting on his Ma's knee, *White Heat*)? Isn't, that is, an historical and ideological dimension of analysis always necessary in the very discussion of how aesthetic conventions and codes are used and re-used, shaped and reshaped?

Further, in terms of consumption or reception, how do people receive films? What of the audiences themselves, given that they are divided in terms of class, gender, ethnic community, subculture, formal education, age, regions? Do audiences passively accept the film's conventions and meanings? Or do people actively participate – for example, in terms of psychoanalytic theory, do people 'identify' with characters, values, events in the film, as a way of satisfying various repressed wishes and anxieties, a way of gaining a momentary harmony of subconscious desire and conscious enjoyment of the narrative of the film before them? What of other aspects of the question of pleasure in the consumption of film: for example, do people gain pleasure from recognising the conventions of genre (as in a western or spy movie) being employed, anticipating/being surprised by how such conventions are being used and changed? Aren't audiences (and not only critics) always recognising allusions in this text to similar codes and conventions and themes in other texts?

But what of the question of displeasure? Why do audiences *not* like films? Are they disappointed, for example – as I was disappointed in viewing the CIA-parody film *Hopscotch* – that the degree of suspense and danger appropriate to the conventions of the chase were not being met, that the protagonist 'won' too easily? This raises the whole question of value-judgements, of the play of pleasure and displeasure by the viewer, of how much people judge both the use of conventions in a work, as well as the reshaping of these conventions in terms of contextual (historical, political, ideological, metaphysical, class, age, etc.) situations and pressures. For if these kinds of context are always helping to shape the way conventions are used and appropriated – are altered and made new – then context is always inscribed *in* the text, part of its very aesthetic shape: and value-judgements are then simultaneously about text and context-in-text.

If such a multifaceted approach to text/context seems clearly appropriate for the history of film, it certainly hasn't struck literary critics as irresistible – and the institutional dominance of formalist, textcentric criticism has been the story of this book. Yet we've also noticed that formalism, in the guise of New Criticism as a teaching practice, was most strong and persuasive in the Cold War years, and that since then, and particularly from the latter 1970s, it's been losing its grip on the profession.

I've also asked in this book: is there a new formalism developing called 'deconstruction',[1] that particular North American appropriation of the later Roland Barthes and the linguistic philosophy of Jacques Derrida – where New Critical principles have been restored in the light of a theory of language as the play of infinite difference – which will sweep all before it? Will it rejuvenate New Criticism as an effective, persuasive, and intellectually formidable force just as it is waning? Further, will Marxists and so-called post-Marxists become attracted to this kind of semiology, so that a new formalist orthodoxy will embrace right and left, and hence be so heterogeneous as not to appear an orthodoxy at all (the moment when an orthodoxy, as we saw in chapter four, is at its strongest)?

A formalist textcentred approach also seems most attractive when contextualist criticism denies the inner reality of the text. This has frequently happened in popular culture studies, where the main Marxist schools (the Frankfurt school and the English *Screen* group in the 1970s) have tended to ignore the specificity of popular culture in favour of analyses of supposed effects on the psychology of mass audiences.[2] Don't look at the text, look at what it's doing to the poor buggers who watch Hollywood films or TV – they just get sucked into society's dominant ideologies, don't they? (No, they don't.) Other Marxist students of popular culture and the mass media will interest themselves only in processes of production like ownership and control, as if the specific character of texts will automatically follow from such an analysis (however worthy in itself).

In this situation late-Barthes-style semiology and deconstruction can seem very attractive. In too much Marxist analysis the meanings of a text are seen as securing the force and pervasiveness of a dominant ideology. The late-Barthes-style semiologists and deconstructionists can reply that this approach reduces the text to a single overall meaning (relationship to ideology), and is hence inadequate to *any* text's richness, the full play of its meaning, its signs and codes. Rather than revealing ideology, texts are seen as part of a great sea of 'textuality' and 'intertextuality' – of language where meanings are unbounded and unconstrained. And because language is structured on differences – where everything refers to what it's different from, what it isn't – then texts are always ambiguous, multivalent, and paradoxical, and hence too plural to be tied to a single dominant meaning as in ideology-centred analysis.

Popular culture study in general, and not just at the hands of Marxists, has suffered from the reverse of the textcentredness that has afflicted 'high' literature study. It's been all study of production and/or reception, not study of texts as also a necessary moment of analysis. In effect, there's been a sociological imperialism at work, with criticism moving in to take up the space of textual analysis. Yet to prefer analysis only of the texts of popular culture – the tendency of this kind of semiology and deconstruction – will, again, mean instituting an anti-historical criticism. It will bring popular culture studies into line with the dominant formalist 20th-century 'high' culture teaching practices.

Overall, the argument of *In a Critical Condition* is that there is at the moment no clear dominance, no hegemony, of formalist criticism. And it is in this context, as an intervention in the debate, that I've written this book.

# Epilogue
# A doubter meets the devotees

(The following adventure is not written in the manner of a *roman à clef*. All places and personages are purely imaginary. And don't ask how many children have these people. All the characters are but spaces where codes and symbols intersect.)

My mother is wonderful. She gets a name or a title wrong seconds after one has told it to her. I told her I would be travelling interstate for a few days, that I had been invited to give a lecture and seminar paper at — University. Ah, you're going to Fletcher University, she immediately said.

An old friend of mine, at Fletcher University, was visiting Sydney and dropped in to tell me what to expect. The Monday of my visit was routine, a lecture on the 1890s, but on the Wednesday I had to offer something for the staff-postgraduate seminar. 'You'll have to perform, John, I'm afraid, you'll really have to perform.' I muttered something about a paper on the number of times crows are mentioned in Australian literature, when, suddenly, 'This will be fabulous, this will be great, you must give this . . .' This 'friend' had spied the just completed draft of the foregoing chapter on Roland Barthes. 'This'll bring 'em along. It's a hornet's nest there, everyone's divided about all this semiotics and semiology. But I'm warning you, they'll try and mince you up, they're fierce, our young semioticians, they're fierce. So if you want to do it on the crows . . . No, no, it's all right.'

I won't bore you with the preliminaries – hearing in the first half hour different accounts of every conflict in the place, admiring the campus, small buildings set in beautiful bush, giving the lecture to a friendly looking group of students, and, with the Nice People there – mainly those interested in a more historical approach to things – pubbing and restauranting the night before the dread seminar, to which gladiatorial occasion I turned up the next day feeling decidedly seedy, drawn, and jittery. I hoped the braincells that had remained would get me through.

A large number of people, it appeared, had turned up to see the fun, the dissection (deconstruction) of an Upstart Name from Sydney. Seats filled up and people spilled round the sides and behind me. Since my paper was called, precisely, 'Dr Who, Leela, and the Death of the Author: Roland Barthes', I protested to the chairperson, my erstwhile 'friend', about my back being so exposed. Various pleasantries were exchanged, a lighthearted mood seemed to prevail, jokes flew, mainly concerning the imminent death of the author, coffee, and one of the Nice People had brought a cheesecake, which people gobbled before my hungover eyes. (The chairperson, my 'friend', pinched my piece during question time.) I explained the conditions of producing this discourse. I was on a Literature Board grant, and trying to write more relaxedly and freely and less academically. At the same time, I insisted, there would be no whimsy, no jokes, no levity, in the presentation. I recounted going down to give a seminar paper at the Melbourne history department a few weeks before, and foolishly including jokes etc. in the paper, only to be met with twenty or so immovably unsmiling unflinching unblinking faces, where not a lip twitched and where I spent most of the paper, as it went on, trying to anticipate jokes and cut them out. Humiliation and misery. From this I decided, I told my present hearers, never to include a whimsical note again, and this paper will be unrelievedly solemn.

I therefore solemnly explained who Dr Who and Leela were and what an Android was for those who mightn't know, and then gave the paper – in general convicting Barthes and his kind of semiology of intellectual imperialism. For the most part I read out the

T. S. Eliot/Roland Barthes section of the chapter, which surprised even me by its degree of intellectual passion. Impressed by this, or by my foolish plea for Seminar Solemnity, as soon as question time started, *it* started – no time now for the pleasantries of social life and smiles in corridors; things were to be approached with a high provincial seriousness. As the Russian formalists might have said, the Nice People immediately backgrounded themselves, while the bright young lads with gimlet eyes shot to the argumentative foreground. For the next hour and twenty minutes, from one-thirty to ten-to-three, the paper-giver was bombarded one after the other rat-a-tat with hostile questions. It was the kind of atmosphere that would have made a bear-pit seem gracious. (Or, how does it go, it would have made a fox-hunt look like a social tennis game at a Vicar's teaparty.) As Mrs Thatcher would have said, one was not delighted.

It's not that things started slowly, that people took a while to hit their stride. Nor had the cheesecake worked, sweetening their tempers. Too much lemon. The first question was delivered by a smooth greybearded gent, the elder statesman of the semiotic tribe, I learnt later. Memory of hectic encounters of this kind can never be convicted of being clear, but his question went something like – I'm interested in (read appalled by) the way you're writing this for the Literature Board (it sounded like a threat to report me), this anecdotal style, what's the use of it, what's it do for your argument (I'd opened with an anecdote about a friend saying semiotics is just like practical criticism), it's rather like, don't you think, those physics textbooks where the author dedicates the book to his wife Martha thanking her for looking after the kids and doing all the washing up. I'm interested in (winding up) why you think there's anything interesting in this kind of thing.

A veteran from English universities then quickly foregrounded himself. After correcting my pronunciation of 'Roland Barthes', he said, yes, he'd heard this kind of jibe before in English universities about Barthes and S/Z, it was just practical criticism. This is old stuff surely. And you say semiotics will or might take over French departments – it already had, it already had (this said as if it refuted my point).

Then someone sitting behind me this time actually strode to the foreground, with a sort of agitated hunting gait, and attacked my flank. What interests me is the way you say throughout your paper you're irritated by Barthes, or you're not impressed by Barthes – I mean, who are *you*, why should we be interested in *your* opinion of anything, who are *you* to tell us this, why should we care what *you* think. (This pleasant inquirer after the truth of things, or rather the nature of discourses, had been particularly smiling towards me during my visit so far, even unctuous in his attentions. I wondered if Brutus had laughed and joked with Caesar only hours before . . .)

This high standard of questioning was maintained for the duration. I tried to answer as firmly and quickly as possible, and to return some shafts and score a few palpable hits. In some ways it was a usual question-time performance: you get accused of neglecting some point or other that in fact you'd spent almost overlong covering and going over; you're accused of neglecting complex differences between (say) New Critics, when such complexity couldn't possibly be covered in a short seminar paper and doesn't contradict your main point anyway, only extends it. What distinguished the occasion was the energy, intensity, waspishness and, most remarkably, anger of the grilling I was being exposed to.

The only pleasant note – for the paper-giver – the semioticians and high New Critics appeared to be thoroughly enjoying themselves, in a contorted kind of way – was when a German hermeneutics person suddenly broke in and expostulated that he couldn't see anything in all this Barthes and French semiology stuff, he'd glanced that morning at the first few pages of S/Z, and its reliance on Saussure and simple notions of linguistics, of connotation and denotation and so on, were so simple, so crude, so old-fashioned. He couldn't, he wound up, see anything in semiotics at all. (Apparently this person had given a paper a few months before on the German hermeneutic tradition, and French or French-loving semioticians had come from miles around to put all this German stuff through the grater.) No one supported this intervention, but he at least was determined to be *freundlich*.

After an hour, by two-thirty, I was exhausted. Trying to answer one question I even began to stutter, and said, sorry, I'm becoming rather tired. The chairperson, however, my 'friend', who knows how to take a hint, said nothing, and let things go on. (She told me later she couldn't stop at that point, 'they' would have accused her of being authoritarian; she also said one of the Nice People had handed her a note during question time saying: 'Do you usually do this to your friends?')

Now things really started – or ended for me. Discussion devolved on to just three of the pack, sitting in a line on the floor – one who sounded like a Walking Glossary of Semiotic Terms, another who looked like a bitter refugee from Carlton, reality, and all things Melbourne – who for the last twenty minutes starting grinding their teeth, coming out with desperate arguments why they and their version of semiotics (whatever it was) were right and shouldn't be challenged, getting openly nastier and nastier, and finally setting the third of the trio, a kind of trained postgraduate hound, to bark and bite at me. He accused me of being 'reactionary': because I was criticising a major semiotics text in public, then this was reactionary – people wouldn't read Barthes any more, and semiotics wouldn't ever get a chance.

The conclusion having been reached that rather than Barthes' approach in S/Z being a form of intellectual imperialism, I on the contrary was a fascist, the chairperson allowed the meeting to end.

I retired exhausted and didn't feel altogether exalted. No one, except the German hermeneutics person, had supported me. The room had seemed to shimmer with hostility and near-hatred, and it was little comfort, for the moment, to feel that the semioticians were obviously totally threatened. I wondered if the bear retains its dignity in the pit while the dogs howl and snarl and grip its flanks, or do the excited spectators admire only the curs for their energy and persistence. At afternoon tea a little later some of the Nice People came up and said they'd enjoyed it. Buck up, they said, you were treated lightly, compared to some seminars we've had. Then the semioticians came up smiling, and began again, in a strange and obviously endless monotone, justifying themselves. And then, finally, I could get to the airport and get Home, to Sydney where no one listens to a word anyone ever says.

What this little episode reveals I'm not sure. These particular semioticians were young and male and had an extraordinarily aggressive macho intellectual style – and we can recall here Barthes the macho rapist of texts. All the non-semioticians – except the

English high New Critic – were cowed, sitting there (apparently) silent and afraid; and indeed that I could give the paper at all was a tribute to my own massive male intellectual confidence. (Only one woman spoke, and she told me later that she'd had to tense herself to do it.)

The nightmare of history seems to be hanging over a new generation: like the New Critics and especially the Leavisites of old, some semioticians at least, in attempting to establish a distinct discipline with its own (small) vocabulary and approach, are creating an enclosed speech, which yet is aggressively claimed to apply to all cultural and communication studies as the only proper method. Everyone else is to be held in contempt, and their intellectual energy, will, and confidence sapped.

Semioticians like this would presumably think of themselves as anti-élitist and as anarchistic, as positing always the multiplicity of discourses, and how discourses are not natural, but constructed, and this can be exposed (as in Russian formalism's defamiliarising). Aren't they dealing with mass popular culture like film, whereas the Leavisites despised mass civilisation? And aren't the Leavisites conservative, whereas they (like Barthes) are or were of the left? The Leavisites certainly did have a dislike of modern industrial society and its cultural products, but as for conservatism – the semioticians would do well to recall that in the 1930s the Leavisites conceded a great deal to contemporary Marxists in terms of the necessity of an historical context for literature (as in L. C. Knights' *Drama and Society in the Age of Jonson*, published in 1937) or in terms of 'economic communism' as a social ideal (Leavis in *Scrutiny*).

The extreme conservatism was to come later, particularly in the Cold War 1950s and '60s. Perhaps, as we enter Cold War II, we might be discerning a similar trajectory in semiology/semiotics. Some of them, at least, are becoming just like the Leavisites at their worst used to be, élitist, arrogant, intimidating, verbally bullying, and massively ignorant of everything in the world except their own interests.

Further, like all colonial servants of an overseas cultural dominance (the theoretical majesty of Paris, France) local semioticians such as these are more enthusiastic about doing the work of intellectual imperialism than their metropolitan heroes are themselves. For our local lads are obviously neocolonials, cultural cringers, of a most violent kind. (At tea one of the pack said someone had come up the year before to give a paper on an Australian short story writer, but he couldn't think of the name. Lawson, I asked. No. Oh, Frank Moorhouse. Yes, that's the one. Moorfoot, or something.)

It may be that some young male semioticians somewhere in Australia, if they ever read an Australian text and think they recognise themselves in this portrait, will feel enraged by the paper-giver's treachery in recording these anecdotes. It just shows – never trust a person with a Literature Board grant, hiding his notebook under the table. But also rest assured that I also have experienced their plight – I went to a conference some years ago and before giving my paper changed the chairs from rows to a semi-circle, to make discussion easier. This vile act found me convicted of Marxist authoritarianism by a character in a story written not long after by an Australian short story writer. Moorfoot, or someone.

# Notes and References

## Prologue

1. Cf. Pierre van den Berghe's delightful little counter-manual, *Academic Gamesmanship* (New York: Abelard-Schuman, 1970).

2. Cf. John Docker, *Australian Cultural Elites* (Sydney: Angus and Robertson, 1974), chapters on *Meanjin* and *Southerly*.

3. This bore fruit in Ian Lennie's superb article, 'English Studies in Australia', *Arena*, No. 20, 1969.

4. Cf. René Wellek, *Concepts of Criticism* (New Haven and London: Yale University Press, 1963), 'Concepts of Form and Structure in Twentieth-Century Criticism', p. 59.

## 1  The Australian Background

1. This chapter is a heavily revised version of a paper given to the Inaugural Conference of the Association for the Study of Australian Literature, Monash University, May 1978.

2. J. B. Hirst, 'The Pioneer Legend', *Historical Studies*, XVIII (1978), 316-337.

3. Russel Ward, *The Australian Legend* (1958; Melbourne: Oxford University Press, 1966), pp. 1-2.

4. René Wellek, *Confrontations* (Princeton University Press, New Jersey, 1965); see also Wellek's essay on Herder in *A History of Modern Criticism*, I (1955). For Herder's stress on individuality in history, see

Ernst Cassirer, *The Philosophy of the Enlightenment*, translated by Fritz C. A. Koelln and James C. Pettegrove (Princeton University Press, New Jersey, 1951), pp. 230-233.

5. For this aspect of Herder see Elie Kedourie, *Nationalism* (Hutchinson, London, 1960). See also J. A. Moses, 'The Crisis in West German Historiography: Origins and Trends', *Historical Studies*, vol. 13, no. 52, April 1969, pp. 445-459.

6. Wellek, *Confrontations*, p. 89.

7. Ibid., pp. 97-99.

8. Marcus Clarke, Preface to Gordon's *Poems*, in John Barnes (ed.), *The Writer in Australia 1856-1964* (Melbourne: Oxford University Press, 1969), pp. 34-36.

9. For a more detailed account of Stephens' rural eugenics, see John Docker, 'Can the Centre Hold?' in Sydney Labour History Group, *What Rough Beast? The State and Social Order in Australian History* (Sydney: George Allen and Unwin, 1982), pp. 71-78.

10. S. A. Rosa, *The Coming Terror; or, the Australian Revolution* (published by the Author, Sydney, 1894), pp. 19, 29.

11. See Brian Elliott, 'Jindyworobaks and Aborigines', *Australian Literary Studies*, No. 1, 1977; H. McQueen, 'Rex Ingamells and the Quest for Environmental Values', *Meanjin*, No. 1, 1978; Brian Elliott (ed.), *The Jindyworobaks* (St Lucia: University of Queensland Press, 1979), and John Dally, 'The Quest for the Jindyworobaks', *Meanjin*, No. 3, 1980.

12. *Sydney Morning Herald*, 4 February, 1978, p. 19.

13. Cf. Brian Elliott (ed.), *The Jindyworobaks*, Introduction.

14. *Jindyworobak Review 1938-1948* (Melbourne: Jindyworobak Publications, 1948), p. 45. Judith Wright also contributed a short essay 'Perspective' (pp. 71-73), where she acknowledges the historical importance of the Jindies.

15. See *Refractory Girl*, No. 8, 1975, pp. 60-64, which focuses on the work of Grace Cossington-Smith, Margaret Preston, Thea Proctor, and Grace Crowley in the period from the early 1920s to the mid-1940s. See also Janine Burke, *Australian Women Artists 1840-1940* (Melbourne: Greenhouse Publications, 1980), and Humphrey McQueen, *The Black Swan of Trespass* (Sydney: Alternative Publishing Cooperative Ltd., 1979). See also Drusilla Modjeska, *Exiles at Home. Australian Women Writers 1925-1945* (Sydney: Angus and Robertson, 1981).

16. J. J. Healey, *Literature and the Aborigine in Australia 1770-1975* (St Lucia: University of Queensland Press, 1978), chapters, 6, 7, 8, esp. pp. 139-180.

17. Ibid., p. 140.

18. Bernard Smith, *Place, Taste, and Tradition* (1945; Melbourne: Oxford University Press, 1979), pp. 195-199.

19. Editorial, *Art in Australia*, March 1925.

20. Ibid. Preston's article was accompanied by illustrations of Aboriginal art.

21. Editorial, *Art in Australia*, March 1930.

22. Margaret Preston, 'Some Aspects of Painting in Australia', in John Ingamells (ed.), *Cultural Cross-Section* (Adelaide: Jindyworobak Publication, 1941), pp. 39-41.

23. *Art of Australia 1788-1941* (New York: Published for the Carnegie Corporation by the Museum of Modern Art, 1941), edited and compiled by Sydney Ure Smith, pp. 16-17.

24. A. D. Hope, *Native Companions* (Sydney: Angus and Robertson, 1974), p. 45.

25. Bernard Smith, *Place, Taste, and Tradition*, pp. 176, 197-198, 260.

26. *Sydney Morning Herald*, 2 September 1980. See also, however, Blaikie's *Remember Smith's Weekly?* (1966; Adelaide: Rigby, 1975), p. 106, which is almost completely celebratory of Stan Cross's cartoons, as of everything else in the paper's history.

27. Katharine Susannah Prichard, *Coonardoo* (1929; Sydney: Angus and Robertson, 1975), pp. 2, 20-21, 53, 55, 59, 60-64, 71, 108-109, 133.

28. *Art in Australia*, March 1925.

29. *Art in Australia*, March 1930.

30. Cf. John Docker, 'The Organicist Fallacy: Jack Lindsay, Romanticism and Marxist Aesthetics', *Arena* 47-48, 1977.

31. *Art of Australia 1788-1941*, p. 16.

32. Compare the importance of the 'analogy between human and plant life' and of the role of organicist metaphor generally in Herder's philosophy of history: Hayden White, *Metahistory: The Historical Imagination in Nineteenth-Century Europe* (Baltimore: John Hopkins University Press, 1973), p. 79.

33. A. A. Phillips, *The Australian Tradition* (Melbourne: Cheshire, 1958), pp. 48-49.

34. Vance Palmer, *The Legend of the Nineties* (1954; Melbourne University Press, Melbourne, 1966), chapter three, 'Myth-Making', pp. 52-55.

35. Ibid., chapter nine, pp. 169, 172.

36. Geoffrey Serle, *From Deserts the Prophets Come* (Melbourne: Heinemann, 1973), pp. 61-62.

37. Nettie Palmer, 'The Growth of Latin American Literature: As an Australian sees it', *Meanjin*, No. 2, 1947, pp. 118-119.

38. A. A. Phillips, *The Australian Tradition*, pp. 54-55.

39. Russel Ward, *The Australian Legend*, pp. 13, 254-255.

40. A. A. Phillips, *The Australian Tradition*, p. 54.

41. See Vance Palmer's editorial in *Meanjin*, No. 2, 1957, pp. 100, 223. For a fuller analysis, see John Docker, *Australian Cultural Elites*, pp. 103-107.

## 2 The International Context

1. T. S. Eliot, *The Sacred Wood* (London: Methuen, 1957), pp. 47-59.

2. See 'Postscript: 1976' to his *William Morris. Romantic to Revolutionary* (1955; London: Merlin Press, 1977), pp. 769-770, 779, 784-785, 787-794; 'Outside the Whale', in E. P. Thompson (ed.), *Out of Apathy* (1960), reprinted in Thompson's *The Poverty of Theory* (London: Merlin Press, 1978); 'The Politics of Theory', in Raphael Samuel (ed.), *People's History and Socialist Theory* (London: Routledge and Kegan Paul, 1981), pp. 396-400. See also Stuart Hall, 'Cultural Studies and the Centre: some problematics and problems', in Stuart Hall, Dorothy Hobson, Andrew Lowe and Paul Willis (eds.), *Culture, Media, Language* (London: Hutchinson, 1980), pp. 16-19.

3. Christopher Lasch, *The Agony of the American Left* (New York: Vintage, 1969), p. 107.

4. Frank Kermode, *Romantic Image* (1957; London: Fontana, 1971), p. 176.

5. Francis Mulhern, *The Moment of 'Scrutiny'* (London: New Left Books, 1979), p. 324.

6. Ibid., p. 311.

7. See L. C. Knights and Basil Cottle (eds.), *Metaphor and Symbol* (London: Butterworth Scientific Publications, 1960).

8. S. L. Goldberg, *F. R. Leavis. The Modern Mind* (CAB booklet) Vol. 36, No. 3, 1965, pp. 45-46. Vincent Buckley, *Poetry and Morality. Studies on the Criticism of Matthew Arnold, T. S. Eliot and F. R. Leavis* (London: Chatto and Windus, 1959), pp. 139-205.

9. John Fekete, *The Critical Twilight. Explorations in the Ideology of Anglo-American Literary Theory from Eliot to McLuhan* (London: Routledge and Kegan Paul, 1977), pp. 61-103. For a more sympathetic study of the southern agrarians and Ransom, see Richard Gray, *The Literature of Memory. Modern Writers of the American South* (London: Edward Arnold, 1977), pp. 55-63. For New Criticism in general see also Richard Ohmann, *English in America* (New York: Oxford University Press, 1976), pp. 69-91.

10. Quoted in Fekete, pp. 68-69.

11. Quoted in ibid., p. 67.

12. See Fekete, chapter seven, 'New Criticism', pp. 85-98.

13. Fekete, p. 242, n. 13. See Daniel Aaron, *Writers on the Left* (1965; New York: Oxford University Press, 1977), for *Partisan Review* in the 1930s, and Lasch, *The Agony of the American Left*, for the journal in the 1940s and '50s.

14. Lionel Trilling, *The Liberal Imagination* (1950; New York: Viking Press, 1951), Preface, pp. ix-xv.

15. Ibid., 'Manners, Morals, and the Novel', pp. 208-209, 219-222.

16. Trilling, *Beyond Culture*,'On the Teaching of Modern Literature', p. 27.

17. 'On the Teaching of Modern Literature', pp. 8-9.

3 The Cold War

1. See, for example, John V. Kelleher, 'Matthew Arnold and the Celtic Revival', in H. Levin (ed.), *Perspectives of Criticism* (Cambridge, Mass.: Harvard University Press, 1950), and Frederic E. Faverty, *Matthew Arnold: The Ethnologist* (1951; New York: AMS Press, 1968).

2. Pieter Geyl, *Debates with Historians* (1955; London: Fontana, 1962), chapter three, 'Carlyle: his Significance and Reputation', pp. 51, 66-67.

3. Ibid., chapter one, 'Ranke in the Light of the Catastrophe'.

4. Cf. René Wellek, *Confrontations* (Princeton: Princeton University Press, 1965), chapter on 'Carlyle and the Philosophy of History', p. 104.

5. A revised version, given the title 'James McAuley: the Poetry and the Attitude', appeared in *Arena*, No. 26, 1971. (The particular analysis of McAuley that follows in this chapter is lifted from this long ago piece.)

6. *Manchester Guardian*, 10 July, 1950, reprinted in *Meanjin*, Vol. XIII, No. 4, 1954, pp. 612-615.

7. Christopher Lasch, *The Agony of the American Left* (New York: Vintage, 1969), chapter three, 'The Cultural Cold War: A Short History of the Congress for Cultural Freedom', pp. 70, 107. For CIA funding of and influence on *Encounter* and other Cultural Freedom organisations, see pp. 98-110.

8. Ibid., pp. 70-75.

9. See Noam Chomsky and Edward S. Herman, *The Washington Connection and Third World Fascism* (Boston: South End Press, 1979).

10. Lasch, *The Agony of the American Left*, pp. 66, 80-82.

11. Nor into opposition to the Cold War in figures like Brian Fitzpatrick, a founder of the Australian Council for Civil Liberties. See Fitzpatrick's 'The Importance of Being Earnest About Liberty', *Meanjin*, Vol. XV, No. 1, 1956, pp. 92-96; Don Watson, *Brian Fitzpatrick* (Sydney: Hale and

Iremonger, 1979); Robin Gollan, *Revolutionaries and Reformists* (Canberra: Australian National University Press, 1975).

12. Cf. Despina Balzidis, 'James McAuley's Radical Ingredients', *Meanjin*, Vol. XXXIX, No. 3, 1980, pp. 374-382.

13. *The End of Modernity* (Sydney: Angus and Robertson, 1959), p. 8.

14. Ibid., p. 59.

15. Terry Sturm, 'The Social Context of Brennan's Thought', *Southerly*, No. 4, 1968, pp. 270-271.

16. Cf. Tim Rowse, *Australian Liberalism and National Character* (Melbourne: Kibble Press, 1978), pp. 232-239.

## 4   The Metaphysical Ascendancy

1. Francis Mulhern, *The Moment of 'Scrutiny'* (London: New Left Books, 1979), pp. 326-328.

2. G. A. Wilkes, 'The Eighteen Nineties', *Arts* I (1958), reprinted in Grahame Johnston (ed.), *Australian Literary Criticism* (Melbourne: Oxford University Press, 1962.)

3. Ibid., pp. 36-39.

4. W. M. Maidment, 'Australian Literary Criticism', *Southerly*, No. 1, 1964, p. 30.

5. G. A. Wilkes, 'Going Over the Terrain in a Different Way: An Alternative View of Australian Literary History', *Southerly*, No. 2, 1975.

6. Cf. John Docker, 'Commonwealth Literature and the Universities', *New Literature Review*, No. 2, 1977.

7. G. A. Wilkes, 'The Eighteen Nineties', p. 40.

8. Leon Cantrell (ed.), *The 1890s. Stories, Verse, and Essays* (St Lucia: University of Queensland Press, 1977), introduction, p. xv.

9. See Bertolt Brecht, 'Against Georg Lukács', in *Aesthetics and Politics* (London: New Left Books, 1977).

10. Reprinted in John Barnes (ed.), *The Writer in Australia* (Melbourne: Oxford University Press, 1969), pp. 273-296.

11. 'The Image of Man . . .', pp. 275-279. We learn (p. 278) that Henry Kendall 'gave us the amazing anomaly of an Australian with an almost completely English sensibility'.

12. Ibid., p. 279.

13. I must confess that 'The Image of Man in Australian Poetry' inspired the title of the chapter 'The Image of Woman in A. D. Hope's Poetry' in *Australian Cultural Elites*.

14. 'The Image of Man . . .', p. 284.

15. 'Utopianism and Vitalism', *Quadrant*, No. 2, 1958-59, reprinted in

Grahame Johnston (ed.), *Australian Literary Criticism* (Melbourne: Oxford University Press, 1962), pp. 16-29.

16. In his review of Johnston's collection W. M. Maidment asks of Buckley's dismissal of Lindsay's ideas, how then *could Creative Effort* have influenced poets like Slessor, FitzGerald, and Douglas Stewart? Further, Maidment demonstrates, Buckley gets completely wrong Lindsay's alleged acceptance of Nietzsche's political theory. See 'Australian Literary Criticism', *Southerly*, No. 1, 1964, pp. 40-41. My own article in *Australian Literary Studies* (No. 1, 1973), 'Norman Lindsay's *Creative Effort*: Manifesto for an Urban Intelligentsia', was also an attempt to argue against Buckley's view that Norman Lindsay's ideas were negligible and influenced poets like Slessor only in their early, immature work.

17. 'The Image of Man . . .', pp. 285-287.

18. For the debate about utopianism, see Frank Manuel (ed.), *Utopias and Utopian Thought* (Boston: Houghton, Mifflin Company, 1966). See also chapter two of the present work.

19. 'Utopianism and Vitalism', pp. 17-23.

20. 'The Image of Man . . .', pp. 274, 289-296.

21. 'Utopianism and Vitalism', p. 27.

22. Ibid.

23. W. M. Maidment, 'Australian Literary Criticism', *Southerly*, No. 1, 1964, p. 24.

24. Vincent Buckley, '*Capricornia*', in Grahame Johnston, *Australian Literary Criticism*, pp. 169-176.

25. A. A. Phillips, 'Barbara Baynton's Stories', in Barbara Baynton, *Bush Studies* (1902; Sydney: Angus and Robertson, 1965), pp. 29-42. The essay was first published in *Overland*, and reprinted in A. A. Phillips' recent edition of *The Australian Tradition* (edited by Brian Kiernan).

26. 'The Democratic Theme', *The Australian Tradition*, pp. 44-48.

## 5   The Gloom Thesis

1. Manning Clark, 'Re-writing Australian History', in T. A. G. Hungerford (ed.), *Australian Signpost* (Melbourne: Cheshire, 1956), reprinted in Manning Clark, *Occasional Writings and Speeches* (Melbourne: Fontana / Collins, 1980).

2. Michael Roe, 'Challenges to Australian Identity', *Quadrant*, April 1978, pp. 34-40.

3. See R. A. Gollan, 'The Australian Impact', in S. E. Bowman (ed.), *Edward Bellamy Abroad* (New York: Twayne, 1962); 'American Populism and Australian Utopianism', *Labour History*, No. 9, 1965.

4. *Meanjin*, No. 1, 1962, p. 49.

5. Leon Cantrell (ed.), *The 1890s. Stories, Verse, and Essays* (St Lucia: University of Queensland Press, 1977).

6. G. A. Wilkes, 'The Eighteen Nineties', pp. 30-32.

7. A. A. Phillips, *The Australian Tradition* (Melbourne: Cheshire, 1958), p. 48.

8. Arthur Jose, *The Romantic Nineties* (Sydney: Angus and Robertson, 1933), pp. 4, 33, 34.

9. Ibid., pp. 38, 19.

10. See P. J. Keating (ed.), *Working Class Stories of the 1890s* (London: Routledge and Kegan Paul, 1971).

11. Jose, *The Romantic Nineties*, p. 13.

12. Graeme Davison, 'Explanations of Urban Radicalism: Old Theories and New Histories', *Historical Studies*, April 1978; 'Sydney and the Bush: An Urban Context for the Australian Legend', ibid., October 1978.

13. William Lane, *The Workingman's Paradise* (Brisbane: Dunlop and Co., 1892), p. 82.

14. P. J. Keating, *The Working Classes in Victorian Fiction* (London: Routledge and Kegan Paul, 1971), chapter one.

15. The passage is quoted in ibid., pp. 19-20. For disagreement on this point see Michael Wilding's introduction to William Lane, *The Workingman's Paradise* (Sydney: Sydney University Press facsimile edition, 1980), pp. 18-20. See also Brian Kiernan, 'Sydney or the Bush', in Jill Roe (ed.), *Twentieth Century Sydney* (Sydney: Hale and Iremonger, 1980), concerning literary images of Paddy's Market.

16. Miles Franklin, *My Brilliant Career* (1901; Sydney: Angus and Robertson, 1974), p. 147.

17. See Brian Matthews, 'Henry Lawson and the Work Ethic', *The Literary Criterion*, Vol. XV, Nos. 3 and 4, 1980, Special Australian Literature Number, pp. 108-116.

## 6 The New Right and the New Left in the Same Trap

1. Manning Clark, 'Re-writing Australian History', in T. A. G. Hungerford (ed.), *Australian Signpost* (Melbourne: Cheshire, 1956). Reprinted in Manning Clark, *Occasional Writings and Speeches* (Melbourne: Fontana/Collins, 1980).

2. See John Docker, *Australian Cultural Elites*, chapter two, 'Norman Lindsay, Kenneth Slessor and the Artist-Aristocracy'.

3. 'Utopianism and Vitalism', *Quadrant*, No. 2, 1958-59.

4. *Australian Liberalism and National Character*, p. 192.

5. Warren Osmond, *The Dilemma of an Australian Sociology* (Melbourne: Arena Publications, 1972), pp. 6-7.

6. See *Australian Liberalism and National Character*, pp. 192-239 for Rowse's discussion.

7. Peter Coleman (ed.), *Australian Civilization* (Melbourne: Cheshire, 1962), pp. 1-11.

8. See David Marr, *Barwick* (Sydney: George Allen and Unwin, 1980), pp. 21-25.

9. Mayer quoted in Rowse, *Australian Liberalism and National Character*, p. 226, n. 53.

10. Ibid., p. 214.

11. Ibid., pp. 226, 231-232, 238-239.

12. *The Old Mole*, No. 7, 26 October 1970, pp. 6-7. For discussion of the way the working class and the union movement have been miscast as the main protagonists of the White Australia policy and racism in Australia, see Verity Burgmann, Revolutionaries and Racists, 1887-1917, Phd thesis, Australian National University, 1980, pp. 20-21.

13. Humphrey McQueen, 'Australo-Marximus: On Some Reactions to *A New Britannia*', *Politics*, May 1972, p. 48.

14. Humphrey McQueen, *Australia's Media Monopolies* (Melbourne: Widescope, 1977), and *The Black Swan of Trespass* (Sydney: Alternative Publishing Cooperative Ltd., 1979).

7   New Criticism Grows Old

1. Much of this chapter was first published as a review-article, 'Leonie Kramer in the Prison House of Criticism', in *Overland* 85, October 1981.

2. Leonie Kramer (ed.), *The Oxford History of Australian Literature* (Melbourne: Oxford University Press, 1981).

3. As we saw in chapter four, W. M. Maidment, in a review of Grahame Johnston's collection *Australian Literary Criticism* in *Southerly*, No. 1, 1964, raised exactly these kinds of methodological questions against G. A. Wilkes's chapter 'The Eighteen Nineties': questions which the orthodoxy has never tried to answer. So much for intellectual openness.

4. Dorothy Green, 'Approved Writers in a Void', *The National Times*, April 5-11, 1981.

5. See also Richard Fotheringham, 'Sport and Nationalism on Australian stage and screen: From *Australia Felix* to *Gallipoli*, *Australasian Drama Studies*, Vol, I, No. 1, 1982, pp. 65-88.

## 8 A New Formalism?

1. Boris Eykhenbaum, 'Concerning the Question of the "Formalists"', in Christopher Pike (ed.), *The Futurists, the Formalists, and the Marxist Critique* (London: Ink Links Ltd., 1979), p. 52.

2. Roland Barthes, *Image-Music-Text* (Glasgow: Fontana/Collins, 1979), 'The Death of the Author', p. 147.

3. Terence Hawkes, *Structuralism and Semiotics* (London: Methuen, 1977), pp. 111-112.

4. See Howard Felperin, 'Leavisism Revisited or the Mystifications of Plain-Talk', *Meanjin*, Vol. 41, No. 2, 1982, pp. 171-179.

5. Peter Sanderson, 'The Secret of X-Appeal', *The Comics Journal*, No. 74, August 1982, pp. 64, 66.

6. Victor Erlich, *Russian Formalism* (The Hague: Mouton, 1955), p. 243. See also Ewa M. Thompson, *Russian Formalism and Anglo-American New Criticism* (The Hague: Mouton, 1971).

7. Roland Barthes, *S/Z* (New York: Hill and Wang, 1974).

8. See also the essay 'From Work to Text' in *Image-Music-Text*.

9. 'The Death of the Author', p. 148.

10. Cf. Barthes in 'From Work to Text' (p. 164): 'the text is that space where no language has a hold over any other, where languages circulate (keeping the circular sense of the term).'

11. *Structuralism and Semiotics*, p. 113.

12. Ibid., p. 118.

13. In *Image-Music-Text* (p. 156) Barthes salutes Marxism, but his anti-contextualism is clearly leading away from it in *S/Z*.

14. Hawkes, *Structuralism and Semiotics*, p. 121; Barthes, 'The Death of the Author', p. 147.

15. *Structuralism and Semiotics*, p. 121.

16. See also 'From Work to Text', p. 161.

17. Ibid., pp. 163-164.

18. Ibid., p. 161.

19. C. Levi-Strauss, 'The Story of Asdiwal', in E. R. Leach (ed.), *The Structural Study of Myth and Totemism* (London: Tavistock, 1967).

## 9 Conclusion

1. For a sympathetic account see Christopher Norris, *Deconstruction. Theory and Practice* (London: Methuen, 1982). For a critical account see Frank Lentricchia, *After the New Criticism* (London: The Athlone Press, 1980), chapters four and five.

2. Cf. John Docker, 'In Defence of Popular Culture', *Arena*, No. 60, 1982.

# Index